McElhaney's
LITIGATION
James W. McElhaney

Joseph C. Hostetler Professor of Trial Practice and Advocacy
Case Western Reserve University School of Law

Section of Litigation • ABA Journal
American Bar Association

© 1995 American Bar Association
and James W. McElhaney

Library of Congress Catalog Card Number 93-74905
ISBN 0-89707-954-X

The cover illustration is by W. B. Park of Winter Park, Florida.

The material contained herein represents the opinions of the author and should not be construed to be the action of either the American Bar Association or the Section of Litigation unless adopted pursuant to the Bylaws of the Association.

Discounts are available for books ordered in bulk. Special consideration is given to state bars, CLE programs, and other bar-related organizations. Inquire at Publications Planning & Marketing, American Bar Association, 750 North Lake Shore Drive, Chicago, Illinois 60611.

14 13 12 11 10   9 8 7 6 5 4

To MJM
who listened to every word

CONTENTS

Acknowledgments ix
Foreword xi

Part One Starting Out   1

1 The Guide 3
2 The Most Important Witness 8
3 Jury Voir Dire 13
4 The Risk of Confusion 18
5 The Golden Rule 23
6 Taking Sides 27

Part Two Trial Preparation   33

7 The Discovery Plan 35
8 Preparing Witnesses for Depositions 40
9 Focusing the Deposition 45
10 Pit-Bull Depositions 51
11 Presenting Depositions 56
12 Preparing Experts 61
13 Summary Judgments 66
14 Composting Files 71
15 Working the File 77

Part Three Direct Examination   83

16 Organizing Direct Examination 85
17 The Paragraph Method 90
18 Emphasis on Direct 94
19 Leading Questions 99
20 Freeze 104
21 Helping the Witness 108

Part Four Cross-Examination   115

22	The Language of Cross-Examination	117
23	The Weasel Factor	123
24	The Runaway	128
25	Pressure Points	133
26	Careful Cross-Examination	138
27	An Impeachment Checklist	143
28	Prior Inconsistent Statements	149
29	Phantom Impeachment	154
30	Refreshing Recollection	159
31	Nine Ways to Cross-Examine an Expert	164
32	Blind Cross-Examination	169
33	Liar!	175
34	Breaking the Rules of Cross	181

Part Five Foundations and Objections   187

35	The Evidence Steps	189
36	Laying Foundations	194
37	Authentication	199
38	The Objection List	204
39	When to Object	210
40	The Art of Objecting	215
41	Making the Record	220

Part Six Evidence   225

42	The Real Witness	227
43	It's Not for Its Truth	231
44	The Big Four	236
45	Hidden Rules	241
46	The Best Evidence	246
47	Limited Admissibility	251
48	Using the Wrong Deposition	256
49	Understanding Character Evidence	261
50	The Catch in Character Evidence	266
51	One Size Fits All	271
52	Publishing the Exhibit	276

Part Seven Lawyers, Judges, and Ethics   281

53	Talking to Judges	283
54	Judge Trials	288
55	Games Judges Play	293
56	Staying Out of Jail	298

Part Eight Tactics   305

57	Seeing the Facts	307
58	It's Happening Now	312
59	Creating Tension	318
60	Say It Again	323
61	Focus	328
62	Highlighting	332
63	Clutter	338
64	Cover Yourself	343
65	Taking the Blame	348
66	Mootcourtitis	353
67	The Giggle Test	358
68	Rehabilitation	362

Part Nine The Language of Persuasion   369

69	Professionally Speaking	371
70	Reading Out Loud	376
71	Bilingual	380
72	Key Words	385
73	Bad Words	390
74	Hollow Words	396
75	The Real Message	401

Part Ten Final Argument   407

76	Peck	409
77	The Cat and the Mouse	414
78	The Greased Pig	418
79	Jumping to Conclusions	422
80	The Trial of Henry Sweet	426

Parallel Table   431

ACKNOWLEDGMENTS

This is a book for trial lawyers.

Everything in it came from someone else. That kind of massive appropriation of other people's material is called scholarship.

I have tried to acknowledge the people who shared their ideas with me in the text itself, and so will not repeat their names here. But I am grateful for their willingness to talk to me and to let other people in on what they have found successful. In every instance I have gotten more from them than they from me.

Lawyers who try cases are a special breed. They work harder and play harder and care more than any other lawyers I know. They are voracious readers. They not only want to know, they want to understand. And they have a passionate need to communicate their understanding to other people—friends and families, colleagues and acquaintances, judges and juries.

Why this need to explain, to show, to tell, to persuade?

Because it is an essential part of the force that drives them. No matter what you hear about trial lawyers, the truth is they are closet idealists. Every trial lawyer is a dragon-slayer at heart—a Quixote who needs to right wrongs, to fight injustice.

I believe in lawyers—especially those who are willing to risk themselves in pursuit of a worthy cause. Which is why I want to thank them for what they have contributed to this book.

James W. McElhaney
Cleveland, Ohio
January 1995

FOREWORD

This book translates the wisdom of hundreds of trial lawyers through the judgment of a superb advocate to produce in one place a thesaurus of litigation practice in which humor and grace are never far away. Jim McElhaney is well known to the members of the American trial bar for his lectures (performances) on advocacy and for his great works in *Trial Notebook*. The chapters in this new collection live up to our expectations of McElhaney and the book is a matched companion for *Trial Notebook*, which mainly describes trial parts and slices of litigation technique. *McElhaney's Litigation* expands on the subject to include in greater detail and variety all aspects of litigation, and it more nearly exhausts each aspect. Both books include the real and frequently funny vignettes of trials and courtroom incidents that are the McElhaney trademarks. *Litigation* provides an explanation of techniques, strategies, and rationales to complete any particular trial topic under discussion. For example, cross-examination is presented in some seventy-two pages with such chapter headings as "The Runaway," "Pressure Points," "Breaking the Rules of Cross," and "Liar." Who can resist reading with those hooks, and nine additional chapters on cross-examination, to capture the imagination?

So McElhaney has done it again. A delightful and extraordinarily useful collection of the best writings of the best writer of our generation on litigation to join *Trial Notebook*. And if you are a man or a woman of steel, you can resist turning to "Games Judges Play" like "Simon Says" (p. 295) and "ZAP" (p. 296). But I could not resist reading and reading and reading just a little bit more.

Benjamin R. Civiletti

PART ONE

Starting Out

Even though you cannot take the stand and testify on behalf of your client, you are the most important witness in the case. Understanding that is key to everything you do, and is especially important at the start of the trial.

CHAPTER 1
The Guide

CHAPTER 2
The Most Important Witness

CHAPTER 3
Jury Voir Dire

CHAPTER 4
The Risk of Confusion

CHAPTER 5
The Golden Rule

CHAPTER 6
Taking Sides

CHAPTER I

The Guide

After the verdict, a number of jurors went over to Flash Magruder. Several of them asked for his card and said that if they ever needed a lawyer, they would call him. The foreman took even greater pains.

"Mr. Magruder," she said, "you were wonderful. You made excellent arguments. We all agreed that you were the best lawyer. The only thing was, the defense had the stronger case. If you had better facts, we would have decided in your favor." A moment of solace that takes some of the edge off an unhappy defeat?

Certainly. But there is something else at work as well. Whenever the jury compliments the losing lawyer, there is a problem. It means that what he did and how he did it intruded on the case. The jurors were all too aware of how he tried to shape their view of the facts.

It is a problem that can trouble even very good lawyers. When the jury is too taken with the skill of one of the lawyers, it can push the case in the wrong direction.

Avoid Conspicuous Virtuosity

It usually happens when the lawyer concentrates more on persuasive techniques than on the underlying human drama being played out in the trial. It is not the product of any one particular thing that the lawyer says or does, but rather comes from a whole series of acts that reflects how the lawyer approaches the business of trying the case.

Some lawyers over-think their cases, so they have fancy answers for everything. Like a street-corner salesman with a black suitcase on collapsible legs and a roll-down banner, some lawyers seem to set up their displays right in front of the jury. And like the huckster with both forearms covered with $20 "Rolexes," if the jury doesn't seem to like one argument, they are ready to roll up their sleeves to reveal another one that might look more attractive.

The mind-set of the advocate makes a tremendous difference. While positive thinking is important, the belief that you can talk the birds out of the trees or sell ice to Eskimos is the wrong approach. It produces conspicuous courtroom virtuosity—arguments that convince the jury that you are the better lawyer.

You should not care who they think is the better lawyer. You should care who they think has the better case.

Understanding that you do not want to look slick leads some lawyers to do a little creative bumbling—just so they won't look too good. They deliberately drop things or bump into chairs so the jury will think they are "human." It is not a particularly good idea. It certainly never helped Gerald Ford. "Bumbling" may be inconsistent with "slick," but it does not do anything to convince the jury that you have the better case.

Be the Guide

There is another mind-set that is more likely to do the job. You are the guide who knows the territory, the one who can be trusted to steer the jury straight throughout the entire trial.

Does it work? Imagine for a moment: Suddenly you find yourself in the middle of an unknown swamp. You don't know where you are or how you got there. All you know is that somehow you have to find your way out. You have no compass. There are no roads or trails, no signs or maps, no shadows or guiding stars. As you look around, you see two people, each saying there is only one way out. The problem is, each one is pointing in a different direction.

Which one do you follow—the one who has the suitcase with the collapsible legs, who wants to sell you one of the watches on his wrist; or the one who is pointing out landmarks and is helping you understand the terrain?

Thinking of yourself as the guide is an approach that will affect everything you do.

You will want to understand everything in the case

Edward Bennett Williams used to say, "There is no substitute for knowing everything." He was not just talking about taking depositions and going through the motions of formal discovery. Informal discovery—immersing yourself in the business of the case and learning everything you can about it—is the key to understanding what the facts really mean. You do not have to be a pilot to try an aviation case—but it helps. Neither do you have to be a railroad engineer to try a train-crash case. But it is certainly worthwhile spending time riding in the cab of a locomotive and talking to dispatchers and conductors down at the railroad yards. You will learn things you will never even hear about in a deposition.

Look at it this way. You are not Nero Wolfe the detective. No Archie Goodwin is going to bring you all the facts as you sit in your big leather chair. It is not your job to solve the case by sitting and thinking about the facts.

You are the guide—a teacher. You are going to show the way. But before you can do that, you need to learn the territory yourself. And the right way to do that is both literally and figuratively to get out of the office and do your own investigation.

You will become dedicated to making things clear

Legal scholarship—as practiced by judges, teachers, and lawyers—assumes that precision brings clarity and minutiae produce understanding. It is an assumption that is tied to the hope that the law is actually a science, and that legal principles are best discussed as abstractions, with all of the humanity carefully removed.

It is a tradition that concentrates on teaching lawyers to talk to each other. It teaches the language of the law, and then pays no attention to whether we are capable of communicating our ideas to anyone else.

That is not enough. Good trial lawyers speak English as well as law. They are committed to the elegance of simplicity.

You will realize that your legal education did not prepare you to be the professional communicator your work requires you to be. Instead of concentrating on creative hedging, you will become the master of the declarative sentence, the advocate of clear organization, the champion of simple language.

You will care about facts

Facts win cases. Make that even stronger. Facts, not arguments, win cases.

As a general rule, the more intricate and complicated a legal argument is, the less persuasive power it has. And the more you think like a guide, the more you will be convinced that facts are the key to persuasion.

It is hard for young lawyers to believe, but there was a time when law was practiced without the photocopy machine. When you had an important point to make (and did not have time to have it typed into a brief), you sometimes took the books to court. That is what Edward Bennett Williams did one morning in the 1950s.

He was on his way to argue a motion in the federal district court in Washington, D.C. He was walking up the courthouse steps, carrying a pile of books that went all the way up his fully extended arms to his chin, with page markers in every book.

An older lawyer was walking down the stairs and saw Williams with his books. "Young man," he said to Williams, "what you need is a witness."

You will guide the jury through the facts—not through the courthouse

Some lawyers, sensing that they should assume the role of the guide, get sidetracked onto the wrong tour. Instead of taking the jury through the facts, they give them a tour of the law and courthouse procedure.

Depending on the jurisdiction, the jury has probably seen a film or a videotape about their role in the case as well as what they should expect from the lawyers and the judge. Then before you rise to give your opening statement, the judge explains what you are going to do. Why in the world should you explain it a second or a third time—to prove you know what an opening statement is? This is the time to introduce them to the facts, not to take them on the wrong trip.

You will show, not tell

Have I said this before? Well, it is still important. The difference between showing and telling is the key to the work of the guide.

Showing means making your points with facts, not with arguments. Lawyers who look for clever characterizations do not understand. Characterization is the enemy of persuasion.

Showing means letting the witness testify on direct examination instead of telling her what to say with leading questions.

Showing means helping expert witnesses become teachers whose job it is to explain, rather than advocates whose job it is to argue.

Showing means making the case come alive with demonstrative evidence so the judge and the jury can see for themselves what happened.

You will never mislead the judge or the jury

A guide worth following is someone you can trust. If the judge and the jury feel they cannot believe what you say or rely on your word, they will not pick you as their guide. They will find their own way out of the swamp.

CHAPTER 2

The Most Important Witness

Beth Golden was representing the plaintiff in a product liability case and asked Angus to help her get ready for trial. They spent hours on the law, the theory of the case, evaluating the witnesses, and planning direct and cross-examinations.

"Who are you going to call first?" Angus asked Beth.

"My product design expert," Beth said. "Liability comes first, and everything hinges on him. If the jury goes with my expert, I've got a winner. He's the most important witness in my case."

Angus smiled. "Well, one out of three isn't bad," he said.

"One out of three," Beth said, "what are you talking about?"

"The three things you told me," said Angus. "I agree with one of them. You said if the jury goes with your expert, you've got a winner. I agree with that—although I would put it the other way around. I would say if you've got a winner, the jury will go with your expert.

"But you also said liability comes first, and that's not necessarily true—especially in this case. Maybe you should start with damages so the jury will want you to win and want to believe your expert.

"And then you said that your expert is the most important witness in your case. That's where I really disagree. He's not your most important witness—you are."

"Angus," said Beth, "this is not like you. You don't expect me to go around playing these little trial tricks—trying to sneak in facts without a real witness, or bend the edge of the rule that says you cannot state your personal belief in the justice of your cause."

"You're right," said Angus. "Not only are those kinds of tricks improper, they're needless. Look what your presence says to the jury without your saying a word:

- I have studied the facts and understand what this dispute is all about. You can trust me to steer you straight.
- I have carefully screened the witnesses. I will only call those who will tell you the truth.
- I know the law that governs this case. Justice is on our side."

"The lawyer says all that just by being there?" asked Beth.

"Right," said Angus. "And there is more:

- If I introduce evidence, it is because it is important.
- If I leave something out, it is because it is not important.
- And if I attack a witness, it is because he is not telling the truth."

"Angus," said Beth, "all that sounds impressive. But there is no way the jury is sitting there, thinking all those great thoughts before anything happens. They are caught up in what is to them a strange situation, trying to sort out just what is going on, and trying to understand what the case is all about. They are not philosophizing about the role of the lawyers."

"You're right," said Angus. "They don't think those things at the beginning. And they never think of some of them—at least not consciously. But all of them have an influence on how they look at you and what they think of your case."

Angus is right. Thinking of yourself as a witness—the most important witness in the case—has a profound effect on what you do and how you do it.

The Lawyer "Testifies"

To begin with, there are four times in the trial when you really do act like a witness—you talk directly to the judge and jury, without having to go through anyone else.

First is jury voir dire

To be sure, you are sizing them up, and they know that. But they are also sizing you up—getting a sense of what kind of person you are, how you put your ideas, whether you get right to the point or only dance around it. And they get glimpses of other things, too, such as how much you believe in your case, and how you feel about your client, the judge, and the other lawyer.

Second is the opening statement

By now the jury has a little notion of what the case is all about, but this is their first opportunity to hear a coherent statement of the case. Whatever label you put on it, you are the first real witness for your cause. What are they to think of you? Do you know the facts, or do you hedge around with vague legalisms such as "my client" and "the day in question"? Do you tell the story with simple words, or do you lard it with purple prose in an obvious tug at their heartstrings?

Third is cross-examination

And now you may be tempted to disagree with the idea that you are really a witness. This time it is the witness on the stand who is doing the testifying, isn't it?

Not if you do it right. It is a mistake to think of destructive cross-examination as an opportunity for the witness to give more information. Cross-examination is your opportunity to tell your side of the witness's story. And you should do all the talking. When it is done well, all the witness can do is reluctantly agree that what you say is true.

Fourth is final argument

Here, in a sense, is when the jurors are most critical. What kind of witness are you now that they know the case? Are you careful and reasonable? Or are you asking them to speculate on little bits and pieces, and jump to unjustified conclusions? Do you unreasonably reject obvious points that you ought to give away? Worse, are there some points you do not seem to understand?

The Jury Is Watching

Once you start thinking of yourself as the most important witness in the case, you will realize that you are never really off the stand. The jury is watching you all the time, seeing how you react to adverse testimony, noticing whether you are courteous to the court and the other lawyer. Just as you do not like witnesses who constantly quibble or try to score points with nasty comments, jurors do not like lawyers who act that way, either.

By the way, have you noticed recently how many lawyers say they are *on trial* instead of being *in trial*? When a lawyer tells me he is *on trial* I am always tempted to say I did not even know he had been indicted—but then I think how you really are on trial when you are in trial.

The truth is, everything you do during the course of the trial conveys an impression of how you view your case. Take witness choice, for example. When you put a weak witness on the stand, it tends to cut the case down to his level. Lawsuits, like chains, tend to be no stronger than the weakest link.

Why?

Because the very act of putting the witness on the stand implies that you are vouching for his credibility. In fact, that used to be the law, and you could not impeach your own witness unless you were both surprised and hurt by his testimony. The common law had the same instinctive reaction that jurors do today.

Whom do the jurors blame for a bad witness? Listen closely to the comments clerks and bailiffs hear every day. "I wonder where she got that guy?" "Where did he dig him up?" "Can't he find someone better than that?" Then comes direct examination, and the lawyer is still responsible for what happens. A confused, rambling examination suggests a disorganized understanding of the facts. Not only does it fail to tell the story effectively, a poor direct examination is the living picture of a guide who cannot be trusted to lead the jury through the thicket of facts in the case.

Dwelling at length on small points is a little different. At first it suggests that the seemingly insignificant detail will become important later on.

Why? Just putting it in the case says it is worth the jury's while.

So the first time the fact that took so long to explain turns out to be meaningless, the jury feels cheated. When it happens again, they wonder whether the lawyer is trying to kick sand in their faces or is just inept.

The witness theory also explains why clever arguments and plays on words can be self-defeating. They focus on your ability as a speaker rather than the underlying facts.

Don't Hide Anything

It also shows why you need to think carefully about whether you should bring out harmful information yourself or leave it to the other side.

It is an article of faith with a lot of lawyers that you ought to steal the other side's thunder when you can. But recently Robert Klonoff and Paul Colby have challenged that idea in their book *Sponsorship Strategy* (Michie 1990). They suggest that putting on unfavorable evidence gives it additional weight and ought to be avoided except in exceptional circumstances.

On the other hand, some lawyers, such as Tom Demetrio of Chicago, feel that the credibility that comes with open candor is the most important attribute any lawyer can have.

Whatever your starting point, the witness theory sharpens the issue. What will the jury think when your opponent finally brings out the harmful information? Nothing devastates your credibility more than looking like you deliberately created a false impression.

There is one last question.

How do you feel about your case?

You already know it is improper to tell the jury you believe in the justice of your cause, or to personally vouch for the credibility of any witness.

But the law does not say you cannot believe in your case; it only says you cannot say so. And if you do not believe in the justice of your cause, you cannot fake it. It will show in everything you do or say.

As R. Eugene Pincham said at a National Institute for Trial Advocacy Program, "You can't sell what you don't buy."

CHAPTER 3

Jury Voir Dire

One of those "litigation reformers" was out at the law school, and Judge Wallop was sitting next to me in the audience.

"Lawyers are losing the right to conduct jury voir dire because they are abusing it," the reformer said. "Instead of making a rational inquiry to determine whether a prospective juror should sit in judgment on a case, lawyers are perverting voir dire by trying to use it to persuade juries before the case even starts."

Judge Wallop looked right at the speaker.

"Humbug!" said the judge.

The speaker rose to the bait. "Oh, sir," he said, "surely you are not questioning whether lawyers are losing the right to conduct jury voir dire?"

"Nope," said Judge Wallop, "I'm not. It's happening."

"And surely," said the speaker, "you are not arguing that lawyers do not use voir dire to try to sell their cases even before the opening statements are made?"

"No question," said Judge Wallop. "Some lawyers try to use voir dire to persuade. But that is not why they are losing it. Any judge worth his or her salt can put a stop to improper argumentation during jury selection. Easiest thing in the world.

"Lawyers are losing voir dire," the judge continued, "because of something that is much harder to deal with. It is because they waste huge amounts of time and make it incredibly boring. Just this morning a lawyer in my courtroom took nearly three hours to accomplish almost nothing. He had a list of sixty-two questions that he put to every potential juror—one at a time. Juror after juror, he asked the identical questions.

"He did the whole thing from his counsel table," said Wallop. "He never got out of his seat. He never smiled. He never looked at any of the jurors, except to glance at them at the start of one of his sixty-two–question series. He took detailed notes on all of their answers—as if they were laboratory animals responding to some experimental stimulus—and he never looked up from his notes.

"I would have welcomed a little persuasion, just for variation," concluded Judge Wallop.

I am afraid the judge is right. We have already lost voir dire in most federal district courts, and it is on its way out in a number of state courts. And the real reason is not abuse—that is easy to fix. The real reason is most of us are wasting our time. It is a shame, because it is an important part of the trial, and there is a lot you can accomplish on voir dire, even in a short time.

The Jury Picks a Lawyer

First is establishing a relationship with the jury. Tom Demetrio of Chicago says that while the lawyers are sizing up the jurors, the jurors are sizing up the lawyers. "Voir dire is just as much lawyer selection as it is jury selection," says Demetrio. "Jurors use voir dire to pick a lawyer they can trust to explain what the case is all about. Stop this silliness of trying to argue the case before the jury even knows what it is.

"Be open and friendly," says Demetrio. "Smile; be polite, considerate. Burying your head in your notes is unforgivable. If you aren't likable, they aren't going to select you. Most cases are won on the facts and the law, but it is possible to lose a case in voir dire."

Steve Miller of Cleveland says most lawyers talk too much in voir dire. "Get the jury talking," says Miller. "There are only two times during the trial that the jury gets to talk. First in on voir dire—if you let them. Second is in their verdict.

"You can learn a tremendous amount about the jury if you just listen," says Miller. "No rule says you have to ask jurors only leading questions. There is no requirement that you preach to the jury—as a lot of prosecutors do—and try to get 'commitments' from them about particular points."

There is a lot to what Miller says. Jurors are quick to figure out the "judicially correct" answers to the questions you put to one juror after another. They can tell what is the right thing to say. The result is that you get very little useful information out of a tightly structured judicial catechism.

Let Them Talk

On the other hand, open-ended questions that encourage the jurors to talk are more likely to let you know how they really feel. And the more you know about the jury, the better. Later on it will be invaluable in deciding which witnesses to emphasize and how to present your arguments.

But a lot of lawyers are uncomfortable about jurors expressing their opinions very openly. They are afraid that one of the jurors may blurt out something outrageous that will poison the whole panel. Does that make sense?

Suppose you represent a chiropractor in a malpractice case. Should you keep a lid on things so that no juror feels encouraged to let fly at chiropractors?

A juror's hate for chiropractors will do a lot more harm in the deliberation room (where you can't hear what he or she says) than it will during voir dire. So unless the juror is talking specifically about your client, there is no problem letting everyone hear what the juror has to say.

Jean Maclean Snyder of Chicago says that how you talk about the case at the very beginning makes a big difference. You have to tell the jury a little about it just so you can ask intelligent questions.

"Voir dire is an opportunity to give the jurors the essence of what your case is all about without too many details," says Snyder. "You can make a clear statement about the underlying rights and wrongs that will shape their attitude about the entire case."

Snyder's case of the rock star in Comiskey Park is a good example. The plaintiff attended a rock concert and claimed he got hurt when the crowd got unruly. He said the crowd's conduct was all the rock star's fault.

The rock star's behavior was more than a little bit salty, and his language had been outrageous. Snyder didn't try to hide any of her client's warts in voir dire. He was a rowdy man whose behavior was not likely to appeal to anyone on the jury—and yet that behavior wasn't really the cause of anything that had happened to the plaintiff.

When Snyder talked to some of the potential jurors who had been excused from the case, she was impressed at how strong their opinions were concerning what had happened and their feeling that it was not the defendant's fault.

Damage Assessment

Eric Kennedy of Cleveland likes to use voir dire to warm up the jury on damages. In a big case, Kennedy says, it is important to let the jury know early on that he may suggest, for example, a verdict in excess of $2 million.

"They also need to realize that they have to work within an imperfect system," says Kennedy, "particularly in a death case. In a perfect system, Mrs. Williams might be able to get back what was taken from her. But nothing will replace Mr. Williams, and she is not going to get him back. It is an imperfect system, so the only thing that they can award is money damages.

"Understanding that the system is imperfect takes the blame off the client for seeking money damages and places it on the legal system, because there is no other way for righting a wrong."

Kennedy also uses voir dire to discuss whether the jury will hesitate to return a large verdict—say, $3 million—even though they are sure it is the right amount. "The very first car I ever bought," Kennedy tells the jury, "was a used car that cost $1,000. I knew it was worth that much because I had it appraised by a mechanic I trusted, and because the blue books said it was worth at least that much. But when it came time to sign the check for the car, it was hard to do because $1,000 was so much money to me. It was hard for me to even think about that much money."

Who Do You Want?

Bill Pannill of Houston focuses on the kind of juror you want in the case. Say you represent the plaintiff in a difficult business case that involves expert witnesses who are going to testify about metallurgy. Do you look for the successful, sophisticated person who can easily grasp these difficult issues?

"No," says Pannill. "You are for the plaintiff—the one who has been stepped on. So look for the traditional plaintiff's juror. The blue-collar worker. The person with an injury. The one who knows what it's like to be stepped on. It is the lawyer's job to explain metallurgy—it is the jury's job to appreciate the underlying situation."

"Right," says Jo Ann Harris of New York, who both prosecutes and defends. "If you are prosecuting a bank case, you don't even want a bank teller on the panel. He will impose his own ideas on the rest of the jury. If he disagrees with one of your witnesses on even a minor point, it can twist the whole case in knots."

Finally, Steve Miller says listen to your clients when making your peremptory challenges. They have cultural insights about what is going on that you may not be able to appreciate.

Miller has a great example. He was representing Harley-Davidson, the motorcycle manufacturer. One of the potential jurors was a motorcyclist who owned a small Honda motorcycle. Years ago he had taken a tour through the Harley-Davidson plant in Milwaukee.

What should Miller do, keep him or strike him? After all, he owned a competing motorcycle. "Keep him," said Miller's client, the head of Harley-Davidson's customer service. "He's a 'wannabe.' He'd love to ride a Harley, but he can't afford one yet."

It was the right call.

CHAPTER 4

The Risk of Confusion

Two young lawyers assigned to work up a case for trial were arguing about which side had the burden of proof, and what that meant. They were in the middle of the "burden of producing evidence" and the "risk of non-persuasion" when they were interrupted by a senior partner who had been listening in.

"I don't want to minimize your discussion," he said, "but you're missing the most important point. Of course you can have a directed verdict against you if you fail to prove part of your case. That's what happens when you do not carry the 'burden of producing evidence.' And at the end of the trial the judge has to instruct the jury who must convince them. That is the significance of the 'risk of non-persuasion.'

"But unless you have an unusual case or are badly inattentive, you are not likely to run afoul of either burden. The important question is, who bears the 'risk of confusion'?"

"The what?" they asked.

Small wonder they were not familiar with the term. It is not current among judges and scholars. And yet the senior partner was right. The "risk of confusion" is probably the most important burden in a trial.

The phrase was used by Kevin McMunigal of Case Western Reserve University School of Law when he was an assistant United States attorney in San Francisco. It means what it says. Even though you have introduced all the necessary evidence and have met all the formal burdens, you will not prevail if you have not overcome the risk of confusion. It is a practical burden imposed by all fact-finders. They instinctively put the obligation of making things clear on one of the parties.

The one who bears the risk of confusion is usually the one who has the obligation to persuade—but not always. In criminal cases, the risk of confusion is usually on the prosecution. In white-collar and economic crimes in particular, it can be very difficult to get a jury to convict unless they clearly understand what was done and why it is a crime. But in some products liability cases, the risk of confusion may rest with the defendant, no matter who has the burden of proof.

It can be on either party in any kind of case, switching back and forth from one point to another. So the important task is not to create a theory that will tell you when you are likely to bear the risk of confusion. Your sense of human nature should tell you that. The important job is to figure out how to meet it.

The first step is to understand that we are all operating under the disadvantage of a legal education.

Am I serious?

Absolutely. Think back to your first year of law school. You had to learn how to make sense out of what were usually very poorly written decisions. Then you had to defend your understanding in a "Socratic" dialogue that actually amounted to a stream of ideas bandied back and forth. While the intention may have been to force you to learn how to create order out of confusion, you actually learned how to mimic your mentors. You learned how to write like a judge and how to talk like a law professor. Law school does many wonderful things, but it usually does not create good communicators.

When you try a case, you are a teacher. You teach the facts that support your position and try to expose the fallacies of your opponent's case. If you are going to do it well, you must be more effective than most of your teachers were. You will have to be clear.

Clarity—the antidote to the poison of confusion—has no single formula. It is too often neglected by judges and lawyers, even scorned by some academics. While you will never completely master it, clarity is worth pursuing your entire life. There are some things you can do that will help you overcome the risk of confusion in trying cases.

Use simple words

It took a long time to learn to talk like a lawyer, and it seemed worth the effort. But now that you are trying cases, you need to talk like a real person again.

How can you do that?

It is said that Dr. Karl Menninger of the Menninger Clinic would insist that the psychiatric residents in the clinic discuss their cases, even the most difficult and arcane, in simple street language. It is not a bad idea. If you are talking to a jury, it is essential. There is only one way you can be sure you will do it well—practice all the time.

Stop using words like *prior* and *subsequent* when you can use *before* and *after*. Do not use *observe* when *see* or *hear* would work as well. There is no reason to ask a witness, "Would you indicate, please, what next, if anything, you did on that occasion?" when you can ask, "Would you tell us what you did next?"

Plain language is especially important in opening statements and closing arguments, when the jury's attention is on you, and not on a witness, the judge, or the other lawyer. If you fear that you need fancy language to impress the jury, take heart. Winston Churchill inspired all of England with simple words, like "blood, toil, tears, and sweat."

Make one point at a time

The superior mind is the one that sees the interrelationships among different ideas. That is why some very intelligent people are hard to follow. They constantly interrupt one point with another. If you have that tendency, fight it off. You must learn the self-discipline that will let you talk about one point at a time.

The risk of confusion works with the judge as well as the jury. The fascinating thing is that some lawyers who are always prepared when they talk to a jury do not think about what they are going to say to the judge. Stuck without a plan, they simply argue. Soon one point interrupts another, and none of them is persuasive.

Organize your material effectively

How do you do that? There are hundreds of different ways to organize the simplest case. Obviously, there is no one right way to do it. But there are some things that will help. It should be easy to understand. It should be interesting. It should have a central focus.

The theme, the focal point around which everything turns, is worth a lot of attention. Without it, the case starts to fragment into little pieces your opponent can scatter in final argument. As Fred Bartlit of Chicago says, "Every time I have a single focal point in a case, I win. Every time I do a fabulous job on ten different issues, I lose."

When you present your material, let your organization show. Everyone has heard about the U.S. Army system of education: "Tell them what you are going to tell them, tell them, and tell them you told them." Does it work?

Without a doubt. For example, if you write the outline of your opening statement or final argument on the blackboard, or check off the points that you put on a screen with an overhead projector, you are letting your organization show. It can do a lot of good.

First, the judge and jury can see where you have been and where you are going. Second, you are a more effective teacher, since you are using a demonstrative aid that lets the fact-finder both see and hear. Third, you seem more credible, because you are literally showing that you know (and have thought about) what you are saying.

Think about credibility for a moment. The side that undertakes to make things clear has a special advantage. Being the explainer creates a sense of reliability that extends to your witnesses and your arguments.

Eliminate unnecessary details

Spend your time where it counts. For some reason, the smaller the detail, the longer it takes to tell about it. Fight that tendency, because the jury will assume that the longer you spend on a point, the more important it is.

If you are going to teach the facts of your case, you need to think about good teaching materials. Of course, you will use real and demonstrative evidence—photographs, maps, drawings, even the things themselves. They lend an air of reality to the entire business.

But there is another kind of exhibit, one which Deanne Siemer calls "testimony aids" in her book *Tangible Evidence* (Law and Business, 1984). Testimony aids are things that did not play any part in the transaction itself—a checklist with the key points of an expert's opinion, or a chart that shows how the defendant created a screen of dummy corporations. They are teaching materials, and their only claim to admissibility is that they help the jury understand what the witnesses say.

Just how much of this sort of thing do you use? Be sparing. One picture may be worth a thousand words, but that does not mean one thousand pictures are worth one million words.

Finally, you have probably already guessed that if you have the risk of confusion, it is a real mistake to tell the jury you think the case is complicated. That kind of negative message can cause real trouble.

Only the one who is sure his opponent bears the risk of confusion should try to muddy the water. Even then there are dangers. It gives the opponent the chance to talk about the squid on final argument—who scuttles backward when attacked and hides behind a cloud of ink.

CHAPTER 5

The Golden Rule

There is a lawyer in a small town near Cleveland who does it all the time. On final argument he stands in front of the jury, a pair of shoes in his hands. He holds them out for the jury to see and says:

"These are the defendant's shoes; size 10 brown oxfords, worn at the heels. They say Thom McAn inside, but they belong to Michael Williamson. You are about to be asked to judge Mike Williamson, and I want you to understand it would be wrong to do that, wrong to judge a man, wrong to evaluate him and what he has done, unless you had first stood in his shoes."

If you are tempted to try that yourself, do not. Not that it is ineffective. On the contrary. The lawyer who uses it is said to get good results. The trouble is, an argument that asks the jurors to put themselves in the place of one of the parties is improper. Perversely, lawyers call it the Golden Rule, for the very reason that it forbids you to ask the jurors to do unto the parties as they would have done unto themselves.

Why would we have such a rule?

It is thought that asking the jury to stand in the shoes of one of the parties is an appeal to passion and prejudice. And sometimes it is—especially in personal injury cases. *Smith v. Merzolf*, 375 N.E.2d 995 (Ill. 1978).

But notice something crucial. The law only says that it is improper to *ask* the jury to put themselves in the shoes of one of the parties. It does not say they cannot do it on their own. And it does not say you cannot try your case so they instinctively stand in his shoes. It only says you cannot ask them to do it.

It should not surprise you that one of the most persuasive ways to present your case is so the jury identifies with your client and looks at all of the evidence from his point of view.

The question is, how do you do that without running afoul of the rule?

Use Every Part of the Trial

Every part of the trial gives some opportunity to create a sense of identification with your client. Start with the opening statement. One way to heighten the sense of identification is to put the jury right in the center of the action. Even though it is the dead of winter, you begin by saying:

"Ladies and gentlemen, it is July 23, 1993. You are standing on the corner of 5th and Wells, in downtown Milwaukee. It is 2:30 in the afternoon. There, on the southeast corner, is an elderly gentlemen with a cane, waiting for the light to turn green. Off to his left, a block away, a black and silver Chevrolet Corvette is approaching the intersection of 5th and Wells at a high rate of speed.

"You are about to see what will happen when those two forces—the man and the car—come together. Let me tell you about the man who is about to step off the curb. . . ."

No one said, "That could have been you, about to be hit by a speeding car." Merely taking the jury to the scene, together with foreshadowing the injury that is about to take place, creates a subtle sense of identification. Donald H. Beskind of Durham, North Carolina, says there is a natural tendency for juries to identify with the plaintiff. So unless there is something about the plaintiff or what he did that alienates the jury, subtle identification is all that is required.

It is harder to create identification with the defendant. Take the opposite side of a similar case. Suppose we are representing a truck driver who struck a young woman as she was walking across the street. She was thrown into the air by the impact and fractured her skull when she hit the pavement. She was knocked unconscious and never came to. She died three days later.

Our defense is that the woman was not in the crosswalk when she crossed the street, and that she was negligent in failing to look out for traffic. The plaintiff's lawyer has just made a marvelous opening statement, and we have to do what we can for the defendant. If you think we have the short end of this case, you have good instincts. Yet maybe we can do something more than just keep the damages down.

The Human Defense

"Ladies and gentlemen, this is a case about something that everyone who has ever driven a car has feared. This is a case about jaywalking—and the young man that fate chose to be behind the wheel when a pedestrian darted into his path, right in the middle of the street.

"A few minutes ago, the judge told you that the official name of this case is Walker versus the Mason Construction Company, Incorporated. I would like you to meet the Mason Construction Company, Incorporated. Ken, would you stand up, please?

"Ladies and gentlemen, this is Ken Mason. He and his wife, Helen, *are* the Mason Construction Company. Kenneth and Helen Mason have a business that builds porches and patios and does simple home repairs. Ken is the carpenter and bricklayer. Helen handles the books, answers the phone, and helps schedule the work. Thank you, Ken, you can sit down now."

There are some things worth noticing about this introduction to the opening statement. The beginning draws on what really is a common fear. We all know that we could be driving when someone darts out in front of us, and there would be nothing we could do. Even if we knew it was not our fault, it would haunt us. The introduction evokes those feelings without saying, "it could have been you behind the wheel of that car." And fate choosing the defendant suggests it was not Ken Mason's fault, but that he, too, was a victim.

Second, introducing the defendant is a gracious thing to do, the kind of good manners we sometimes forget in the courtroom. It is a human act, like calling him by his real name rather than "the defendant," or even worse, "my client."

Humanizing a large corporation is an even bigger challenge, but it can be done. Take the time to select the personal representative for the company yourself. Do not just accept whomever they send. Often the company will assign someone who may do a fine job representing the company to a buyer or a group of stockholders, but who will create an awful impression before a jury.

There is no formula for who to pick, but the chances are someone with hands-on experience with what is in issue and who knows how to communicate with ordinary people will be a good choice.

Details on Direct

Now turn to direct examination. Of course you will go through the events, but you also will have your party tell the jury something about himself. Pick the details carefully. Take the elderly man crossing the street in Milwaukee as an example.

Suppose he is a retired machinist who used to be a union steward in the shop where he worked. Should he tell the jury about that? In an industrial town like Milwaukee, with a large number of skilled workers who are union members, the risk is not very great. Still, the chances are you would like to know who is actually on the jury before you decide.

Go a little further. Should he tell the jury why he was downtown in the first place? On the one hand, suppose he was going to a department store to return some merchandise he was unhappy with. While some jurors might identify with that, there is the danger that others might think he is a cranky old geezer who is prone to complain.

On the other hand, suppose he was looking for a model airplane (like the kind he used to make when he was a boy) to buy for his grandson's birthday. What are the risks? There could be some juror on the panel who harbors a pathological hatred for all grandparents, but the chances of that are slim. There is some good reason why both lemonade and oatmeal manufacturers use grandfathers to advertise their products.

One of the most creative ways to make the jury identify with your client is with an analogy in final argument. Bill Colson, of Miami, tells about seeing a young boy who is buried up to his head in sand.

He is one of a group that was taking turns being buried by the others. But he becomes absolutely terrified when his friends pretend to desert him there in the sand. He feels—just for a few seconds—what it is like to be a quadriplegic.

So does the jury.

CHAPTER 6

Taking Sides

Dick Mudger was starting to raise his voice. "Juries do not always make up their minds in the opening statements," he said. "Give people a little credit. Juries are perfectly capable of reserving judgment until they have heard all the evidence. And in my experience, they do it all the time."

Flash Magruder raised his voice, too. "If you would ever read instead of just pontificating, you would know that 80 percent of jurors make up their minds during opening statement."

Dick Mudger (the insurance defense lawyer), Flash Magruder (the plaintiff's lawyer), and Angus were out at the law school to give a demonstration in opening statements to my class in trial tactics, and we were having a "discussion" on the importance of openings before they did the demonstration.

Angus joined in. "It is an article of faith with a lot of lawyers—particularly the plaintiff's bar—that jurors decide the case during the openings. And for years, speakers and writers have been citing Kalven and Zeisel, *The American Jury* (1966), as saying that 80 percent of all jurors make up their minds during the opening—before they have heard any evidence.

"But the problem with that theory," said Angus, "is that there is nothing like that in *The American Jury*—as Hans Zeisel pointed out in a recent *Ligation Journal*.

"Which doesn't mean that opening statements aren't important," said Angus, "or that some jurors don't make up their minds at the start of the case. But it does mean that it's not in *The American Jury*."

"Which sounds like you're not taking a position about jurors making up their minds at the start," I said. "You're not saying they do, and you're not saying they don't."

Angus smiled. "Tell you what," he said. "Let's do a little experiment after the demonstration."

The demonstration turned out to be exciting—not because it was perfect, but because both Mudger and Magruder are good lawyers, and because they cared about the case.

After the demonstration, Angus said, "Jimmy, before your critique, let me do my little experiment.

"All right," said Angus, talking to the class, "let me see the hands of those who have made up their minds in this case."

No hands went up.

Mudger started gloating. "See," he said to Magruder. "I told you."

Angus continued asking questions. "Why not? Why didn't anybody decide the case?"

"Too close to call," said one student.

"We were concentrating on the lawyers' techniques," said the next student.

"Too soon," said another. "We haven't heard the facts."

"Maybe we're just self-conscious," said the next. "I mean we were talking about when jurors made up their minds, and maybe that made us too self-aware."

"Maybe this is the same point," said another, "but we knew we weren't supposed to decide until the end of the case."

"Excellent," said Angus. "Now I'm going to ask another question—totally different. I am not interested in how you would vote in jury deliberations. Instead, I want to know who you want to win this case. Who are you pulling for? Let's go right down the line." Then Angus pointed to each of the students, and everyone responded.

"Plaintiff" . . . "Plaintiff" . . . "Plaintiff" . . . "Defendant" . . . "Plaintiff" . . . "Definitely Defendant" . . . "Plaintiff" . . . "Unsure" . . . "Plaintiff" . . . "Defendant" . . . "Plaintiff."

"Okay," said Angus. "Seven for the plaintiff, three for the defense, and one uncertain. Not one of you had 'decided' the case after the opening statements, but 10 out of 11 knew who you wanted to win. No one was ready to vote, but almost all of you had taken sides.

"That," said Angus, "is what jurors do during the opening statements. They take sides—just like when you're watching an interesting football game. Even if you have no reason to favor either side, there is a good chance you will be rooting for one team or the other by the kickoff."

The Right Point of View

There is a lot to be said for the way Angus looks at it. Jurors typically do not "decide" the case on the basis of the opening statements. But pulling for one side or another—even just slightly—gives them a point of view. From then on, they tend to look at everything that happens from the vantage point of the side they favor.

The juror's "point of view" is one of the most powerful persuasive forces in the case. When you look at the evidence from one side of the case, it tends to support that side. And that feeling tends to strengthen your commitment—which in turn makes their evidence seem even stronger.

That process should make you ask the basic question: Why do jurors take sides? What makes them pull for the plaintiff or the defendant?

There is an old industry, which recently has turned its attention to litigation, that undertakes to deal with the question. As in Robert Lewis Taylor's *Journey to Matecumbe* (1961), there are a lot of medicine men floating down the Mississippi of Litigation, selling bottles of "Litigation Elixir" to lawyers who thirst for ways to make jurors want them to win. They offer everything from magic words for opening statements and final arguments to zip code analysis for jury voir dire. And if you have ever priced this medicine, you already know it is easy to spend $20,000 or $30,000 for just a few bottles.

Before you spend your money on Swamp Water, there is a commonsense approach you ought to think about.

Injustice Stirs Us to Action

The idea comes from Edmond Nathaniel Cahn's *The Sense of Injustice* (1949). Justice, said Cahn, does not move people to passion. Appeals to justice simply produce thoughtful contemplation. And "contemplation," said Cahn, "bakes no loaves." Perhaps that is because justice is an ideal, and not a concept capable of precise definition. But if justice is not something you can put your finger on, Cahn said, injustice is. Everyone has suffered injustice. And injustice has the power to stir people's blood.

Cahn was on to something. The most powerful call is not to do right, but to undo wrong. It is not justice that motivates judges and juries—it is injustice, and the power to right a wrong.

Looking at the trial from the standpoint of righting a wrong shows you what to do with the opening statement.

- Comprehension is important. The jury will see no injustice if they cannot understand the facts.
- Identification is important. It is easier to understand an injustice if you can see it happening to yourself.
- Credibility is important. There will be no sense of injustice if the jury cannot trust what they hear.
- Impact is important. You want people to remember what you said, and you want the facts to make a vivid picture in their minds.

But none of those things makes the jury want you to win. The motivation for taking sides is the sense of injustice.

That means your opening statement should be a simple statement of the case that paints the picture of the wrong that has brought you to court.

Taking sides shows why it is so important not to exaggerate, misstate evidence, or promise facts you cannot deliver. If a juror takes your side believing something you said that turns out to be untrue, he will feel betrayed. What might not matter so much if jurors really waited until the end to decide makes a big difference when they feel they were lured into an emotional commitment based on a false representation.

"If You Break It, You Pay"

You must not think that the tendency to take sides means that everything must be done in the beginning of the case. Sometimes the sense of injustice is stronger in final argument than anywhere else in the trial. A good example is the defense argument, "If you break it, you pay." Here it is in a products liability case:

"You know how lawn mowers are supposed to work. They are supposed to spin. They are supposed to cut. And you are not supposed to reach underneath a mower when it is still spinning. Which is just what the plaintiff did.

"But if you feel that this Martin Lawn Mower was defective—and that's what hurt the plaintiff—then it's our fault, and we pay. It's that simple. If you break it, you pay. That's the American way. You are responsible for what you do.

"You see it in all kinds of stores and in every turnpike gift shop: 'Lovely to Look at, a Pleasure to Hold; But if it is Broken, then it is Sold.'

"If you break it, you pay.

"There is another side to that: If you didn't break it, you don't pay. It is wrong—it is an injustice—to pay for something you didn't do.

"When I was a boy growing up in Milwaukee, my father was a traveling salesman. Worked for a corrugated box company, selling corrugated boxes all throughout Illinois and as far down as St. Louis. That meant he left town on Monday morning before my brother, John, and I got up for school. And he wasn't home until Friday evening.

"That put my mother in charge of discipline. And she was not really a disciplinarian. So when I did something really wrong, she would say, 'Wait 'til your father comes home, young man.'

"And my father never wanted to make his homecoming part of punishment so we never got spanked on Friday night.

"That came on Saturday—with the flat side of a big wooden clothesbrush.

"But of all the things I did and all the punishments I got, there is only one that I still remember. It's when my brother moved the car. He was 12 and I was 9, and he started up the car—the green Pontiac—and moved it down the drive. Then he drove it back and tried to put it where it had been. But he didn't quite succeed—and I got the blame.

"I got the punishment for what my brother did, and my father wouldn't listen to me when I tried to tell him I didn't do it. And the injustice of that still gives me a lump in my throat even though Dad has been gone for more than five years.

"Don't you be part of injustice like that."

PART TWO

Trial Preparation

The point is not to make it complex; anyone can do that. The idea is to follow a simple, well-organized system that will actually help get cases ready for trial.

CHAPTER 7
The Discovery Plan

CHAPTER 8
Preparing Witnesses for Depositions

CHAPTER 9
Focusing the Deposition

CHAPTER 10
Pit-Bull Depositions

CHAPTER 11
Presenting Depositions

CHAPTER 12
Preparing Experts

CHAPTER 13
Summary Judgments

CHAPTER 14
Composting Files

CHAPTER 15
Working the File

CHAPTER 7

The Discovery Plan

Angus was not just annoyed with his new associate—he was hot. "Michael," he said, "trial preparation doesn't mean taking depositions pointlessly. Before you do anything else, read the file and start working on your discovery plan."

"Discovery plan?" asked Michael.

"Discovery plan," said Angus. "If you just start taking depositions when you get a new case, you will be like all those other 'litigators' who spend years in mindless discovery. They fight for weeks over the answers to hundreds of useless interrogatories. They take depositions of people who would never testify if the case went to trial. They order up warehouses full of irrelevant documents and have their junior associates spend months sifting through them.

"Some of them do it on purpose," Angus continued. "They are trying to crush their opponents with paper, bore them to death with tedium. But unfortunately, even more lawyers flail around in pretrial preparation simply because they never have a discovery plan."

The truth is, Angus is right. But the problem is, how do you put together a discovery plan that will make trial preparation efficient? The stumbling block seems obvious. Every case is different. How can a plan devised for a products liability case have anything to do with an antitrust case or a corporate contract dispute?

The answer is simple. Start with a basic framework and modify it to fit the case you are working on. And one of the best basic frameworks is the one hammered out by David M. Malone of Washington, D.C., and the late Robert F. Hanley of Chicago. Of course, it does not fit every case. It is designed with business litigation in mind. But it makes a lot of sense, and it is remarkably flexible.

Before we start, time out for an important warning. This is a discovery plan. And discovery is not the best way to learn the basic facts of a case. In fact, it is probably the most expensive and inefficient way to gather information. The way to learn the facts is through informal investigation—calling and digging and writing and talking—but that is a topic for another day.

Look at it this way. If you prepare a case properly, you actually should not discover very much information with discovery. You should know most of it already. Instead, use discovery to nail down information so it will shift and change as little as possible before trial.

And now, back to the framework. It has four basic steps:

- Written interrogatories.
- Document production.
- Depositions.
- Requests for admissions.

The order can be changed, but at a price. It is an important part of the plan. And pay particular attention to what each step is designed to do. If you use discovery this way, it will minimize any potential troubles.

Use written interrogatories to find out whose depositions you want to take and where the documents you want are located.

Use documents for information, to refine the list of depositions you will take, and to help figure out what questions to ask.

Use depositions to nail down what you have learned, to get some important admissions, and to evaluate the witnesses.

Use requests for admissions to fill in any gaps.

Each of these steps is worth some discussion.

Interrogatories

Start with written interrogatories. They can give you names, numbers, addresses, titles, locations, and other bits of solid information. Use what you learn to help decide which depositions to take.

A lot of lawyers disagree. They hate interrogatories and hate even more the idea of starting discovery with a list of questions that will obviously be answered by the lawyers for the other side. They say interrogatories are an invitation to a long fight about what is a proper question, how many questions you can ask, and whether an answer is responsive to the question. "Interrogatories?" they say. "No thanks."

And if you write long interrogatories—or a lot of interrogatories—or interrogatories that call for interpretational opinions or admissions, the lawyers who hate them are right. They will cause you nothing but trouble.

But Timothy C. Klenk is a champion of using interrogatories the right way. He explained his system in "Using and Abusing Interrogatories," *Litigation*, Vol. 11, No. 2, page 25 (Winter 1985).

Klenk's list of uses for interrogatories includes identifying documents, people who know the facts, financial information such as income and sales, and information about experts. (You should use depositions for information *from* experts.)

Klenk warns against using interrogatories for information about conversations, questions that call for explanations, complex transactions or events, or identifying trial witnesses.

Documents

The second step is the request for documents. And now for a genuinely valuable tip. Except in the simplest cases, do not combine a request for the production of documents with a deposition.

Why not?

Because you will waste time and let important points go by. As David Malone says, thousands of depositions are conducted each year in which the questioner starts with a pile of documents on the left side of the table and is finished when all the documents have been moved to the right side of the table. The documents have been produced on the very morning of the deposition. The questioner often only verifies that the document was written by the deponent, is on the deponent's letterhead, and is a record kept in the ordinary course of business. Page by page, the painful progression proceeds.

Don't do it that way. Get the documents well before the deposition so you will have time to study them first.

And another point. Except in unusual cases, it is silly to use deposition time to verify that the records and other documents came from the opponent and qualify as business records. As Malone says, if you frame your request properly, your opponent will automatically be admitting that the documents are authentic business records just by producing them. Later you can ask your opponent for any other documents that pertain to the case.

Depositions

After you have gone over the documents, you are ready to begin taking depositions.

Where do you start, the top or the bottom—with the chief executive or the people on the assembly line? Bob Hanley liked to start at the top, and to stop as soon as he had everything he needed. If you start at the bottom, the logic of your choice forces you to keep on taking depositions until you reach the top.

But there are times when you want to start at the bottom. If you represent the plaintiff in a medical malpractice case, for example, you may want to save the doctor's deposition for last—after all the nurses, interns, and residents have had a chance to point to the center of the circle (and away from themselves) to explain what went wrong.

Requests for Admissions

Next come requests for admissions under Rule 36 of the Federal Rules of Civil Procedure. Admissions are wonderfully flexible:

- Requests are served on parties, not witnesses.
- They can be served any time, and there is no limit on the number of requests you can make.
- If they are not denied, they are admitted.
- If the other party denies the request, you can recover the cost of proving it under Rule 37(c) of the Federal Rules of Civil Procedure.
- While admissions are for the present case only, they are not merely admissible, but binding on the party who makes them.

Everyone knows that requests for admissions are a good way to clear away clutter from a case. Say you want to introduce a letter sent to your opponent by someone who is not a party or a witness in the case. You can use a request for an admission to establish its authenticity.

But it does not stop there.

Requests for admissions can fill some holes left in your case.

When you go back through discovery, the question you forgot in an early deposition will loom larger than before. Places where the defendant's witness weaseled will suddenly jump out at you. Something you learn in the last deposition makes you want to go back and talk to one of the first witnesses again.

But instead of taking supplementary depositions, you can use requests for admissions. You know how you want those additional questions answered. Answer them that way in your request for admissions.

There are good reasons for making your requests simple and direct.

First, you want to give your opponent as little leeway as possible. The more argumentative your request, the more opportunity he has to escape. Just to make sure he does not, couple your request for admissions with interrogatories he must answer if he denies the request. Then if the request is denied, at least you have some idea of what you need and where to look.

Second, every time you write a request for an admission, you are not writing just for your opponent—you are writing also for the jury, and you want them to understand what your opponent has admitted.

CHAPTER 8

Preparing Witnesses for Depositions

"Okay, Angus," said Mike. "What do you think?"

"It depends," said Angus. "What should I be—honest or supportive?"

"Was it that bad?" asked Mike.

"Pretty bad," said Angus.

Mike Pirelli had hung up his own shingle when he graduated from law school last year and has been starting to build a litigation practice. When one of Mike's first cases started to heat up, Mike asked Angus if he would sit in on the plaintiff's deposition and help him evaluate how everything went.

"The truth is," said Angus, "your plaintiff didn't make a very good impression."

"You're right," said Mike. "But don't worry. He'll come around. You'll see. By the time of trial, he's going to be great."

"Mike," said Angus, "I don't know how to tell you this, but, chances are, that deposition you just participated in was the trial."

"What are you talking about?" asked Mike.

"Come on," said Angus. "You know the statistics—90 to 95 percent of all cases settle before trial. So in more than nine cases out of ten, the depositions are the only trial you get.

"And the settlements reflect the impressions that you and your clients—and your other witnesses—make in the depositions."

"Look, Angus," said Pirelli, "I know that prepping witnesses for depositions is important, but it takes time, and . . . ."

"Wait a second," said Angus. "Did you ever have your wisdom teeth pulled?"

"What does that have to do with prepping witnesses for depositions?" asked Mike.

"Easy," said Angus. "Did the dentist give you a handout that explained what to expect, how to take care of yourself, and what to do if something went wrong?"

"Yeah," said Mike, "so what?"

"If the dentist can do it," said Angus, "so can you."

"Wait a minute," said Mike. "I may have not done the world's best prep job on Emil Sanders, but it sure was better than giving him some dumb handout and then hoping he would get everything right."

"Giving a witness a handout is not a substitute for live witness preparation," said Angus. "It's part of it. The handout—the letter—is useful in all kinds of ways.

"First, make it short and simple. One of the advantages of a simple checklist is that your witness can read it over several times before the deposition—and some people really need the repeated exposure. Use the handout to explain what the deposition is all about, to help put the witness at ease, to set the ground rules for how to answer questions, to explain what to do if you object, and even make some suggestions for how to dress.

"But the handout is just the start. Next, you should make your own videotaped instructions. You can do it yourself in your own office, if you want. You can have a friend or an associate serve as the person you talk to, so you won't have to look right in the camera lens the whole time. Besides, having someone to talk to makes the whole thing go easier.

"If you aren't ready for a videotape yet, you can make a simple audiotape. Work from notes, rather than reading a prepared script, and it will sound a lot more natural. Even if you make the videotape, you should make an audiotape as well. Some clients—especially business people—would rather listen to a tape in a car than be a captive who is forced to sit in front of a video screen. And maybe some of your clients do not read well—if at all. You want to do something for them.

"You will do a better job with the basics if you put it in writing and on tape, rather than making it something that you do every time from rote memory."

"Well, maybe," said Mike, "but I still think the personal touch is better."

"Of course," said Angus, "which is why you are going to such lengths to get the basics nailed down. This way you can concentrate on the real problems in the case. Because after the witness reads the handout or watches the videotape, you are ready to go to work."

The Conference

"Now comes the conference with the witness. And there are a number of points you need to make—which are based on an outline developed by Steven M. Kaufmann from Denver and the late Bob Hanley from Chicago," said Angus.

1. Tell the truth. No fudging, no shading, no exceptions to the rule.
2. Explain why the witness's testimony is important to your case. What may seem obvious to you may be a revelation to the witness, and will almost always have a good effect. Witnesses who feel they have an important role in the case tend to take it seriously and want to do well in the deposition.
3. Go over what the witness should expect. Touch on some of the points from the handout, and see how well they have sunk in. If the witness seems exceptionally concerned, you may want to actually go to the deposition room a day or so early, to get the feel of things (as you might take a witness to the courtroom before trial).
4. Tell the witness this is serious business. No chit-chat or small talk with the other lawyer. No sarcasm, no facetious remarks. The cold record will not get the joke, so wait until the deposition is over. Remember: No matter what, no matter how nice he or she may seem, the other lawyer is not your friend.
5. Listen to the question. Take your time. Make sure you understand before you answer. If there is any part of it you do not understand, say so.
6. Answer the question—not some other question—just the question you are asked. Say no more than is necessary to answer the question. Do not volunteer extra information or explanations.
7. Do not guess. If you don't know the answer, say so. If you don't remember, say so. It is your job to give the answers you know—not to speculate about the answer you don't know.
8. You are the witness—not the lawyer. Do not argue with the lawyer for the other side. Do not object. Do not try to sell the case. Just answer the questions.
9. Watch out for questions that paraphrase your answers. Lots of times the lawyer may take your ideas and put them in other words—changing your meaning in ways that you might not catch

at the time. If the lawyer asks if his paraphrasing is accurate, you are entitled to say that you would rather stand on your answer and stick with the way you put it.

10. Beware of absolutes. Watch out for questions that use the words *always* and *never*.

11. Admit preparing for the deposition. There is nothing wrong in going over your testimony in advance. It would be irresponsible not to.

12. If I object—listen. If you are talking when I object, stop talking at once. An objection is a danger signal. It says you should put your mouth in low gear and your brain in high gear.

13. If you discover you have made a mistake in your testimony, let me know before the deposition is over. We will fix it. Mistakes do not correct themselves.

14. If you get tired, ask for a break. If you need to go to the bathroom or to get a cup of coffee, say so. And if you start to get argumentative or talkative—which is natural when you get tired— I will ask for a break myself.

Practice Depositions

"Next," said Angus, "comes the practice deposition."

"Oh, come on," said Pirelli, "practice deposition?"

"Absolutely," said Angus. "You don't learn to ski by listening to a lecture. It just gives some initial pointers. Same thing with testifying at a deposition.

"The best way to do it is with another lawyer asking the questions so you can do the objecting. You don't have to go through the whole thing—but with a key witness, it's not a bad idea.

"Another thing," said Angus. "Consider videotaping the practice deposition. It's no great expense. You can have a secretary or a paralegal run the camera, or if you don't have anybody, you can just put the camcorder on a tripod, set it on wide angle, and let it run.

"It's something Bob Hanley used to do with great results. The videotape does a far better job than you will in critiquing the witness. It picks up on hedging and evading better than written notes, and it remembers unfortunate little mannerisms so that all you have to do is mention them and the tape will do the rest. You don't even have to replay the whole thing. Usually fifteen or twenty minutes is enough."

"But wait a minute," said Pirelli. "Won't the video be discoverable?"

"Not very often," said Angus. "It's protected by the attorney-client privilege as well as by the attorney work product rule. Hanley never had to turn over a videotape, but he always kept them until after the case was settled or the trial was over, lest anyone accuse him of destroying any evidence.

"One last point," said Angus. "There is another benefit when your witnesses are well-prepared. Your stock goes up, too."

CHAPTER 9

Focusing the Deposition

Most of us learned how to take depositions by watching other lawyers do it. The problem is, we were usually watching lawyers who did not have a clear plan of what they wanted to accomplish or how to go about doing it.

The result is that thousands of lawyers mimic the mediocrity of their mentors. So what ought to be interesting episodes of witness examination often turn into endless days (and sometimes weeks) of unstructured interrogation.

Most depositions lack focus. And if you try telling that to a lawyer who is taking one, you are likely to get the standard response—"this is discovery"—as if that were an excuse for a rambling, disjointed examination that seems to take forever.

But there are some simple principles that make the whole business more productive and (believe it or not) more fun.

- Know as many of the pertinent facts as you can before you take the deposition.

    Maybe it would have been better if the drafters of the Federal Rules of Civil Procedure had never said that depositions were part of discovery in the first place, because the truth is, a deposition is a poor way to learn what a case is all about. You will save a lot of time, money, and pain if you learn as much as you can through formal discovery before you start putting witnesses under oath.

- Go to the scene. Study the pictures. Read the correspondence. Talk to your clients. Do everything you can to get educated before you start formal discovery.

    When you do start, do not begin with depositions unless you must. Start with written interrogatories to get names, addresses, telephone numbers, product names, and production dates—"hard" data—information no one can argue about. This is the kind of information that will help you decide which witnesses you want to depose and which documents you want to request.

    But don't use interrogatories as a substitute for depositions. When you use interrogatories to ask about conversations or other "soft" information, you are asking for a discovery war that will add months or years to the life of the case.
- Next, get the documents. Study them to sharpen your understanding of the case and to decide which witnesses you are going to depose and what you are going to ask them.
- Learn as much as you can about the witness before you take the deposition. You need to know something about the person you will be talking to before you walk into the deposition room; it will affect everything you do. One of the easiest ways to miss something big is to go to the deposition cold.
- Know what kind of deposition you are going to take.

As far as the rules are concerned, a deposition is a deposition. But as far as you are concerned, every one is different, and what you do depends on what you want to accomplish.

1. Testing the witness and the lawyers

Nearly every deposition involves evaluating the witness. You want to know how she holds up under fire. Does she have a short temper? Is she likely to lose her cool in the stress of a trial? How credible does she seem? Does she make the facts seem simple and clear, or fuzzy and complex? Is she the kind of person the jury is likely to identify with?

This is essential information. These are the kinds of questions that are answered by your personal observation, not by reading the cold transcript.

While you are testing and evaluating the witness (and her lawyer), the other side is testing and evaluating you. Wanting to see how witnesses and lawyers respond is one reason why some litigants refuse to even discuss settlement until all the parties and the principal witnesses have been deposed.

2. Getting information

No matter how much you do before the deposition, there are always some facts you will not know until you ask the questions at the deposition.

How do you ask those questions? Not by leading or browbeating the witness.

Ask open-ended questions that invite explanations. Ask the witness to help you understand the facts. Of course it takes time before this will produce results. After all the predeposition preparation the witness went through, it may take twenty minutes or half an hour before he is relaxed enough so you can ask him important questions. And if there is any need for getting tough with the witness, do it later—after you have your information.

Through all of this, keep your mind on the record. As Steve Miller of Cleveland says, "The only usable product of the deposition is the transcript. What seems so powerfully implicit in the deposition room goes away unless you make it explicit on the record. Lawyers who brag about surgically rearranging a witness in a deposition are usually disappointed when they read the transcript."

3. Building your case

When you are learning the facts, you ask open-ended questions and encourage the witness to talk. It's different when you know the facts and want to nail them down. Then *you* do the talking—very carefully—so the witness must agree with what you say. You break the story into simple facts and put them to the witness one at a time. Systematically, you take away his weasel words. You need persistence and strength of character to do this well, but it can be worth the effort.

Building your case is something you should usually do at the end of the deposition, not at the start. If you begin with a stiff cross-examination of the witness, you will have a hard time getting him to respond to open-ended questions later on. Why should he relax and open up when he knows that you are his enemy?

4. Testing your theory

When you take the deposition of the other side's expert, your first job is usually to find out what the witness is going to say at trial. You want to figure out your opponent's theory of the case as well as find its weak spots and contradictions, if you can.

But some lawyers like to do more. They want to get double-duty out of the other side's expert by using him as a testing ground for their own theory of the case. It can be a helpful thing to do. Approached carefully, you can get a feeling for how much respect the opposing expert has for the ideas that underpin your case.

But as David Malone of Washington, D.C., points out, there can be a serious cost. Using the deposition to test your theory of the case necessarily involves educating your opponent about your basic trial strategy. And even if the expert cannot shoot your case down now, you can count on his doing a better job by the time of trial.

5. Boxing the witness

It is the stuff nightmares are made of. You are cross-examining the opponent's expert:

> Q. But doctor, you didn't say anything about the possibility of peritonitis in your deposition, did you?
> A. That's because you didn't ask.

There it is. The hole you leave unplugged turns out to be the most attractive escape hatch for the witness. That is why containment, or boxing in the witness, is one of the most important deposition techniques.

Boxing in the witness is a two-step process. The first step is to measure the contents; the second is to build the box around it.

Measuring the contents—learning what the witness does and doesn't know—involves more than just asking open-ended questions. It means asking follow-up questions, exploring what the witness hasn't said as well as what he has said. It is one of the reasons why writing out your questions in advance almost guarantees disaster—it tends to cut off follow-up questions.

And there is more. Jean Maclean Snyder of Chicago says, "A deposition is one time when you can ask a witness 'why?' In fact, it's a great question in a deposition. If there is a good answer to 'why?' you might as well know what it is. And if there isn't a good answer, then that can devastate the other side at trial."

The next step is building the box. The point is to establish that the witness has gone to the end of the line on every inquiry—that there is nothing left. And the technique is never to do this by implication, but always to make it explicit. "Is there anything else that happened?" "Are there any other theories for analyzing why this loss took place?" "What facts would change your opinion?" "Was anyone else there?" "Do you remember anything else about this transaction?" "Is there anything that would refresh your recollection?"

6. Evidence

As far as the rules of procedure are concerned, you can use any deposition to prove facts at trial. But using the typical deposition is one of the worst possible ways to prove anything. The questions are usually long, rambling, and unartfully put. The answers often miss the point, or are fragmented, hesitant, and incomplete. Sometimes they are deliberately misleading. When you are busy digging to find what is there, you are not thinking about how to explain it all to someone else.

That is why an "evidence deposition" should be done entirely differently from a "discovery deposition."

Now the entire examination is outlined and practiced before you get there, just as in a trial. Keep it short, simple, and interesting. Use exhibits that can be put in front of the jury when the deposition is read (or shown) during the trial. Think of the court reporter as the jury. Is everything the jury needs to know in the record?

Understanding the importance of evidence depositions explains why periodically you need to do some of that in discovery depositions. Every now and then in any deposition you should take a mental step backward to assess where you are and what has been established. Pick out the essential points, clean them off with the brush of plain English, and restate them to the witness so that he agrees you've got them all straight. Those are the points you will pull out if you have to use the discovery deposition at trial.

7. Settlement

Some depositions are taken not because any facts are in doubt, but because they can encourage settlement. There are chief executives of some companies who know their hands were in the cookie jar, but who are convinced that no mere lawyer could ever pin it on them. There are doctors who know they botched the operation but who insist that any settlement would be morally wrong. And sometimes your own clients cling to unrealistic expectations until they have had to answer questions under oath. A settlement deposition can be useful.

But be careful. Do not use settlement as an excuse for browbeating and bullyragging the witness, the other party, or his lawyer.

And if the other side does it to you, don't put up with it. Randi McGinn of Albuquerque has a simple way to deal with abuse from lawyers: three strikes and they're out. The first time the other lawyer raises her voice or stands over the witness, McGinn objects and reads into the record what the other lawyer did. The second time it happens, McGinn records it again and warns the opposition that it won't be tolerated anymore.

The third time, McGinn and her witness walk out, headed for the court to get an order.

It works.

CHAPTER 10

Pit-Bull Depositions

Beth Golden is one of those quiet, competent professionals whom everyone seems to respect. So when she came storming into the Brief Bag the other evening, it was clear that something was wrong. She walked over to where Angus and I were seated, and dropped her law-firm issued, catalog-size, leather briefcase on the floor with a clunk.

"Angus," she said, "something has got to be done."

"Undoubtedly," said Angus, "but about what?"

"About the outrageous way some lawyers conduct themselves at depositions," Beth said. "It used to be that only a few lawyers from big, out-of-town firms and a handful of local loonies would interrupt every question, coach their witnesses with improper objections, answer questions for the witnesses, and instruct their witnesses not to answer perfectly proper questions.

"But not anymore," she continued. "Now everybody is doing it, and it's got to stop. What's more, the whole business is made worse by the judges. They're reluctant to give rulings even when it's obvious that the other side is totally out of line.

"Angus," she said, "it's about time you and some of the so-called heavy hitters around here did something about it."

"Beth," said Angus, "you are absolutely right. The situation is appalling. And I am trying to do something about it. But I'm afraid that what I'm doing will help the practice of law about as much as a bumper sticker helps a whale."

"The problem is nationwide," Angus said. "And it is not limited to depositions. It runs throughout pretrial practice. Discovery has become like the trench battles of World War I—an unending war of attrition."

"Well, if that's the case," said Beth, "why don't these people come to their senses and stop it?"

"Some lawyers do it," said Angus, "because they are able to make it pay. And until clients become educated enough to know that these so-called 'litigators' are not real trial lawyers and that discovery abuse keeps the meter running, the problem will continue.

"Other lawyers do it because it actually helps their clients. They have found that hardball pretrial practice makes some opponents fold up and go away.

"One way or another, a lot of lawyers use abusive pretrial tactics because they think those tactics work."

"Angus," said Beth, "you've made it worse. When I came in, I was just mad. Now I'm depressed."

"That's no help," said Angus. "Whether or not you can solve the problem, at least you can learn how to deal with it."

I could tell Angus was about to give one of his famous performances, so I got out my pencil. Here are my notes.

The Test

The situation is classic. You are taking the deposition of an expert witness. Because he is your witness and you arranged the deposition, it is being held in your office. Opposing counsel is late, and when he gets there, he sweeps into the room and starts to take over. First, he tries to rearrange where everyone—including the witness and the court reporter—is sitting. Then he instructs your secretary to switch all his calls into the deposition room. Next he complains that it is too hot (or too cold) and starts to readjust the thermostat and maybe opens or closes the curtains and blinds. Then he sits down and pulls out a big cigar.

What is happening?

You are being tested. Whether or not your opponent knows what he is doing (and he usually does), he is attempting to see how far you can be pushed.

There are lots of ways to flunk the test. One way is to try to ignore what is going on. Another is to lose your cool and blow up.

The way to pass the test is to put a stop to it. "Bill," you say, "you're too good a lawyer to play games like this. Let's get down to work." Then if he persists, you can tell him, "Bill, when we're in your house, we'll do it your way, but you're in my house now, so we're going to do it my way."

The Wedge

There are two things to know about a lawyer who tries to coach a deposition witness through his objections or who even tries to answer the questions himself.

First, what he is doing is wrong. Everyone knows that witnesses need to be prepared to testify, but that should be done before the deposition.

Second, the lawyer is coaching the witness because he is afraid of what the witness might say. That means he has not adequately prepared the witness for the deposition. It also means he is afraid you are getting close to something that might help your case or hurt his.

Understanding why your opponent is coaching the witness helps you deal with the problem. Every time he does it, you should call him on it. Make an objection for the record. If it gets bad enough, you can even get the judge to order him to stop.

But there are probably better things to do than run to the judge when a lawyer coaches a witness during a deposition. One of them is to drive a wedge between the lawyer and the witness.

The idea comes from Patricia Hynes of New York City. Here is how it works. The usual objection just makes it clear that you are not getting what you want—the witness's testimony. But the wedge focuses on how your opponent is treating the witness.

Some appropriate responses are: "I object. You're not being fair to the witness. You're cutting him off before he has a chance to finish." Or, "Objection. Give the witness a chance to tell his story." Then say to the witness, "Have you finished what you were going to say?" Or, "Is there something you would like to add?"

Keep it up as long as your opponent keeps coaching the witness. The witness has a story and wants to tell it—which is exactly what your opponent is afraid of.

You May Answer

When opposing counsel objects, too many lawyers think they either have to withdraw the question or argue about it.

Not so.

The objection does not mean you have been caught with your hand in the cookie jar. There is no need to back off and withdraw the question—unless you want to.

First, remember that the information you are seeking does not need to be admissible as evidence in order for you to demand an answer. It only needs to be reasonably calculated to lead to admissible evidence.

Second, note that if an error can be cured at the deposition, the objection must be made or else it is waived. So lots of objections are made at depositions. And because typically the judge isn't present, there has to be a way to deal with the objection later. The only practical solution is to have the court reporter record the objection and then allow the witness to answer the question, unless the answer is privileged. Incidentally, this is exactly what the rules require.

But a surprising number of lawyers—and most witnesses—do not know this. They think that an objection brings the line of questions to a halt.

That is where your knowledge of procedure gives you an advantage. Unless you feel like it, you do not even need to respond.

After the objection, you can simply look at the witness and say, "You may answer the question."

The nice thing is, it works.

Three Strikes

Some lawyers have the notion that they can simply tell a witness not to answer a particular question. You already know that idea is wrong.

Now suppose your opponent suddenly tells the witness not to answer an important question. What do you do—run to the phone and call the judge?

Not yet. First, have your opponent state the reason he has asked the deponent not to answer. Unless there is a good-faith assertion of a privilege, tell the witness, "You may answer the question."

Second, Deanne Seimer of Washington, D.C., has a marvelous technique. Instead of arguing about an objection or an instruction not to answer a question, she says, "Maybe I can get this some other way." Then she rephrases the question. It is amazing how often the other side does not object when the question is put a little differently.

Third, if those tactics don't work, finish making your record. Explain that the witness refuses to answer because of the other lawyer's instruction. This, by the way, is not a legal requirement, and if you forget to do this, all is not lost.

On the other hand, it does make your record more impressive when you go to the judge.

But you will not go to the judge after the first road is blocked. Wait until there are at least three solid, unjustified instructions to the witness not to answer questions before you suspend the deposition.

Say Cheese

There are some attorneys who object to virtually every question during a deposition. This is where staying power really counts, and knowing that the other side is trying to make you mad makes it easier to stay calm.

Even so, there are times when you must ask the judge for help. The trouble is, the written page tends to take a lot of the snarling and barking out of the opponent's objections. What is offensive in the deposition room can look almost reasonable on paper.

One cure is the video deposition. Fifteen minutes of pain played back for the judge is more persuasive than a whole book of rules.

CHAPTER 11

Presenting Depositions

By all rights it should have been fascinating. One of the nation's most respected military leaders was actually suing a major television network for defamation. A federal district court in New York was trying the war in Vietnam in *Westmoreland v. CBS*.

Judge Pierre Leval, aware that the issues were complex, had imposed thoughtful time limits on each side to keep the case from getting out of hand. And in an innovative move, he gave the lawyers the right to make periodic statements to the jury to help them keep track of the proceedings.

Yet none of it was a match for one of the most potent forces of boredom in modern civilization. Whenever the lawyers announced another deposition—whether it was written or on videotape—there would be audible groans from the jury.

The lesson of the *Westmoreland* case is simple. All other things being equal, live witnesses are more interesting than depositions. But there is another lesson that is not quite so simple. All other things are not equal.

The question is how to present depositions. The place to begin is the changing role of deposition practice in modern litigation.

Depositions started as a way to preserve the testimony of witnesses who would not be able to attend trial—because they were gravely ill, dying, or outside the subpoena power of the court. But then the dream of academics and law reformers for surprise-free trials changed the way we think about depositions. Instead of only being able to take depositions on court order for good cause, the rules were changed so that virtually any witness's deposition could be taken as a matter of right. What began as a way of preserving testimony became a means of gathering information.

The result is that most depositions are not aimed at the courtroom, but at painstakingly gathering facts or laboriously containing a witness. We have moved so far from the original purpose of depositions that when one is actually used in court, we are likely to make a bad job of it.

Meanwhile, it has become easier to get depositions admitted in evidence. At one time a deposition was admissible as a substitute for live testimony only when the witness was actually unavailable. But the practice in most courts (whatever the words of the rule) is becoming convenience instead of necessity, especially with expert witnesses.

That means you often can choose whether to present a deposition instead of a live witness. And despite the *Westmoreland* case, there are times when a deposition is a better choice.

Unattractive Witnesses

Unfortunately, some people make a better impression on paper than they do in person. Serious problems with language, demeanor, or appearance may be reason enough to prefer a deposition over live testimony. It is what Tom Heffernan of Cleveland calls the "Ode to a Grecian Urn" theory of witness credibility: "Beauty is truth; truth, beauty."

Heffernan says that attractive, well-dressed, and groomed people are more likely to be believed than are unattractive people. Once, when Heffernan was taking the deposition of a particularly disagreeable doctor, he was struck by how much better it would be if the witness looked and acted like the court reporter, who was pleasant and attractive. That gave him an idea.

At trial he used the deposition instead of the doctor, saying, "Your Honor, at this time plaintiff would like to introduce the deposition of Dr. Marcia Williams (not her real name), and is asking the very court reporter who wrote down her words to take the witness stand and read her testimony to the jury."

Appearance is not all there is to it. Besides looking for an "affidavit" face, you should choose someone who is a good reader, says Bill Colson of Miami. And reading is an art. Sometimes, Colson warns, good speakers are not good readers. The only way to tell is to practice before trial. In fact, the ability to read aloud is so crucial that some lawyers entrust the job only to professionals, like actors or radio and television announcers.

Virtually everyone agrees that the best way to make a deposition transcript come alive is for you to deliver the questions and let someone else answer from the witness stand. Most judges are happy to cooperate, figuring that what helps keep the jury awake ultimately aids the cause of justice. But one misguided judge in Cleveland did not agree. One of the rules for his courtroom specifically forbade using "voice inflection" in reading deposition—a rule that was literally incapable of being obeyed unless the reading was done by a computer.

Timing is another reason why you might want to use a deposition instead of a live witness. A number of good trial lawyers like to have a deposition on hold in case a star witness is late or they want to move a crucial direct examination to the next morning when the jury is fresh.

Video Depositions

What about video depositions? Ask ten lawyers who have used them, and nine will express disappointment. There are reasons for that. Tom Murray of Sandusky, Ohio, is one of the pioneers of videotaped depositions. Murray says that unless you are careful, the typical video deposition is an hour or two of a talking head on a video screen answering questions from a disembodied voice. What lawyers need to do, says Murray, is realize that video is more than just another recording device.

Once you think about it, his point is simple. We are used to taking depositions with coats off, relaxing in a conference room with a cup of coffee and some notes about the questions we are going to ask. Everything we do is shaped by our knowledge that we are not in front of the judge and jury—that the written transcript is the jury's only impression of the deposition room.

But a video deposition is different. To do it right you must think of the camera as the judge and jury. You would never dream of letting them watch only the head of a live witness while you asked questions from outside the courtroom, so why should you do it that way on video? There are some rules worth following for videotaping depositions.

Prepare the witness

Video depositions are evidence depositions. And even though the law in most jurisdictions does not distinguish between them, evidence depositions are different from discovery depositions. The point of a discovery deposition is to probe, while the point of an evidence deposition is to present evidence to a judge and jury.

If the deposition is going to be interesting, the witness must be prepared as if for trial, because for him, the deposition *is* the trial. That means that instructions to pause and think for a few seconds before answering each question may be fine for written depositions but ruinous to a video presentation. Not surprisingly, one of the best ways to prepare the witness is in your office, with your own video camera and videocassette recorder, so both of you can see what to improve.

Act like you are at trial

This means a lot of things: keep the pace brisk. Ask short questions. Use simple words. Organize the direct examination as if you were telling a story. Be interested in what the witness says. Ask the follow-up questions you think the jury wants asked. Throughout the entire deposition your mind-set should be, "The jury is watching right now."

Use professionals

Under the rules of some states, you can videotape depositions by taking a video camera to a deposition and letting a clerk or a paralegal tape the proceedings as if they were home movies. And that is what they will look like, too. If your budget will permit it, use professionals who have good microphones, mixers to balance the volume of the different microphones, and professional quality cameras. And to get rid of the talking-head problem, use two cameras—one for the questioner and the other for the witness.

Use exhibits

One way to add interest is with demonstrative evidence. The typical way to handle exhibits is to call them deposition exhibits and have each marked for identification. Make sure you lay the proper foundation for the exhibit during the deposition or have a stipulation to its admissibility. Then, when videotaping, have the witness point to a blowup of the exhibit just as if he were in court.

Later, when the jury is watching the deposition in trial, you can have the exhibit placed on a tripod right next to the video screen. It not only adds to the content of the deposition, it gives the jury someplace else to look besides the screen, and it serves as a realistic link to what is going on in the deposition.

Keep it short

Television has taught us to expect highly sophisticated techniques when the screen lights up. No matter how good they are, video depositions do not live up to those expectations. Worse, television has trained us to have a fifteen- or twenty-minute attention span before we are given a commercial break. Maybe this is one reason why no juror has ever complained that a video deposition was too short.

Besides, if you keep it under half an hour, you won't have to serve popcorn.

CHAPTER 12

Preparing Experts

"Wait a minute," said Angus. "Turn off the machine." Angus and Dick Mudger were watching a videotape of Mudger's direct examination of an expert witness.

"The problem is you are trying to fix the wrong thing," said Angus.

"What are you talking about?" said Mudger. "This examination needs work."

"Look," said Angus. "You wanted me to critique the direct examination of your accident reconstruction expert, right?"

"Exactly," said Mudger.

"Because you think if you do a better job of asking questions, his testimony is going to be more effective," said Angus.

"That's the idea," said Mudger.

"Well," said Angus, "you were right in thinking this examination needs work. The truth is it's awful. It's slow, boring, tedious, confusing—like most expert testimony. But the problem is not with your questions. It's in his answers."

"So all I have to do is tell Dr. Carrington what to say and everything will be fine?" asked Mudger.

"No," said Angus. "You don't tell him what to say—not if you want to keep your license to practice. But you certainly need to help him learn how to be an effective witness if you are going to do a proper job of representing your client."

Angus was about to do another one of his lists, so I got my pencil. Here are my notes.

Pick the Right Witness

The problem is most expert witnesses have no idea what their real role is in a trial. Most of them feel their job is to fill the courtroom with erudition, so the very weight of their knowledge will overwhelm the judge and jury into intellectual submission.

Once they set out on that awful quest, everyone who listens to it is in pain. Overly qualified, redundant, highly technical opinions are expressed in jargon that only people who have studied in the field for years could follow.

To the typical juror, the typical expert—whether medical, scientific, or economic—sounds like someone who truly has the gift of tongues.

But that is not an expert's job. An expert is supposed to teach—to explain. And just as good teachers are rare, so are good expert witnesses.

Since it takes great effort to teach an expert to overcome the verbal habits of a professional lifetime, you are usually better off picking the right one to begin with rather than trying to fix the wrong one.

But because master explainers are so hard to find, there are some things you can do to help make the best you can find be a better witness.

Tell the Witness His Real Role

Let the witness know what the real challenge is—to make a difficult subject matter come alive so that the jury actually enjoys his testimony. If the jury thinks of the expert as a teacher—the fundamental symbol of credibility—they are more likely to accept what he has to say.

Have the Witness Educate You

The first job for the witness is to explain everything to you. You have to keep asking questions and demanding answers until you are satisfied. Do not just rely on the witness, either. Read as much additional literature as you have time for; it is not just background information. Learned treatises that support the witness are admissible under Rule 803(18) of the Federal Rules of Evidence.

Cut the Explanation Down to Size

Now that you are immersed in the subject, you are ready to cut the expert's job down to size. Here the rule is virtually absolute: Despite your temptation, you will not put the jury through the same training course you have just finished. They do not need to know all the concepts you have mastered. They do not need to know all the words you have learned. You have learned more than you need to know precisely because you must cut the expert's testimony down to workable dimensions.

The first thing to go should be unnecessary background.

A fingerprint expert has to be ready to explain how every fingerprint is unique, but he does not need to go through the history of fingerprint analysis to demonstrate that the prints on the gun came from the defendant.

But clues, indications, details—points that are signposts to the expert in solving a problem—can be particularly worth keeping. If the expert makes the jury feel the game is afoot and they are participating in finding the solution, he is likely to lead them to the conclusion you want.

What to keep and what to let go are difficult decisions, but your bias should be on the side of exclusion. Most experts are on the witness stand two or three times as long as they should be.

Work on Vocabulary

The biggest single job—but one that is actually fun—is teaching the expert to be bilingual. And the reward is twofold. By the time you are done with the project, you will both be better communicators.

Start by actually making a list of the special words the expert feels he has to use in his testimony that the average juror is not likely to understand. This is one of those jobs that sounds harder than it is. Relax. In less than half an hour you will have gone through most of the key words for the witness's testimony.

And now you need to know what to do with the list.

You will try to get rid of most of the words that are on it.

Help the witness translate most of the terms—90 percent or more—into ordinary English. Then help him figure out how to deal with the handful that actually have to be used in his testimony.

Keep that final list short. A jury can enjoy learning two or three new words if they are worth the trouble and the jury can learn them in context. The worst way to teach the jury a list of new words is the way you hated when you were in grade school—an actual list of words you had to learn to spell and define.

The most important result of vocabulary work will be to make both you and the witness more sensitive to which words actually help communication and which just get in the way.

The effect on the witness will be startling. Instead of "Mr. Krueger suffered a lesion to the left motor cortex of the cerebrum," you will hear "Ed Krueger's head hit the dashboard so hard that the impact literally caused a tear on the side of his brain that has turned into scar tissue." Instead of "this lesion is the focal point for classic Jacksonian seizures," you will hear "this scar in Ed Krueger's brain sends out abnormal brain waves that cause him to have seizures—epileptic fits."

Make It Come Alive

You are not simply helping an explainer teach a class, you are concerned with making memories. No matter how accurate the explanation is, if no one remembers it in the deliberation room, it is not going to do much good.

You want the key points to stand out—to be memorable.

Of course, demonstrative evidence can help, if it makes things simple. A good example is the neurologist from the Cleveland Clinic who brought a real human skull to court to show the jury how the sharp bony edges on the inside of the skull can actually cut into the brain when a strong-enough blow strikes the head.

No one on the jury had even touched a human skull before. And even though it had been prepared for medical-school use with wires and springs to hold it together, everyone knew it was real. The doctor undid two of the springs and took off the top of the skull so you could see inside. One by one the jurors ran their fingers over the sharp edges, just as the doctor had done.

He made his point.

Organize

Unless you have an unusual witness, do not put him in charge of organizing his own testimony. That is something for you to do. You want simple, functional order. The problem with most experts (and nearly *all* academics) is they want to define everything before they use anything. If the witness insists on explaining something before it is needed, the jury will forget about it before the witness gets to using it and they won't care anymore when he gets there.

Let Your Organization Show

Put it on a chalkboard, write it on a flip chart, show it with an overhead projector, have a commercial artist paint it on a panel that gets mounted on a plastic-foam board.

It should be the actual outline of the expert's testimony. And when you examine the witness, follow the outline.

It is worth the trouble for a lot of reasons.

First, it makes it easier to follow the testimony. Like a program at any kind of professional presentation, it tells everyone where you have been and where you are going.

Second, because it makes the expert's testimony both written and oral, the jury retains much more of it than if they had simply heard him speak.

Third, audible and visible organization conveys the message that the expert has really thought this through and is not just shooting from the hip.

Finally, when you take the blowup of this outline to the pretrial conference, it sends an even more important message. It says you are ready for trial.

CHAPTER 13

Summary Judgments

It's been some time since the Supreme Court decided to breathe new life back into motions for summary judgment under Rule 56 of the Federal Rules of Civil Procedure, and I wanted to see how things were going for the people in the trenches.

First I talked to Judge Wallop.

"Summary judgments are easy to deny," said Wallop. "I've never been reversed for turning down a motion for a summary judgment."

"Wait a minute," I said. "Haven't you heard? Summary judgments are back in style."

"Well, maybe you are right, Jimmy, but the trouble is, too many lawyers haven't gotten the message. Most of them still treat summary judgment motions as routine pretrial practice. They grind out piles of paper, never expecting them to be given any real consideration."

"So what do you do?" I asked.

"I hate to disappoint them," said Judge Wallop. "Most of them would be shocked if their motions were granted. So I try to give them about as much attention as I think they deserve. That means I pay a lot of attention to a few of them and not very much to the rest."

"I was going to ask you for some tips on how to win a motion for a summary judgment," I said.

"I don't know if I can do that, but I sure can tell you some ways to lose."

Here is Judge Wallop's list.

Three Ways to Lose a Summary Judgment Motion

1. File the motion on the eve of trial

Summary judgment is a way to avoid trial. In effect it says, There is no way the other side will be able to prove what it claims, so we might as well call off the trial right now.

Sometimes you know right away that you have a strong case for summary judgment. Other times you may not know until you are well into discovery, or even until discovery is finished. But when you wait well past discovery and file a motion for summary judgment right before trial, it looks like it is just a ploy to put things off.

2. Flood the court with paper

Most summary judgment motions are decided on the briefs. If it takes hundreds of pages to point out a hole in the opponent's case, the judge may well figure there must be some material disputed facts somewhere in all those words. Denver U.S. District Judge Jim Carrigan agrees. Carrigan says large law firms often are the worst offenders, filling their briefs with string citations and prolix and redundant argument.

3. Ignore the rules of evidence

The question is not "What do they claim?" but "Can they prove it?" The proper focus is on what will be admissible at trial, and that means you must do your homework. Federal District Judge John M. Manos of Cleveland makes the point with an instructive products liability case:

The plaintiff was badly burned when his pants caught on fire. His expert, a specialist in fires, said the cloth was defective because a hot ash could cause it to go up in flames.

The defendant, on the other hand, had an expert on clothing.

He said the pants were just fine.

Both of the experts put their opinions in affidavits.

The defendant moved for a summary judgment, saying that the plaintiff had the wrong kind of expert, and needed one on clothing, not just fires. The defendant was so confident of his position, he did not even bother to depose the plaintiff's expert witness.

That turned out to be a mistake.

First the judge decided that an expert on fires could testify about burning pants. Then the defense claimed the plaintiff's expert could not have a sufficient basis for his opinion.

That argument had to lose. Rules 703 and 705 of the Federal Rules of Evidence are different from the common law in two important ways. First, the basis for an expert's opinion need not be admissible in evidence if it is reasonably relied on by experts in the field. Second, the basis for the opinion need not be stated in court before the opinion itself is admitted. It is up to the cross-examiner to show the opinion is not based on proper information.

Because the defendant had not taken the expert's deposition, the court had no way to look behind the affidavit to see if the opinion should be excluded.

Next I talked to Dick Mudger, who specializes in insurance defense. Mudger likes to use motions for partial summary judgment to cut a case down to its core.

He says summary judgment motions can be valuable even when they are denied. It works like discovery. When you challenge your opponent's case, you force him to turn over some of his cards.

This technique often works better for the defense than for the plaintiff. When the defense says the plaintiff cannot prove a particular issue, the plaintiff has to introduce admissible evidence to establish those facts or else suffer a summary judgment on that point. (*Celotex Corp. v. Catrett*, 106 S.Ct. 2548 [1986].)

Of course, the plaintiff can move for a summary judgment, too. And when the defendant has the burden of proof on an issue, the plaintiff gets to see the defendant's hand just as the defendant gets to see his.

But when the plaintiff moves for a summary judgment on facts he has the burden of proving, things can be different. The defendant may say that the credibility of the plaintiff's witnesses is at issue. And because impeaching evidence can lose much of its effect once the other side knows what it is, many judges are reluctant to make the defendant turn over these cards before trial.

Educate the Judge?

Mudger also likes to use summary judgment to educate the trial judge on complex issues—even when it is obvious that the motion will be denied.

Mudger gets serious disagreement on this point, especially from judges. Many of them would rather have a straightforward trial brief than background material disguised as a motion.

Look at it this way. You are not likely to pay much attention to arguments that are made in support of an obviously incorrect conclusion.

Next on my list was Flash Magruder, the plaintiff's personal-injury lawyer.

Magruder more often defends against summary judgment motions than makes them, and these days he takes them a lot more seriously than ever before. But just as defense lawyers say there are too many baseless claims, plaintiffs' lawyers say there are too many groundless motions for summary judgment. Magruder says some defense lawyers like to keep the meter running with their motion practice, while others want to show their clients that they are doing something, even if it doesn't work. Still others try to wage a war of attrition with endless motions and briefs.

Magruder worries about multiple defendants who try to sneak out of the case one at a time. So he fights tooth and nail to keep every defendant in the case as long as possible, whether the defendant belongs there or not.

Chicago plaintiff's lawyer Tom Demetrio disagrees with Magruder's approach. "If it develops that a defendant does not belong in one of my cases, I get rid of him long before he files a motion for summary judgment. As a matter of fact, sometimes defendants call me and ask why I dismissed them so early—they were looking forward to taking a few more depositions and staying in the case a little longer."

Demetrio has a good reason for getting rid of defendants who do not belong in a case. "Your credibility with judges and other members of the bar is the most precious thing you have. The judge club is a small group, and word gets around quickly. If they learn that you make motions you do not believe in, it undercuts every argument you make from then on."

The Right Way

Finally I talked with Angus.

Here are his five points, in the order he gave them to me.

1. Never move for summary judgment unless the facts support it

It is easier to get a summary judgment than it used to be, but it is even easier to get in trouble with a frivolous motion.

2. Pinpoint the holes in your opponent's case

A shotgun motion for a summary judgment is about as effective as a general denial. At best it gets ignored.

3. Be careful with your timing

With documentary cases you may want to move for summary judgment before discovery starts.

Depositions and interrogatories undoubtedly will inject the parties' interpretations of those documents into the case. They can make your questions of law look enough like material questions of fact so that the judge will deny the motion.

On the other hand, in nondocumentary cases, an early motion may only serve to educate your opponent. Then he knows what evidence you think is missing and will argue that he should have full discovery to try to establish it. (See Gregory Wallace's thoughtful article, "Summary Judgment Ascending," *Litigation*, Vol. 14, No. 2, p. 6 [1988], for more ideas on when to file the motion.)

4. Know who is going to really decide the motion

Some judges turn a lot of their motion practice over to their clerks. You may prefer to take the case to trial rather than risk having a recent law school graduate form an adverse opinion that could influence the final outcome.

5. Decide if you really want a partial summary judgment before you file the motion

Rule 56 does not require the court to dispose of the whole case. It can eliminate uncontested issues and leave the rest for trial. That is not always an advantage. There are times when eliminating a strong case on liability, for example, will only soften how the jury feels about damages.

CHAPTER 14

Composting Files

Angus was talking to a group of lawyers about trial preparation and case management.

"There are some powerful traditions in the practice of law," he said. "Like talking to clients and laboriously taking longhand notes on 14-inch yellow legal pads. Another tradition is the way most of us treat new cases when they come into the office.

"There is an initial flurry of activity. We do a conflicts check—formal or informal—depending on the size and kind of practice we have. We open files, set up billing routines, put new names and telephone numbers in our files. Then we take the first procedural steps necessary to keep us out of trouble. We file a summons and complaint if we are for the plaintiff, or make our first dilatory move if we are for the defense.

"Then our secretary puts the file in the filing cabinet—or we leave it on top of the desk or a bookcase with other files just like it—and we let it compost for six months or a year."

Everybody started laughing (because it was so painfully true), and Angus went on.

"And we do nothing with the case because we are busy putting out fires that have started in other files—probably from spontaneous combustion—that have been composting even longer."

Then Angus stopped and looked at everybody before going on. "Let me ask you a serious question," he said. (And it turned out to be one that I have been asking lawyers myself.) "How many of you—let me see your hands—send quarterly reports to all of your clients about their cases?"

No hands.

"Okay," said Angus, "how many of you regularly send quarterly reports to *some* of your clients about their cases?"

Out of 150 lawyers, there were two or three hands raised. Even so, I had my doubts, based on whose hands they were. It was the same kind of result I get when I ask those questions.

Angus went on. "No wonder people like that Miller Beer ad that shows 'Lawyer Roping' in the rodeo," he said. "Even when you're on top of your cases, you're not telling your clients what you're doing."

Angus is uncomfortably accurate. Among the adverse attitudes people have about lawyers is the popular idea that we often do very little to justify our fees. It is reflected in the reasons people go to the bar association to lodge complaints. For example, in Wisconsin last year, there were three times as many charges of lawyer neglect as any other kind of complaint.

Wizard of Ozitis

What a strange situation we have. Exactly when there is a glut of lawyers looking for work, big and little clients are turning from their traditional attorneys in disgust and taking their work in-house, and the pipeline of new lawyers coming from law schools is crammed beyond capacity, lawyers can't figure out how to treat their clients right.

Not that we are bad lawyers. On the contrary, most American lawyers are quite competent, thoroughly honest, and work hard for their fees. But we seem to have something like Wizard of Ozitis. Remember when Dorothy discovered the Wizard of Oz behind the curtain? She said, "You're a very bad man!"

And the wizard said, "No, I'm a very good man. I'm just a bad wizard."

That's the way too many of us are. We're very good lawyers. It's just that we're very bad businessmen and businesswomen.

And the simple truth is, a law practice is a business. That takes nothing away from the professionalism that is involved. We just have to understand that a good law practice is also a well-run business. (That, by the way, shows why it is strange that a number of states that have mandatory continuing legal education do not give CLE credit for office practice courses.)

Now suppose you could stay on top of all of the files in your office. Instead of them controlling you, you were controlling them. Then suppose that every ninety days you took stock of where you were in every case, seeing what you had done and what you had yet to do. Then you would write a short letter to every client, telling what had happened to his or her case in the last three months.

Think of how many clients who were disappointed in the other brand of mousetraps who would beat a path to your door.

But wait a minute, you say. Is this remotely realistic? Good intentions run amok? Utopian ravings of a mad dreamer?

Not hardly. In fact, lots of business experts are shocked when they find that this is not what most lawyers do. If those quick oil-change shops can send their customers a postcard every three months telling them it's time for another oil change, then wills and trusts lawyers should be able to send letters to their clients every year or so telling them it's time to review their wills—and litigators ought to be able to keep up with their clients, too.

But it is truly easier to say than do.

The first step is to control the input of cases into your office. Most of us take on too much work. (I happen to know that Angus is guilty of this too, although he won't admit it.)

When your docket is really too full, a number of things happen. First, your evenings and weekends (already strained) go entirely. Then lesser cases start to cause serious trouble as you concentrate on the bigger ones. Your calendar often lists you in two places at once, and you are able to manage only by figuring which one you can cancel at the last minute.

The costs become unacceptable when you find yourself apologizing to the same federal district judge for the third time in a month when you are late for a hearing or a conference.

Steal a page from Bill Barton's book. Barton practices with another lawyer in Newport, Oregon. They specialize in psychological injury litigation and limit the number of cases they will handle at any one time to thirty. The number obviously depends on the kind of work you do. The idea applies to all kinds of practice.

Second, tell your clients what you are going to do and give them an idea of when you are going to do it (in addition to letting them know what it is going to cost). A simple handout listing the steps that a case has to go through before it gets to trial can go a long way toward putting their minds at ease.

Third, organize the way you prepare cases for trial. Spend an hour next Saturday morning listing all the things you normally do to get a case ready. Don't worry about the order at this point. Just brainstorm your typical case preparation, writing down everything you can think of that you usually do. If you have several different kinds of cases that require different kinds of preparation, make a separate list for each case category.

Systematic Discovery

Now put your list aside for a minute and think about formal discovery. Most of us don't have an organized way of approaching discovery. We just dig in and keep doing it until we can't justify doing any more. That, by the way, winds up costing more money and getting less information than you would get if you used a good discovery plan.

Interrogatories

Start with interrogatories. But instead of firing off hundreds of useless questions, ask for facts—solid information that you know you are entitled to. Get names, addresses, telephone numbers, model numbers, production runs—the kind of hard data that the other side must make available to you. Don't ask for opinions, admissions, information about conversations, and other kinds of soft information.

Using interrogatories for soft information only leads to equivocating answers, angry lawyers, and contested hearings on discovery questions. If you use interrogatories the right way, you will ask only a few questions but you will get useful information.

Documents

Next come document requests. The answers to your interrogatories help point you toward the documents you want and the people whose depositions you will take. But before you take any of those depositions, study the answers to the interrogatories and go through the documents. Few things are less productive than a deposition in which you don't know what to ask because you haven't studied the documents.

Depositions

Now you are ready for depositions, and you should have an idea of what you want to pursue with each witness.

Admissions

Finally come requests for admissions. Use them to clean up what is left over. Here's how that works:

No matter how carefully you conduct discovery, by the time you are through taking depositions, you think of some questions you should have asked—but didn't. The court won't let you take a second deposition of any witness except under highly unusual circumstances, so what do you do?

You know the questions you would like to ask, and you know the answers you would like to get. So write out those answers—in English, not in "legalese"—and submit them as requests for admissions. And if your rules will allow, send supplementary interrogatories that the party must answer for each fact it refuses to admit.

Now you are ready to take that four-part discovery plan and work it together with that list of everything else you do for case preparation that you put aside a minute ago.

Spend some time thinking about timing and case strategy, but don't try to solve every problem in advance. You are after a general approach that you can modify when you need to. The point is to make a system that will work for you—not the other way around.

Now you have a master preparation plan for each of your case categories. If you do it right, it should be only one page long—two pages at the most.

What do you do with it?

Set it up as a checklist and put a copy in the front of every trial notebook (or staple a copy to the inside cover of every file if you still don't believe in notebooks) for each case in your office.

Then, as each step is finished, it is checked off—dated and initialed—by you, your secretary, or your paralegal.

Lean back for a second and think about what you've got—a simple case preparation plan that doubles as an instant status report.

Back to the present. Go ahead and dig into your compost heap and pull out a typical file. Read through it and see how long it takes you to get up to speed on where you are in the case—what you've done and what is yet undone. That twenty or thirty minutes you just took is what the preparation checklist—the instant status report—saves you each time you pick up the file.

Now look ahead and see yourself going over the checklists in all of your active files—dictating your quarterly status reports as you go. Each case takes only four or five minutes, and you are on top of everything in the office.

Maybe you can go skiing next week after all.

CHAPTER 15

Working the File

Angus was out at the school again, this time critiquing final arguments for the mock trial team. One of the students, Sandy Cohen, was displaying what is called "an attitude."

"Ms. Cohen," asked Angus, "don't you like your side of the case? I get the impression you don't believe what you're saying."

"I just don't think it's fair," Sandy replied. "With all the other things we have to do to get ready for the competition, it's ridiculous for us to be arguing the side of the case opposite from the one we're going to do in the contest. It's like a total waste of time."

"You mean you're not going to be on the defense?" asked Angus.

"No, I'm doing the plaintiff. Sean is going to be arguing defense," said Sandy. "Which is why it's so stupid for me to argue for the defendant."

Angus smiled. "Well, I'm impressed," he said.

"I thought you didn't like my argument," Sandy responded.

"Your argument is fine," said Angus. "It's your attitude I don't like. But it wasn't so much the argument that impressed me. It was the assignment that you take the other side in one of the practice rounds."

Everybody was quiet. You don't hear as many people taking students on so directly as you used to a few years ago. Maybe students' skins are just thinner, or maybe it's the big tuitions they're paying these days. Anyway, I was pleased when Sandy asked why arguing the other side was a good idea.

"There are lots of good reasons," explained Angus, "but insight is the most important one. Seeing the other side's strengths helps you understand your weaknesses. And one of the best ways to evaluate their case is to practice giving their opening statement or final argument.

"In fact," Angus said, "arguing the other side is not only a valuable way to prepare your case, it's one of those things that in practice actually helps settle cases."

You can just hear yourself interrupting. "Wait a minute," you say. "I understand the value of seeing the other side's strengths and weaknesses. As a result, you'll probably do better at trial. But how does it help settlement?"

The idea comes from Herbert J. Stern of Roseland, New Jersey, author of *Trying Cases to Win* (Wiley Law 1991). "The hardest thing," says Stern, "is seeing the other side's case. We usually have no trouble believing in our clients' cases. On the contrary. Invariably we get too emotionally involved in our side. We become biased. We become partial. We become like our clients and can see only one side."

Lawyers who can see only one side, says Stern, wind up being polarized, making arguments that juries can't accept. Worse, they don't advise their clients about the weaknesses in their own cases. That means both lawyer and client may find it impossible to make the kinds of accommodations necessary to reach a reasonable settlement.

There is an art to working the file so that it pays off, not only in trial preparation but also in increased settlement value.

It starts with who the lawyers are. As Miriam Kass of Houston, Texas, notes, "Some superstars can say, 'We will settle this case for $12 million—period,' and that becomes the value of the case. The vast majority of us are not in a position to do this."

Kass is right. And just as there are some superstars whose very appearance in the case multiplies its worth, there are also some superclunks who let air out of the case just by taking part in it. There was, for example, a lawyer in an Eastern city who used to hold press conferences in front of the courthouse and jump into the fountain for the photographers to dramatize the importance of his latest case. It was "working the file," but not in the right direction.

You get a lot of mileage out of being a conscientious communicator. Lawyers who send copies of everything to their clients earn a lot of appreciation. Even if they don't understand what everything means, the clients know that the lawyer is doing something on their behalf.

Now translate that into communication with the opponent. Is that something you want to do?

Absolutely. But lots of us are afraid to do it. As Herb Stern points out, "Early settlements are not promoted by the guarded game that most lawyers play in pretrial preparation—when they hold everything close to the vest. Don't do that—trot out your stuff.

"Consider depositions, for example," says Stern. "Everybody says, 'Don't cross-examine the witness. Don't confront him with any inconsistencies. Don't let your theory of the case show. Just let the witness say whatever he wants.'"

Stern says that kind of deposition doesn't produce very much and it doesn't promote settlement. "A vigorous deposition," says Stern, "can let the opponent know you have a case. It can educate the other side, to be sure. But it can also produce some valuable information for trial."

Next, develop the habit of being considerate of the lawyer on the other side. Automatically send her copies of reports and evaluations that are admissible in evidence or are discoverable under the rules of procedure.

This accomplishes several important things.

- First, it keeps her aware of your case. Every time she sees you are doing something, it ratchets the value of your case up another notch. So many lawyers just let cases compost that any sign of activity can be worthwhile.
- Second, sending information automatically lets you pass on material without writing a cover letter that serves as a symbolic dig in the ribs. Remember, when you push too hard, you look hungry—and it doesn't strengthen your case.
- Third, the automatic system keeps the information fresh. Suddenly sending the other side an expert's report that you've had for a year and half doesn't make a very strong impression.

Of course, talk is cheap, and lots of lawyers are so practiced in blustering that they beg to be ignored. Instead of threatening and posturing, there are some little touches that will send the message that you are ready for trial.

- Come to the pretrial conference actually prepared to try the case. Have all your exhibits mounted on foam board and bring them with you in one of those large art portfolios. Whether it's a regular part of your pretrial presentation or not, you want each exhibit pre-marked and pre-admitted into evidence.
- Steal a page from the late Bob Hanley's personal trial notebook. He would time his opening statement before the pretrial conference and then ask the judge whether, say, a 40-minute opening would be all right with the court.
- If you are going to do something like use an overhead projector, ask the judge if you can try it out in the courtroom after the conference.

There are some cases that you can get rid of long before the pre-trial conference. Mark McCarthy of Cleveland, Ohio, has a technique for disposing of cases that the other side simply can't win. Instead of running the meter by taking depositions, answering interrogatories, making document requests, and then filing a motion, McCarthy sends a nice letter to the opponent right after the case is filed. It usually makes five points:

1. Here is what happened.
2. This is what you are going to tell me about the case.
3. This is who your expert will be.
4. This is what your expert is going to say.
5. This is what the court of appeals has said about this area of the law.

As McCarthy says, when the case is a sure loser, his letter saves each side $15,000 to $20,000.

Jean Maclean Snyder of Chicago says that fear of risk plays a large part in settlement psychology. Say you represent the plaintiff in a contract dispute and your investigation shows the defendant was engaged in some doubtful activity that might reflect on his credibility if he takes the stand.

Is the evidence admissible? Its very uncertainty is part of what makes it useful. Instead of saving it for trial or even the pre-trial conference, raising the issue of the questionable evidence at the right time can inject an extra concern for the other side right when it can help nudge them toward settlement.

Then there are settlement files—exhibits, memos, and documents—that are prepared for the other lawyer and his client. A number of the companies that make "day in the life of" presentations also put together settlement videos that say "This is what you're up against."

But Tom Demetrio of Chicago has a different view. "If I were a claims adjuster for Liberty Mutual Insurance Company," says Demetrio, "and the plaintiff's lawyer bombarded me with videotapes and brochures, I would get the message that he wanted to settle the case—not try it. The trial bar is actually a small community, and my credibility depends on my being willing to go to trial."

Until recently, the settlement file technique has been used almost exclusively by personal injury lawyers. But now other lawyers, such as David M. Malone of Washington, D.C., author of *The Effective Deposition* (NITA 1993), are using sophisticated settlement presentations in commercial cases.

Before the quarter-billion-dollar case was even filed in the Southern District of New York, Malone invited the defense lawyers and their principals to a presentation explaining what the case was all about. He had two major objectives:

First, he wanted to be sure that there were no misunderstandings. This was a massive case, not something that was just in the tens of millions.

Second, Malone wanted to show the other side that he was ready to go to trial and knew how to make this case understandable to a jury.

He put together a two-hour presentation that involved photographs, computer monitors, overhead projectors, and exhibits mounted on boards. Malone even invited the other side to ask questions, with the reservation that he would decide which ones to answer. This was all part of his preparation *before* the trial began.

Finally, Loren Kieve of Washington, D.C., says, "Settlement rests on two guiding truths. First, most lawyers procrastinate. Second, most lawyers are optimists and think their case will improve—in time."

Kieve says, "You should file the case—or remove it, if you can—to a fast court like the United States District Court for the Eastern District of Virginia" (which runs the famous "Rocket Docket"). "Two things will happen. First, the opposition will know you're serious. Second, you'll get a trial in four months—and settle the case in even less time.

"If you're not actually in a fast court," says Kieve, "make it seem like one. Press for trial. But understand, this only works when you're prepared. Just remember what Edward Bennet Williams used to say: 'Don't chase justice—you may catch it.'"

PART THREE

Direct Examination

Direct examination is at the heart of every case. Opening statements and closing argument are just hollow words if they are not supported by the evidence. On direct examination, the lawyer is virtually invisible, asking the questions the jury wants answered, painting vivid pictures of the facts with the testimony of the witnesses.

CHAPTER 16
Organizing Direct Examination

CHAPTER 17
The Paragraph Method

CHAPTER 18
Emphasis on Direct

CHAPTER 19
Leading Questions

CHAPTER 20
Freeze

CHAPTER 21
Helping the Witness

CHAPTER 16

Organizing Direct Examination

"Okay, Beth," said Angus, "let's look at the outline for the direct examination of the plaintiff."

"What outline?" asked Beth.

"The outline you're going to use when you do your direct examination tomorrow afternoon."

"I don't know how to tell you this, Angus, but it's all in here," said Beth, tapping her head.

"Like Mozart when he played Salieri's music after hearing it just one time. It's 'in the noodle,' eh?" asked Angus.

"Well, maybe not like Mozart," said Beth, "but I've been over the plaintiff's deposition three times. And besides, I just talked to him yesterday. It's not that big a deal."

Angus looked at Beth Golden over the top of his glasses. "Okay, then tell me how you're going to organize what you've got in the noodle," he said.

"Look, Angus," Beth said. "Our client is a contractor. He was building twelve houses and one of his suppliers breached a contract for the supply of wood. He found another supply that cost $250,000 more, and that's it. What's to organize?"

"Beth," said Angus, "I'm glad you asked."

Here are my notes of what he said.

First, lawyers are professional communicators—teachers who must organize their materials if they are to be effective. As far as Samuel Johnson, the great lexicographer, was concerned, the power to organize was part of the very definition of lawyer.

"As it rarely happens that a man is fit to plead his own cause, lawyers are a class of the community, who, by study and experience, have acquired the art and power of arranging evidence, and of applying to the points at issue what the law has settled." J. Boswell, *A Journal of a Tour to the Hebrides with Samuel Johnson*, Aug. 15, 1773.

Second, there is no part of a trial where good organization is more important than in direct examination. Except in unusual situations (for example, in a criminal defense in which no witnesses are called), direct examination is both more important and more difficult than cross-examination.

Without a plan, the organization of direct is going to be stream of consciousness—a natural way to recall information, but a poor way to transmit it to anyone else. Any lawyer with serious courtroom experience has seen dozens of such direct examinations—flailing, scattered, repetitive excursions that leave the judge and jury confused, bored, or indifferent.

Third, as important as the organization of direct examination is, there is no one right way to do it. Samuel Johnson was right. It is both the art and power of arranging evidence, and it can be done well in any number of ways. Instead of rules, there are choices, each with its own costs and benefits.

Take the introduction of the plaintiff in the lumber-supply case, for example. The standard way to begin a direct examination is to go through a perfunctory set of questions in which you tell the witness to state his full name, spelling his last name "for the record" (as if you did not care, but were required to do it).

To avoid this kind of superficial approach, a number of thoughtful personal-injury and criminal-defense lawyers take the trouble to introduce their clients with the kinds of details that will tend to make the jury identify with them and their situation as much as possible.

Now back to our building-supply case. The chances are that most of the people on the jury are not going to be quick to identify with a building contractor, even if he runs a small operation. But they do identify with injustice and are offended when someone is wronged.

So instead of looking for personal identification first, maybe this is a case where the full introduction of the person should wait until the jury sees the picture—just a snapshot—of injustice.

Here is how it might go. His name is Mark Willis, and he runs the Willis Construction Company. He is the one who is responsible for making sure everything gets done and all of the company's commitments are met. He depends on the steady supply of materials. He made a contract with Tri-City Lumber Company to supply the wood for a dozen houses they were building in a new development. And when Tri-City broke their word, it cost Willis Construction more than $250,000 and put twenty-five people out of work for more than a month.

All of that can be done in a handful of questions and answers. In the first two or three minutes the jury knows who the plaintiff is and what the case is all about. But best of all, they see why he is in court—because he has been wronged.

After an introduction like that, the direct examiner can say:

"Mr. Willis, I'm going to ask you all about what happened when Tri-City did not deliver the lumber. But first I'd like the jury to get a little background information about you, so tell us about yourself, would you please?"

After the introduction, the next question is, how do you organize the body of the direct examination? What kind of system do you use to arrange the testimony?

Chronology is an excellent way to keep things straight, and it probably ought to be what you use unless you have a good reason for doing something else. After all, chronology is the order in which things happened. It implies a sense of cause and effect. It is easy to use and it is generally easy to follow.

But there can be good reasons for using a different plan. Take the psychological effects of primacy and recency, for example.

Primacy—what you hear first—relates to credibility. All other things being equal (which they never are), what you hear first you are more likely to accept as true.

Recency—what you hear last—has a different effect. Instead of relating so strongly to credibility, what you hear last you are more easily able to recall.

So even if you stick to chronology for the rest of your direct examination, there are solid psychological principles for following the old advice, start strong and end strong. And when you *must* cover something damning, rather than letting your opponent get to it first, bury it in the middle so it will not stick out.

But you may not want to use chronological organization at all. When the time line is not important, or when there were too many different things going on at once, using chronology to sort out the facts may do more harm than good. If chronology conveys chaos, you may want to send a different message by choosing another way to put things together.

How?

Highlight key ideas. Good direct examination is good teaching. When there are concepts that must be understood before other things make sense, these key ideas have to come first, especially with expert testimony.

Use functional groups. If the witness has to explain how a machine puts glue on the flaps of envelopes, he does not have to talk about how the paper gets to the factory, or whether it comes in rolls or stacks. The functional group—getting the glue on the flap—determines how you organize his testimony on that point.

Functional grouping is a good reason for making a chart on the chalkboard during the direct examination—right as you ask the questions and get the answers. You can make lists under the titles "Then" and "Now" to show how market conditions have changed. You can list the advantages and disadvantages of diagnostic techniques to show why doing a spinal puncture would have been a dangerous choice in this case. You can make a double-column calendar to show how your client's efforts to solve a problem were met by indifference from his opponent.

Using a flip chart, chalkboard, or overhead projector is a marvelous way to give your direct examination both audible and visible organization. Audible and visible organization not only keeps everyone on track, it also sends the message that both you and the witness have thought this through and know what you are talking about.

Effective organization also includes techniques such as foreshadowing—letting the jury know that something is on the way—and suspense—conspicuously holding something back so everyone will want to know what happens. But while foreshadowing and suspense are valuable, they are best used sparingly. Too much flash and dash makes the jury wonder whether there is any substance to back it all up.

When you work out your organization, write it down in outline form—do not write out your questions word for word. There are some good reasons for this.

First, when you are working from a script, everything sounds a little stilted as you read your questions.

Second, an outline makes it easy to ask follow-up questions when the witness leaves something out of his answer. When you work from a script and things go wrong, you have to unwrite the questions in your mind so that you can rearrange them into a mental outline from which you can frame your next questions. That is a lot of work to do when you are trying to concentrate on how the witness is coming across.

Finally, when you have finished your direct examination and checked off every major point, it is easy to look at your outline and know that you are done.

CHAPTER 17

The Paragraph Method

Ernest Droner was not ready for the simple truth that direct examination is more difficult than cross-examination. So when he was getting ready for his first trial, all he did was read through the depositions and take a few notes. He figured he would have his witnesses just tell their stories when they got on the stand.

The results were awful—disorganized, repetitive, and confusing.

So, the next time, Droner decided to write out all the questions (and expected answers) for every witness. The results were different but not much better. He had a script, but his witnesses did not. So when he got some answers that were not quite what he had expected, Droner had to start rephrasing the questions to fit the situation.

Questions and answers got out of synchronization, and Droner looked hesitant and confused. Often he would ask a question that was designed to get the information the witness had just given. The jury got the idea that Ernie did not understand his own case.

The worst part was that no matter how Ernest Droner approached direct examination, it always came out like a massive run-on sentence. Like an article without a title, headings, paragraph indentations, capital letters, or punctuation (much less a chart or an illustration), it just started and went on and on until it stopped (to the relief of everyone).

One of the cures for Droner's malady is actually simple. It is the Paragraph Method of Direct Examination. Here is how it works. When you organize direct, divide it into separate topics. These are the oral paragraphs that make up the entire direct examination. Just like written paragraphs, they are separate groupings of information and ideas.

But unlike written paragraphs, oral paragraphs do not stand out because of indentation, capitalization, or punctuation. To be sure, you can do some of this with your pace and tone of voice. But if you really want your oral paragraphs to make a difference, they must stand out because of what you say as well as how you say it.

The key is the topic sentence.

The technique is simply to announce each new topic before asking questions about it. For example, suppose you have a case against a hospital that ignored a seriously ill cardiac patient who was waiting in the emergency room. You call an expert to explain that the way the hospital was organized let that happen.

"Doctor, we need to understand how the Mercy Hospital emergency room was set up to handle heart attack victims." Then you start asking specific questions, such as, "Did the emergency room have any specific plan for heart patients?" and, "Was anyone responsible for checking on people who were waiting to talk to the nurse in charge of admissions?"

Wait a minute, you say. You are not a witness. You are not permitted to testify. You are just supposed to ask questions. Isn't a topic sentence an improper comment of counsel?

No.

First, the topic sentence is not an editorial comment on what the witness says. Second, it is not even a leading question. Even if it were, it is preliminary, and you are permitted to lead on preliminary matters on direct examination. (Rule 611(c) Fed. R. Evid.) Third, the topic sentence is proper since it gives meaning to the questions that follow.

Like a boldface headline, the topic sentence stands out. It divides direct examination into manageable bites the jury can chew and digest. It also adds interest to what might otherwise be the continuous drone of direct examination.

But that is just the start. The paragraph method does a lot of other good things that you might not think of right away.

Benefits

First, it helps the witness stay on track. Because of the formality of the courtroom and the stilted way in which many lawyers ask questions, witnesses often wonder what the question is calling for anyway. If on top of that you ask a series of questions without telling the witness the general topic, confusion is almost guaranteed.

Second, the paragraph method helps the judge and jury understand the examination. Unlike you, they are hearing everything for the first time. If they are not told what topic is under discussion, they have to figure it out for themselves, which takes attention away from the details they need to hear. Besides, organizing and labeling information requires some genuine intellectual effort. The chances are, they will not take the trouble to do it. If you do not, why should they?

Third, breaking direct examination down into separate topics helps you keep track of all the information you need to cover. When the subject is finished you know you are ready to move on to the next. Needless repetition is reduced, and testimony becomes lean and more vigorous.

Fourth, topic sentences make it easier for you to ask simple, nonleading questions on direct examination. Go back to the doctor who was telling us about Mercy Hospital's emergency room. You announce a new topic: "Doctor, I want to ask you about your connection with Mercy Hospital." See how easy it is to ask follow-up questions: "Have you ever been on its staff?" "When did you start?" "How long did you stay?" "Why did you leave?" "Where do you practice now?"

Now that you have started thinking about oral paragraphs and headlines, you need to consider how long to make the paragraphs.

That depends. A short, snappy little topic can add interest, but too many of them can make the entire presentation seem choppy. But big topics do not mean you need big paragraphs. Just as readers get tired of looking at gray pages of continuous type, so do jurors tire of the same pattern of words. When you have more than six or seven questions without a verbal topic or a subhead, some listeners will start to stray. Even just announcing a small change in direction can give the new emphasis you need to keep everyone with you.

Snapshots

Think of your oral paragraphs as verbal snapshots—tight groups of information that make a point or two and then are finished. The snapshot idea is particularly valuable, since it will lead you to think about what verbal pictures you want to show the jury.

Choose your pictures carefully, and arrange them so they lead the judge and jury to the conclusion you want. There is more to this advice than you might think. A good picture is not only interesting and easy to understand, it tells an entire story in itself.

For example, suppose you are representing a doctor who is the defendant in a medical malpractice case. Your doctor is charged with failing to diagnose a ruptured spleen. What kind of picture of your doctor do you want to present? That he is competent? Of course. That he did all the right tests? To be sure. Those are expected—and not very exciting.

But suppose you want to show that he really knows his stuff. You want to show your doctor is good enough to teach a course in the spleen. That idea will affect how you phrase your topic sentences—the titles to the pictures you present: "Doctor, teach us about the spleen." "We need to understand how you test to see if the spleen is injured." "Doctor, I am going to ask you to explain how to treat an injured spleen."

All of this is more than justification for using the paragraph method of direct examination. But perhaps the biggest benefit is how it affects your credibility with the judge and jury.

Topic sentences have an effect on the lawyer's credibility? Come on, you say, how can that be?

Visible and audible organization conveys a powerful message. It says that not only do you know the material, you have thought about it. You understand it well enough to make it clear to other people. You are the one who can be counted on to call witnesses who can be believed and make arguments that can be trusted.

Impressions like that are worth developing.

CHAPTER 18

Emphasis on Direct

Some people simply cannot do it right. Former President Harry S Truman was a perfect example. He had trouble reading speeches with the proper emphasis; everything he said had a wonderfully flat Missouri twang. So, according to legend, his speech writers took to putting instructions to the president in his speeches, advising him how to deliver them. The next thing that happened was that Mr. Truman was in the middle of a nationally televised address on the budget, and he found himself saying, "Raise your voice here, Harry."

Emphasis—making something stick out so that it is noticed—is one of the keys to effective persuasion. But in trial, too many lawyers use the Ugly American method of emphasis. Like boorish tourists, they seem to think that if they keep repeating something loudly and slowly, they will get their point across. The results are more painful than effective.

Emphasis on direct examination presents a special challenge. Except in unusual situations, direct examination is the time the spotlight should be on the witness, not the lawyer. The witness, not the lawyer, does the testifying. But when it comes time to make sure that some crucial bit of testimony gets the proper attention, it is the lawyer who must do something about it. Fortunately, there are some techniques that work better than the Truman cure.

Organization

Just as youth is wasted on the young, the beginning of direct examination is usually wasted on introductions. And the beginning is important. The psychological principle of primacy is that what is heard first is more likely to be believed. If you have a point that is truly essential to your case, one place to put it is in the very beginning—followed by the introduction. The end is a special place, too. According to the principle of recency, what is heard last is most easily remembered. And if you must include something that you do not want stressed, bury it in the middle.

Headlines

The traditional way to introduce a new topic on direct examination is to ask a convoluted question in tortured legalese:

> Q. Directing your attention to the evening of October 27, I ask you what, if anything, were you doing on that occasion?

(Nothing that bleak is required. Instead, try using a headline. Tell the witness—and everyone else—what the new topic will be.)

> Q. I want to ask you about the evening of October 27. Tell us, where were you at about 9:00 p.m.?

The headline does a lot of good things. It lets the jury see your organization, so it makes direct examination easier to follow. Second, it keeps the witness on track. Third, it helps you emphasize what is important.

Suspense

Suspense literally means holding something up. People are in suspense when they know something is coming and want to find out what it is. While that definition seems obvious, it is the key to using suspense successfully. The jury will not be kept in suspense unless they know something important is on the way.

Although letting them know that something is coming can be done by implication, probably the easiest way is to do it directly, right in front of everyone. In this example the only extra preparation necessary is to tell your witness (who in this case is an orthopedic surgeon) not to give the plaintiff's prognosis until you ask for it directly. That lets you put it in suspense:

> Q. Doctor Preston, one question before we get started. Will you be able to give us your professional evaluation of Joe Wilson's chances of ever getting out of his wheelchair?

A. Yes, I will.
Q. I want to go into your evaluation of Joe Wilson in just a minute, Doctor, but first I need to ask you some questions about your professional background.

There is nothing fancy about it, but it starts the jury thinking about what is coming next.

Pauses

Silence is one of the most powerful forms of emphasis. As long as you look as if you are doing it on purpose, you can stop for as long as you like and the courtroom will belong to you. But, if you are embarrassed or look confused, the silence will not last long. Someone else will fill it.

Tone of Voice

You do not need to raise your voice; dropping it for emphasis actually works better. When you drop your voice, people have to work harder to listen, and they will, but only for a little while. If listening becomes too much work, they will turn their minds to other things.

Moving

Everyone knows that pacing is distracting. But that does not mean you have to stand in one spot throughout direct examination. Provided you are not appearing before one of those unfortunate judges who thinks it is important for lawyers to stay behind the lectern, purposeful movement helps break the monotony. (And if you are before one of the unfortunate judges who wants you to remain still, use an exhibit as a reason for moving at the right time.)

Repeating the Answer

It is improper just to repeat what the witness says in the hope that will help it sink in. Done to excess, it will bring an objection that should be sustained. Even if there is no objection, habitually echoing the witness annoys the jury. So what in the world is the idea?

James W. Jeans has a marvelous suggestion for how to repeat the answer the right way in his book, *Trial Advocacy* (West, page 224, 1975). When the witness uses a phrase that you want repeated, make that phrase part of your next question:

Q. Did you see the plaintiff before the accident occurred?
A. Yes, I saw her when she darted right in front of my car. *(There's the magic phrase.)*
Q. How fast were you going when she *darted right in front of your car*?
A. Approximately 20 miles per hour.
Q. And where in the street were you traveling when she *darted right in front of your car*?
A. About two feet from the center line.

Exhibits

Pictures, maps, diagrams, and sketches can often make points all on their own. Chosen well, they create their own emphasis. But they can also emphasize testimony. One particularly effective technique is to have the witness go through a segment of his testimony *without* the demonstrative exhibit. Then when the exhibit is introduced, you can have him go over the highlights again, this time using the exhibit.

Reenactments

Reenactments can be powerful—and dangerous, too. The lore of the law is filled with stories about courtroom demonstrations that have backfired. Impulse is the road to disaster. The way to stay out of trouble is to plan reenactments, rehearse them with the witness, and keep them simple. If you want to show that the witness had a good opportunity to see the defendant, have him stand as far away from the defendant as he was on the night of the fight; do not have him reenact the fight.

Present Tense

You may not believe this will work, so try it on someone who does not know what you are about. The results are impressive.

We usually examine witnesses using the past tense. After all, most testimony (other than some expert opinions) deals with the past, not the future. And naturally, our witnesses answer us in the past tense as well. But if you start asking questions in the present tense, about four out of five witnesses will start answering in the present tense.

The effect on the testimony is striking. Everything seems more alive, and it is because the witness is reliving the event, and the jury is going through it with him.

But what if it does not work? About one time out of five the witness will keep talking in the past tense even though your questions are in the present. It does not matter, because the effect of the change in verb tense is subconscious. No one but you will know that the witness has stayed in the past; everyone else will be concentrating on the content of the testimony. But even the present tense of just the questions will have a subtle impact on the jury.

There is a cardinal rule to follow if you use this technique: Never tell the witness you are going to do it. Simply switch to the present tense when you come to the part you want to emphasize.

One final note. Whatever techniques you use, emphasis on direct examination is like underlining in a book. Be sparing. Pick what is worth stressing, but do not overdo it. If you want something to be noticed, you can't underline everything.

CHAPTER 19

Leading Questions

The direct examiner was struggling to make the accountant's background interesting to the jury. The trouble was, the lawyer did not quite understand what all of the witness's qualifications meant, and the witness did not quite understand where the lawyer was going.

Anthony Barker, a barrister from Birmingham, England, leaned over and whispered in my ear, "We would lead through all this, wouldn't you?"

"We should, but we usually don't," I whispered back.

Then, only two or three questions later, the frustrated direct examiner asked a leading question. His opponent objected, the direct examiner did not respond, and the judge sustained the objection.

It took place a few years back at a session on expert witnesses at the Advanced Program of the National Institute for Trial Advocacy in Boulder, Colorado. There were a number of valuable lessons to be drawn, including: It is essential to know exactly what you want to develop on direct examination, and you must be able to defend your line of questioning.

But perhaps the most important lesson is the one that is most often overlooked, precisely because it runs counter to some basic trial instincts: Sometimes that best thing to do on direct examination is to ask leading questions.

The Law of Leading

The place to start is the law of leading. For the most part, the rules are pretty straightforward:

- A leading question is one that suggests the answer to the witness. Its vice is that it tells the witness what to say. If it does not do that, it is not leading. Despite what some trial judges seem to think, there is no other magic formula. A question is not leading just because it calls for a yes or no answer, and inserting the prosecutors' favorite phrase, "what, if anything," is not necessary to make a question nonleading.
- The basic rule is that leading is not permitted on direct examination, but there are lots of exceptions to the rule.
- Leading is permitted on preliminary matters that are not in dispute. The real test of what is preliminary is not whether it comes at the beginning of the witness's testimony, but what function the information serves during the examination.

    Often, a questioner asks for background information for each new direct examination topic. If this background is undisputed, then it is preliminary, even if it is introduced during the middle or at the end of the examination.

    But there is a better way to look at it. If the information is not disputed, then leading questions should be permitted. This approach protects every legitimate interest guarded by the rule against leading questions, but do not expect every trial judge to understand that.
- Leading is permitted with very young or very old witnesses, to keep them on track.
- Leading is permitted with witnesses who have temporary memory lapses and need to be reminded of something before they can go on.
- Leading is permitted with witnesses who have been shown to be hostile in fact.
- Leading is permitted with adverse parties or witnesses who are identified with adverse parties.
- Leading is permitted on cross-examination until it goes outside the scope of direct examination. Then the witness must be questioned "as if on direct examination." (Rule 611(b) of the Federal Rules of Evidence.)

    Understand that going outside the scope of direct examination does not mean you cannot lead—it only means you cannot lead *because* it is cross-examination. If the witness is hostile or an adverse party, for example, then you still

can lead on cross-examination even though you are going outside the scope of direct examination.
- Leading is sometimes permitted on re-direct examination. Here the law is not as well developed as in some other areas. The Federal Rules do not even address the issue.

  Some judges insist that re-direct examination be conducted like direct examination.

  But other judges are more lenient about leading on re-direct examination, because re-direct is in response to cross-examination, and therefore can never be fully anticipated. They believe that leading, as long as it is not too blatant, helps things move more quickly.

  Certainly, there is a good argument for permitting leading during re-direct examination that touches on issues that were "new matters" on cross-examination.
- By local custom in some courts, leading is often permitted during direct examination in questions that are intended to clarify. Interestingly, these questions are often multiple and cumulative in addition to being leading. For example:

  "Let me see if I understand this. You were sitting at the corner in the yellow VW convertible at about 3:30 in the afternoon, when you saw the white Corvette coming around the corner, is that right?"

How can a court permit so many rules of evidence to be broken at one time without sustaining an objection? The idea seems to be that a little creative leading is all right when its real function is to help the jury understand what is already in evidence. Those courts that permit leading in these circumstances instinctively impose two limitations:

First, the question has to start with a phrase that suggests confusion on the part of the lawyer, such as "Let me see if I've got this straight," or "Let me see if I understand this." If you say you are going over something again for the benefit of the jury, an objection is almost guaranteed.

Second, no matter how the question is put, the technique cannot be overworked.

If you ask a clarifying question more frequently than every five or ten minutes, an objection will be sustained, unless something really needs clarification.

Calming a Nervous Witness

Leading on preliminaries is just the ticket to help witnesses overcome their initial nervousness. In addition to putting the witness at ease, it is a lot more civilized to say:

> Q. You are Marsha Adams, aren't you?
> A. Yes.
> Q. And your last name is spelled A-d-a-m-s?
> A. That's right.

This is preferable to asking the witness: "Would you state your full name and address, spelling your last name for the record?"

This question implies that you hardly care what the witness's name is, and you certainly would not bother to get it spelled correctly if it were not for the record.

Leading an Expert

Leading also is an excellent way to cover most of an expert witness's qualifications, especially education, awards, and professional achievements.

The reason is important. The more impressive the witness's background, the more he sounds like he is blowing his own horn when you have him recite the details.

When you lead the witness on his qualifications, he does not sound nearly so pretentious as he does when he goes through all his degrees and honors by himself.

That is why you never want to develop your expert's qualifications by turning him loose with a narrative: When you put him on autopilot, it looks like he enjoys the flight more than anyone else.

And another point. Leading on an expert's qualifications lets you hit just the high points, asking only about what is particularly relevant to the case. It is the kind of touch that spells the difference between a deft and a ponderous examination.

Helping the Witness

When a witness is in trouble, leading is often the easiest way out. Say the witness is confused or has a temporary memory lapse. Of course, you can refresh the witness's recollection or lay the foundation for past recollection recorded.

But before that you should remember to do two things:

First, take the blame for the witness's confusion. Second, restate the question so it leads the witness out of trouble.

The Cost

After all this, you might think that leading is a good way to approach direct examination, at least until there is an objection.

Wrong.

There is a price to pay for leading, even when there is no objection. Too much leading, especially on disputed matters, gives the jury the idea that you do not trust your own witness and must tell him what to say.

And that is the perfect introduction to how to object to leading when you are on the other side.

First, do not object just because your opponent is leading. If he is making the witness look bad by asking only leading questions, you may actually help him by putting a stop to it.

Second, pay attention to how you state your objection. Remember there is no rule that says you must phrase objections so they are incomprehensible to the jury. The simple phrase, "Objection, leading," may get a favorable ruling, but leaves the jury unenlightened.

"Objection, Your Honor, opposing counsel has not taken the oath and is not entitled to testify," may strike the jury more like a gratuitous attack on the other lawyer than an objection they understand.

On the other hand, "Objection, Your Honor, he's putting words in the witness's mouth," or "Objection. He's telling the witness what to say," shows the jury you have a good reason for objecting and are not simply trying to keep them from hearing something important.

CHAPTER 20

Freeze

It was hard to tell who was more rattled—the witness or the lawyer. The witness had frozen on the stand, just as surely as if he had walked out on a narrow ledge high over a city street and was now paralyzed. It was the lawyer's job to rescue him, but he had no idea what to do.

No one would blame the lawyer for wanting to keep the witness from getting into trouble in the first place instead of having to pull him out once he got in. Prevention is better than cure, and there are lots of things you can do that help keep the witness from freezing on the stand—explain the process to him, discuss his testimony, take him to the courthouse and let him see the witness stand; have him practice giving his testimony; even make a videotape of his testimony so he can see himself in action. What you do depends on your evaluation of the witness as you prepare for trial. And steps like these may help. The fear of testifying often melts when the unknown becomes familiar.

There are costs, to be sure. There is always the risk that the edge of spontaneity will be worn off by the grindstone of practice. If the witness sounds downright rehearsed, it can seriously undercut his credibility. Deciding between a witness who can remember nothing and one who sounds coached is not a happy choice. If that looks like the option, you will probably want to see if you can find another witness to take his place.

No matter what you do in trial preparation, prevention does not always work. When things go wrong in the middle of trial, cure is the only option left.

Leading

One of the easiest ways to help a witness who has forgotten something is simply to tell him the answer with a leading question. Before you disagree, think about it for a moment. Leading has a lot of advantages.

First, it is quick. All you have to do is ask the question. Second, it is humane. The witness does not have to sit and squirm while you shuffle through a deposition trying to find what he said before. Neither does he have to agonize over whether he is answering your questions correctly when you try to lay an evidentiary foundation for what he cannot remember.

The question is whether you will be permitted to do it over your opponent's objection.

The answer is, it depends.

Leading is one of four ways the common law has created for helping out a witness who chokes on the witness stand. Normally, of course, leading is not permitted on direct examination, but that is not all there is to it. Leading is permissible for preliminary matters, to help keep very young or very old witnesses on the track, and to help out witnesses who have a memory lapse on the stand.

When you think about it, it is really an informal way to refresh the witness's recollection. Maybe that is why the application of the rule varies so much from one judge to the next. Some judges take a relaxed approach and permit counsel to lead their witnesses when they start to get a little hazy. Others insist on a formal showing of a failed recollection before letting you suggest the answers to the witness.

Whatever the approach, you are more likely to forfend an objection from your opponent if you say something like this to the witness who is having difficulty:

"Mr. Wilson, I sense you are having a little trouble recalling this meeting. Would it help if I told you that it was held in Mr. Evert's office in the first part of July?"

Since it is a discretionary matter, some judges like you to ask them first. Do it like this: "Your Honor, the witness is having some difficulty remembering this point. I think I can save us all some time if I am permitted to clear it up with a few leading questions."

Be careful not to lead more than you must. Even if your opponent does not object, there is a penalty for using leading questions. Every time you have to give the witness the answer, you send the signal to the judge and jury that the witness may not be a good source of information, and that if they want to be certain what really happened, they will have to look to someone else.

Refreshing Recollection

The theory behind present recollection refreshed (as the academics call it) is that the information is somewhere in the witness's mind, but he is having trouble getting to it. Something, however, may tickle or tease the right synapses into life, and the memory will come flooding back.

So the law lets you use virtually anything within reason to help the witness remember: a map, a chart, a picture, a song, a name, a whiff of perfume, an old newspaper, a statement the witness once made.

But it has to be *his* memory that he testifies to, not simply what he was just told in the attempt to bring it back. The difference is important. When the witness actually remembers, his testimony is what counts. He is the real witness, and he is the one the opponent will want to cross-examine. But when the witness merely repeats what he just read, then he is no longer the real witness, and if what he read does not qualify as an exception to the hearsay rule, it should be excluded from evidence.

If you are the opponent, you may want to test whether the witness's recollection is really refreshed before he is permitted to testify to what he was unable to remember just a minute or two before.

Can you do that? Certainly. It is a kind of voir dire examination of the witness, and it is in the discretion of the trial court whether to let you do it now, or make you wait until cross-examination.

Should you do it? That is a more difficult question. Usually the game is not worth the candle—especially if what is being used to refresh the witness's recollection is itself admissible in evidence. Then you would rather have the witness's hazy memory than the certainty of a written document. On the other hand, if the document is not admissible, you might open a hole in the opponent's case that he will be unable to fill.

If you try to test the witness's recollection, you certainly are entitled to have whatever document was used to refresh that recollection at trial, and in the discretion of the court you may even be able to get a document that was used in pre-trial preparation. Rule 612, Federal Rules of Evidence.

Past Recollection Recorded

For the trial lawyer, past recollection recorded is the next thing to try if refreshing the witness's recollection does not work. But for the evidence scholar, it is not even in the same chapter of the book. For the scholar, refreshed recollection is the witness's own sworn testimony, given in court, while past recollection recorded is unsworn evidence that is an exception to the hearsay rule.

While past recollection recorded is one of the "Big Four" ways around problems with business correspondence, it can crop up anywhere. If you have a case that involves a dying declaration, the reputation concerning the boundaries of land, or the facts recited on an ancient gravestone marking, you know the problem is coming. But not with past recollection recorded. You never know when the witness will have a lapse.

Here are the elements:

1. A writing;
2. Made at or near the event;
3. By someone with first-hand knowledge;
4. Who has no present recollection;
5. But who can give a voucher of correctness.

Remember that Rule 803(5) of the Federal Rules of Evidence has made some important changes to the common law approach to past recollection recorded. First, the writing does not have to be made at or near the event, just when the matter was fresh in the witness's memory.

Second, the Federal Rules do not require a full lapse of memory, just enough to prevent the witness from testifying "fully and accurately." Third, to keep juries from giving past recollection recorded disproportionate weight, the writing may be read into evidence, but may not be received as an exhibit unless it is offered by the opponent.

Recess

The fourth thing you can do for a terrified witness is to ask for a recess so he can gather his wits.

There may be times when you need something more heroic than that. You may actually have to call another witness.

CHAPTER 21

Helping the Witness

Direct examination was bad enough. The witness never seemed to know what the plaintiff's lawyer wanted. He hemmed and hawed and stumbled around and constantly corrected himself. He seemed uncertain of the most basic points. When the plaintiff's lawyer started asking leading questions, it didn't help. The impression was that the witness had to be told what to say, and the defense lawyer was wise enough not to object.

Cross-examination was even worse. Every time the defense lawyer asked a tough question, the witness turned and looked at the plaintiff's lawyer as if to say, "Do something for me, will you? How should I answer that question?" At first the plaintiff's lawyer just looked at the counsel table to avoid the witness's gaze. Finally he buried his head in his hands.

When the defense finished his cross-examination and sat down, the plaintiff's counsel quickly said, "No questions, Your Honor." He sounded like was in a hurry to get the witness off the stand.

The witness was the plaintiff's chief executive officer. He had refused to spend more than a few minutes preparing to testify. He said it would be a simple matter of coming in and giving the facts as he knew them. But when he watched the videotape rerun of his testimony in the mock trial, he realized what a mistake he had made. He decided that maybe this mock trial business was worthwhile after all.

The point is that all witnesses, even the most knowledgeable and sophisticated, need help. And the most important help you can give comes before they take the stand.

Even if the witness did fine testifying at a deposition, you should never neglect trial preparation. Courts are fearsome places that have the power of life and death. It is one thing to answer questions in a deposition room; it is quite another to take the oath in front of the flag and give testimony in open court.

Make them part of the team

Most witnesses want to help the party that calls them to the stand. Unless they are adverse witnesses or persons who can cause harm to you or your client, start by explaining why their testimony is important to your case. Just don't overdo it. You don't want them to exaggerate their testimony out of excessive loyalty.

Find out their limitations

Some witnesses are poor readers. Others are weak at math. Some people excel at explaining charts or diagrams, while others find them baffling. If the witness can't handle a piece of chalk and a blackboard, you need to know that before you ask him to draw a diagram for the jury in the middle of a trial. You can only work around a witness's weaknesses when you know what they are.

Tell them not to bluff or guess

Witnesses need to understand that there is nothing wrong with not knowing the answer to a question. But knowing that may not be enough to help some witnesses.

Some people have the tendency to bluff their way through all kinds of situations when they don't know the answer. They just say what they think the answer ought to be. Watch out for these folks. They are guessers—people who don't distinguish carefully enough between what they know and what they suppose.

Don't think you will be able to cure someone of a lifelong guessing habit with a few warnings in a witness preparation session. You need to find out what this witness actually knows and doesn't know about the particular facts in the case and make sure he doesn't speculate. If all else fails, try to get another witness—guessers are trouble.

Ask simple questions

Poor questions are the biggest single cause of witness floundering. So the most important thing you can do for any witness is to learn how to ask good questions.

Easier said than done. One of the primary objectives of the National Institute for Trial Advocacy is to teach the art of asking good questions. It takes practice and effort, but there are some rules that will help.

First, keep your questions short. Very short questions are almost always easier to understand than those that go on for a paragraph or two.

Second, use simple words. Questions that sound like they were asked by a lawyer are usually difficult to follow. Avoid terms like *indicate, with reference to,* and *observe* when you can use *tell, about,* and *see* or *hear.*

Third, start your questions with the classic words that reporters use: *who, what, when, where, how,* and *why.*

Fourth, stay on the subject. Questions and answers do not stand alone. They are part of the overall testimony. When you hop, skip, and jump from one area to another, you will confuse the judge and the jury as well as the witness. Arrange the topics so the testimony paints the picture of what happened. Cover one topic at a time. Then, when you are ready to go on to a new subject, just tell the witness what it is and everybody will be able to follow you.

Watch the witness

You can see a lot in the witnesses' eyes. A word or a phrase throws them off; they don't hear a key part of the question; you leave something out. No matter what the cause, you can read confusion on a witness's face before he says a word.

But you will never even see it if your nose is buried in your notes. So what do you do—write out all your questions and then memorize them?

Absolutely not. Don't write them out in the first place. Instead, outline your examination. List the major topics and key points you want to develop by writing down just a word or two for each one. Then ask your questions from your outline. You will only have to glance at it now and then, so you can concentrate on watching the witness.

Have the witness tell you if he doesn't understand the question

Some people figure it is better to answer a question you didn't ask than to admit they didn't understand what you wanted. They have to realize that there is nothing wrong with asking for clarification before answering a question. It is the kind of care that will enhance their credibility.

Take the blame

When the witness misunderstands the question and starts giving the wrong answer, the natural tendency is to blame the witness: "You didn't understand my question." That response says the witness is flawed—he is not capable of understanding normal questions. At best, he is merely embarrassed or humiliated; at worst, he now resents you and your client.

The point is simple: Don't try to save your own face at the cost of your case. Pride of authorship doesn't belong in your question. Even if your question was a model of simplicity and elegance, if the witness didn't understand it, don't blame her—blame yourself. "I'm sorry, I didn't put that very well. Let me rephrase that question."

Practice direct and cross-examination

Ask any lawyer who has gone to a National Institute for Trial Advocacy program—the video replay is one of the most valuable parts of the experience. And if it works for lawyers, it works for witnesses, too.

It used to be that videotaping witnesses was reserved for full-fledged mock trials conducted by one of those litigation support organizations. But now that new camcorders cost less than $600, even very small firms can afford to have their own equipment.

The idea is that if things are going to go wrong—and they will—it should be when they don't count.

You don't need to videotape the whole trial, just the parts you think will need work. You don't have to make a witness sit through his entire direct examination. Usually ten or fifteen minutes is enough to let him see how he is coming across. And don't ask the same questions the same way each time. You don't want the witness to sound like an automaton who's got everything memorized.

It is usually a good idea to have another lawyer conduct the practice cross-examination. First, you don't want to make the witness afraid of answering your direct examination questions openly and completely. Second, you want the witness to get used to the kinds of things you will do to protect him from an overzealous opponent.

The practice session is the perfect time to work on any tendencies the witness may have to get belligerent or argumentative.

Here are some basic instructions you should give every witness for cross-examination:

- Listen to the question.
- Answer the question that was asked, not some other question.
- Don't volunteer any extra information.
- If you don't know, say so.
- If you don't remember, say so.
- Don't try to sell the case.
- Don't argue with the cross-examiner.
- Don't look to me for help during cross-examination. Unless I object to what the other lawyer is doing or interrupt what's going on, you are doing fine.

Tell them what to wear

Everybody worries about how clothes influence the way others perceive us—which is reason enough to think about what your witnesses should wear. But there is another factor that is just as important: People who are not properly dressed for the occasion don't feel comfortable about themselves and don't perform as well as they should. If you don't advise them, it is amazing what some people will wear to court.

Tell them how to get there

It is also amazing how many lawyers let witnesses find their own way to the courthouse. Testifying is hard enough without worrying about which courthouse to go to, where it is located, how to get there, where to park, and whether there are any nearby bus, subway, or rapid transit lines.

You should make "witness care packages" for both state and federal courts, with maps and all the logistical information a witness needs to get to the right place. Include a form that has a place to write in the name of the judge, which floor of the courthouse, and the room number, as well as the date and time they need to be there.

It is a thoughtful touch to tell them that even though they have to be there on time, it is a good idea to bring a book in case they have to wait.

Keep in touch

Things happen to witnesses just as they do to other people. They die, move away, just disappear. Particularly if you practice in a jurisdiction where it takes a number of years to get to trial, you need to do a periodic check to keep track of important witnesses. It is a lot easier than scrambling around at the last minute, trying to find that guy who puts your plaintiff in the crosswalk.

PART FOUR

Cross-Examination

Effective cross-examination eludes even the finest advocates until they understand its real purpose. The point of cross-examination is not to get information from the witness, to fix what happened on direct, or to try to get the witness to recant his testimony. The purpose of cross-examination is to let you tell your side of the witness's story—your way.

CHAPTER 22
The Language of Cross-Examination

CHAPTER 23
The Weasel Factor

CHAPTER 24
The Runaway

CHAPTER 25
Pressure Points

CHAPTER 26
Careful Cross-Examination

CHAPTER 27
An Impeachment Checklist

CHAPTER 28
Prior Inconsistent Statements

CHAPTER 29
Phantom Impeachment

CHAPTER 30
Refreshing Recollection

CHAPTER 31
Nine Ways to Cross-Examine an Expert

CHAPTER 32
Blind Cross-Examination

CHAPTER 33
Liar!

CHAPTER 34
Breaking the Rules of Cross

CHAPTER 22

The Language of Cross-Examination

The technique does not come naturally, and the reason is simple. Unless you had a very unusual background, you did not learn how to ask good cross-examination questions when you were a child.

Oh sure, maybe a parent or a teacher had a knack for getting the truth from you about the broken candy dish or the missile you launched with a plastic ruler. But that was not cross-examination. That was investigation. The questioner was trying to get information, not present his side of a witness's testimony to a judge or jury. No matter how they made you feel, the questions were all wrong for a courtroom.

Direct examination is different. It sounds more like normal conversation, although there are important differences. The better a direct examination is, the more it gives the impression of being the way people really talk.

But not cross-examination. People simply do not talk that way outside the courtroom. And because you did not do it when you were a child, it is difficult to learn it now.

But you must if you are going to be an effective cross-examiner, and here are some rules that will help. These are rules for destructive cross-examination—the kind intended to attack the witness's testimony on direct examination. Although they are just rules (and not commandments), treat them as absolute until you have enough experience to know when to break them:

- Ask leading questions.
- Ask very short questions.

- Use simple words.
- Use headlines.
- Avoid introductions and tag endings.
- Ask for facts, not evaluations.
- Get one fact straight at a time.

They look simple, but some of them are hard to follow, and all are worth additional discussion.

Ask Leading Questions

Leading is permitted on cross-examination, until you make the witness your own by going beyond the scope of direct examination and those matters touching on the credibility of the witness. Rule 611(b), Federal Rules of Evidence.

So you can ask leading questions on cross-examination and that is the only kind you should ask. The way to follow this rule is by remembering that cross-examination is not designed to get information. Use depositions, sworn statements, interviews, detectives, tea leaves, chicken entrails—anything but cross-examination—to get information.

Cross-examination is not for the witness, it is for you. It is your opportunity to present your side of the witness's story, punctuated by the witness's reluctant agreement that what you say is true.

When you break this rule and ask a witness for information, two important things happen. First, you lose a measure of control over the witness. Second, you send a message to the jury that the witness is reliable. Do it if you must, but understand the cost involved.

Ask Very Short Questions

First, short questions are easier to understand than long questions.

Second, totally aside from their contents, long questions seem to invite long answers. There is a rhythm to any examination and you are the chief force in setting that rhythm. You do not want long answers. You want short answers, so you will ask short questions.

Third, you might think that the more qualifiers you use in a question, the more the question controls the witness. Qualifiers are like slats in a fence, aren't they? Doesn't each one help lock in the witness?

No. Each additional term is an additional invitation to argue or give a nonresponsive reply. Use no more words than you need to ask a question. Mastering this takes serious practice, but it is worth the effort.

Use Simple Words

Simple words are powerful. They are important on direct examination and even more so on cross-examination. Plain language goes with short questions in helping orient the jury and controlling the witness.

Use Headlines

Use topic sentences as verbal headlines to introduce new subjects. "Now I am going to ask you about your gun. It was a .357 Magnum?" The topic sentence is not a question. It requires no response. It simply announces the subject. It is permissible because it gives meaning to the questions that follow.

Use a new headline every time you change subjects. One of the advantages of headlines is that you can frame them to suit the case and the mood of the examination. For example, suppose you want to be terse and businesslike:

Q. Mr. Williams, the subject is the meeting on October 15. You arrived about 10:30 a.m.?
A. Yes.

One the other hand, say you want to be more informal:

Q. Ms. Alexander, I'd like to talk about your correspondence with Dr. Pettigrew. You first heard from him on April 20?
A. Yes.

Headlines help everyone follow your questions. They also tend to keep witnesses from being nonresponsive and changing the subject.

Avoid Introductions and Tag Endings

Cross-examination is better paced and the witness better controlled if you avoid using the following words and phrases:

Introductions
- Let me ask you this question . . .
- Isn't it a fact that . . .
- It is true, is it not . . .
- In fact . . .
- Didn't you testify that . . .
- Am I correct in assuming that . . .
- Would you tell the judge and jury . . .
- Would you tell us, please . . .

Tag endings
- . . . isn't that true?
- . . . isn't that correct?
- . . . right?

All these words, both introductions and endings, might seem to make leading questions stronger, even more leading. But, actually, the reverse is true. Extra words like these just make questions longer. They blunt the force of the question and give the witness more time to think, making it easier for him to squirm out from underneath the question.

And do not respond to a witness by answering "Okay." You may mean only that you have heard and understood the response, but the jury may think you accept what he says as true.

There are two times to break the rule against introductions and endings. First, you can use an occasional introductory phrase for emphasis. "Dr. Pettigrew, this is an important question." Second, you can use a tag ending to prod a witness into answering if he does not respond promptly. But be sparing. Too many lawyers use introductions and tag endings as verbal crutches. You are better off saying nothing than using either of them all the time.

Ask for Facts, Not Evaluations

Any cross-examination question that asks a witness to estimate, evaluate, characterize, or give an opinion (even if it is admissible) is dangerous. "Mr. McKittrick was difficult to work for, wasn't he?" is a poor question. It invites disagreement and sacrifices witness control. Facts are more powerful than opinions:

Q. Mr. McKittrick had six different secretaries in five months?
A. Yes.

Q. Each of them quit after less than a month on the job?
A. Yes.
Q. One stayed only three days?
A. Yes.

There is a time to break this rule, too. If the witness used a memorable characterization in a deposition or a written statement, use his exact words in your question. Then if he argues with your question you can use his statement to hold him to his own words.

Get One Fact at a Time

"On February 22, you saw the police hold William Johnson at gunpoint, right outside his house?"

Technically, of course, you should never ask "multiple" questions on either direct or cross-examination. A question like this, however, that merely specifies time, place, and event might not be seen as multiple. But try breaking down the question into its components. When you do this and follow the other rules, your cross-examination becomes simple, powerful, even elegant:

Q. I am going to ask you about February 22. You were there when William Johnson was arrested?
A. Yes.
Q. You saw them knock on Johnson's door?
A. Yes.
Q. You were only ten to fifteen feet away?
A. Yes.
Q. Johnson came to the door?
A. Yes.
Q. You could see his hands?
A. Yes.
Q. He had no gun?
A. No.
Q. Or any other weapon?
A. That's right.
Q. But the police all had guns?
A. Yes.
Q. All five of them?
A. Yes.
Q. In their hands?
A. Yes.

Q. Pointed at William Johnson?
A. Yes.

For now we do not even care what the cross-examiner is going to do with this. It does not matter. What counts is that he is telling the story his way, and he is in control.

How can you learn to do this, too?

Practice.

It is too late to practice once you get to court, so you will have to practice beforehand. Do not try it on people you are close to, unless you are willing to risk the relationship just to improve your skills. Instead, try it on your desk, a tree, or maybe on your car:

Q. Your engine is knocking again?
A. Yes.
Q. I just took you to the garage last week?
A. Tl.at's right.
Q. It cost $957?
A. I guess so.
Q. Please don't guess. That was the bill, wasn't it?
A. Yes.
Q. And now you're doing it again?
A. That's right.

Just don't let anyone else hear you.

CHAPTER 23

The Weasel Factor

It is a way of looking at witness control.

You ask a question on cross-examination, and instead of a straightforward answer, you get something else. The witness evades, argues, or answers some question other than the one you asked. Barbara Caulfield of San Francisco explained it to a young lawyer who was struggling for control of a difficult witness at a National Institute for Trial Advocacy training program.

"Don't you see what is happening?" she asked. "When you ask this witness a question, he is evading you. It's just as if he were holding up a weasel in your face and saying, 'I can't answer your question because I've got this weasel with me.'

"What you've got to do is take away his weasel. In effect, your response has to say, 'Let me hold the weasel so you can answer the question.' "

Barbara Caulfield was on to something. There is a weasel transaction in almost every problem of witness control.

Initial Control

Some witnesses challenge a cross-examination on the very first series of questions. It is usually a mistake not to use this opportunity to show the witness that you are in control. Not that you have to be loud, rude, offensive, or overbearing. Far from it. Cross-examination does not mean angry examination.

But on the other hand, once you lose control of a witness, it is hard to get it back. So if you are going to maintain control, do it from the very start, even on preliminary matters. For example:

Q. You are married, aren't you?
A. *(In a flippant tone)* You could say that.

In weasel terms, the witness has said, "Watch out, I may have a weasel here."

Your response has got to be: "It doesn't matter whether you have a weasel. You need to answer the question." And one of the easiest ways to do that is to just restate the question.

Q. Are you married?
A. Yes.

Yes, But

"Yes, But" is a weasel game that experts like to play. Here is how it works. Instead of answering your question directly, the witness gives a lengthy "explanation" that is an effort to get around your point. Even though the "explanation" is not responsive, far too many judges refuse to strike the extra information, saying "the witness can explain his answer."

Watch "Yes, But" in action.

Q. Doctor, can we agree that the spinal tap can be a useful medical test?
A. Yes, it can be.
Q. Doctor, when you examined Mr. Murphy, did you do a spinal tap on him?
A. I'm afraid you don't understand the distinct risk involved in an invasive diagnostic procedure such as a lumbar puncture or spinal tap, as it is called. In addition to considerable expense and pain, there is a real possibility of permanent neurological injury.

What do you do? Look at the underlying weasel transaction:

Q. Did you do the test?
A. I'm not going to talk about tests, I'm going to talk about weasels.

You respond by saying,

> Q. That's a weasel you've got in your hands, isn't it?

Which translates into:

> Q. Pardon me, Doctor, does that mean you *didn't* do the spinal tap on Mr. Murphy?

That question not only makes it clear that the witness did *not* do the test, it shows the jury that he has been holding up a weasel instead of answering the question.

Change the Subject

When a witness answers a different question on cross-examination than the one asked, it is a special type of weasel game—"Change the Subject."

> Q. Sergeant Michaelson, you did not hear about Bill Dowland's arrest until April 13, did you?
> A. I was initially assigned to the Dowland case in February and worked on it until the middle of May. Because it involved both wiretaps and coordinating several undercover agents, I was put in charge of a special communications task force.

What he has said is true. While it does not particularly hurt you, it does not answer the question, either. In weasel terms, it is basic: "I asked you about cats and dogs, but you told me about weasels."

The translation is a little bit different than merely repeating the question. It *tells* the witness you are repeating the question.

> Q. Sergeant Michaelson, my question was, you did not hear about Dowland's arrest until April 13, did you?
> A. No.

The difference between just repeating the question and *saying* you are repeating the question becomes important if you have to escalate the battle. Say, for example, the witness does not answer the question the second time. Then you can say:

> Q. Sergeant Michaelson, the subject is Mr. Dowland's arrest. My question is, you did not hear about it until April 13, did you?

A. Oh, I'm sorry. That's right. I didn't hear about it until April 13.

Open-Ended Questions

If you ask a witness to explain something on cross-examination, you usually are asking for trouble. You will get the explanation, but chances are you will not like it. One of the reasons why questions that ask for information are dangerous on cross-examination is the unintended message you send: This witness can be trusted to give reliable information.

You will not ask open-ended questions if you think about the underlying weasel transaction: "Would you like to talk about weasels? That's fine with me, ladies and gentlemen of the jury. He's an expert on weasels."

Long Questions

The weasel theory shows why it is a mistake to ask long questions on cross-examination. The longer the question, the more qualifiers it contains. And the more qualifiers it contains, the more opportunities it offers to disagree. In weasel terms, a long question is like saying: "Here is a whole box of weasels. See if you can find one you like."

Prior Inconsistent Statements

One of the most effective ways to undercut the testimony of a witness is to show that what he said before trial contradicts what he is saying now. Yet there is something doubly unfortunate about the way we usually finish an impeachment with a prior inconsistent statement from a deposition. After confronting the witness with the inconsistent questions and answers, we ask:

Q. Did I ask those questions and did you give those answers on that occasion?

What is wrong with that question?
Two things.
First, it appears as if you are testing the witness's recollection about the exact words he used at the deposition. You get to look at

the script, but he has to rely on memory. While it may reveal an inconsistency, it seems somehow unfair.

Second (and far worse) is the weasel message it sends: "This contradiction is not as bad as it looks—have a weasel."

It is an open invitation to challenge whether the statement you have read was really what was said at the deposition.

So instead of asking the traditional question, let the witness look at the deposition as you read the questions and answers that are inconsistent with his testimony. Then ask:

Q. Did I read that correctly?

You know he will have to answer yes.

Boilerplate

Finally, the weasel theory shows why the boilerplate questions that some lawyers use at the beginning of depositions are so important. Those questions should get the witness to acknowledge on the record that:

- He is under oath.
- He has no medical condition that will keep him from answering questions.
- He should not answer if he does not hear the entire question.
- He should not answer if he does not understand the entire question.
- If he needs to take a break or even recess for the day, he should say so.
- If he remembers something that means he should change an answer to make it truthful, all he needs to do is say so.

With questions like that at the beginning of the deposition, the lawyer is protected if the witness tries to pull a weasel when he is impeached with his deposition testimony. If he says he was tired or confused, the lawyer can read the boilerplate to the witness. Its message in weasel terms is simple: "I'm sorry, but your weasel is in a trap."

CHAPTER 24

The Runaway

He was thoroughly prepared for the cross-examination. He had gone over the facts again and again. He knew where the witness was vulnerable, and he had practiced asking the key questions in just the right way.

But when the questioning began, something went wrong. The witness dodged his question and started talking about something else. The cross-examiner did not know what to do, so he started asking another question while the witness was still answering the last one. In a few minutes, the cross-examiner had lost all control. Instead of scoring the points he had planned on, he was arguing with the witness and trying to shout him down.

It did not work. In a nine-minute interview of then Vice President George Bush, Dan Rather learned firsthand what good trial lawyers already know. It does not pay to be rude to a witness. If you try to interrupt by arguing or talking at the same time or just plain browbeating him into submission, the jury will side with the witness—not the cross-examiner.

Does that mean you are stuck listening to a runaway witness argue your opponent's case? Not necessarily. There are things you can do besides plugging your ears or begging the judge for help. Not surprisingly, the best cure is prevention, and the way to do that is to ask short, leading questions on cross-examination.

But prevention does not always work. Then the decision is whether to respond before the situation gets out of control. Fortunately, there are a number of ways to do that. If you look closely, you will notice that of the seven ways to interrupt a witness, only one actually involves interruption.

What Would You *Like* to Call It?

James Jeans of the University of Missouri at Kansas City was cross-examining a key witness in a drug case at the National Institute for Trial Advocacy. The witness, Laura Hobson, had been promised immunity from prosecution if she would testify against her ex-boyfriend, Fred Peters. First Jeans asked her about some of her drug dealings, and then he turned to the immunity agreement:

>   Q. Then you made a deal with the prosecutor, didn't you?
>   A. I don't know if I would call it a *deal*.
>   Q. Well what would you like to call it—*an arrangement?*

It was a beautiful little interchange, and Jeans won it instantly. It rests on a principle that can be applied whenever a witness argues with your choice of words: Do not insist on a particular word. Offer the witness a neutral term instead. That way you are not arguing with the witness, the witness is arguing with you.

I'm Sorry, But the Rules of Evidence . . .

Some witnesses try to turn the tables and fire questions back at the lawyer.

>   Q. When you saw the tire coming at you, you did not stop, did you?
>   A. Well, counselor, what was I supposed to do? The truck was on my right, the car was on my left, and then this huge truck tire came bouncing down the road, right in my path.

Do not answer his question. The next one will be even worse.

Unfortunately, the typical response to questions from the witness is almost as bad as answering the question, because it sounds overbearing and seems to take unfair advantage of the lectern:

"I'm afraid you don't understand the procedure. I'm the lawyer and you're the witness. I ask the questions and you give the answers. Got it?"

But if this is offensive, what should you do instead? Try giving the real reason for not answering.

"I'm sorry, but the rules of evidence don't permit me to answer your question. If they did, I'd be happy to explain exactly what you should have done."

It stops the witness without being rude. And the real advantage is that you have the rest of the trial to think of an answer, which you can give during final argument—when the witness cannot talk back.

The Loop Back

The witness tries to avoid your question in any number of different ways. Say he is starting an argument or explaining "why" when the question called for "what." Looping back lets you show the judge and jury what the witness is up to:

- Q. You say you never signed Mr. Wood's offer?
- A. Absolutely not. We rejected it out of hand.
- Q. Then on May 20, Mr. Wood asked you to send his offer back to him?
- A. That's right.
- Q. But you did not return his offer, did you?
- A. That is one of the most ridiculous assumptions I have ever heard. Just because someone asks you to send back a piece of paper doesn't mean there is a legal obligation to do that. It is absurd to think you're supposed to rummage through all of your paperwork just to satisfy the odd whim of someone who sent you a letter three or four weeks earlier.
- Q. Pardon me, Mr. Dorf, but a moment ago I asked if Mr. Wood wanted his offer back, and you said yes?
- A. That's right.
- Q. And then I asked if you sent his offer back to him, but you didn't answer that question, did you?
- A. No, I guess not.

We Will Get to That

Now suppose that instead of arguing about Mr. Wood's letter, the witness tries to change the subject:

- Q. But you did not return Mr. Wood's offer, did you?
- A. Counsel, what matters in this case is not the letter, but the oral agreement that Wood made with us just three weeks later.

Q. Mr. Dorf, you want to talk about oral agreements, don't you?
A. Yes, that's right.
Q. We're going to get to oral agreements in just a minute. But before we do that, you need to answer my question.
A. What's your question?
Q. You didn't return Mr. Wood's offer, did you?
A. No.
Q. Even though he asked you to?
A. That's right.

Does That Mean No?

Another way to deal with an argumentative answer is to explain that it really means yes or no. For example:

Q. You did not return Mr. Wood's offer, did you?
A. Counsel, what matters in this case is not the letter, but the oral agreement Mr. Wood made with us just three weeks later.
Q. Pardon me, Mr. Dorf, does that mean no?
A. Ah, er, what do you mean?
Q. You did not return the letter, did you?
A. No.

David Malone's Follow-up Interruption

Now let's make things a little tougher. The witness has a full speech prepared for cross-examination and is intent on delivering it. The judge has already told you three times during your examination that "the witness may explain his answer."

So you have decided to cut your losses and finish the cross-examination. But you need to stop the witness and he is right in the middle of his speech.

If the judge will not help, is it finally time to interrupt? Maybe, but it does not need to be intrusive. First try holding up the palm of your hand in the universal stop sign of the traffic policeman. Interestingly, it will make some people stop talking.

If that does not work, then try David Malone's follow-up technique. Malone practices in Washington, D.C., and is a NITA instructor. His method works on runaway witnesses during either direct or cross-examination. If you pick up on something the witness says and ask a follow-up question, no one will notice that you are interrupting. That is because we accept follow-up interruptions all the time in normal conversation.

Watch the technique at work as the witness keeps talking:

A. ... And then, before we were able to turn off the road, our way was suddenly blocked by an entire troop of Boy Scouts who were carrying backpacks and portaging these huge aluminum canoes. And of course they stopped all the traffic when ...
Q. Pardon me, you say they had canoes?
A. Yes, that's right.
Q. Thank you. I have no further questions, Your Honor.

That's Up to the Jury

Finally, say the witness is not content to argue or change the subject. Suppose that he gives some self-serving opinion. This is the time to invoke the name of the jury:

Q. Did you tell Mrs. Franklin what had happened?
A. Under the circumstances, that was not really necessary. We were more interested in being fair than anything else.
Q. Mr. Michaelson, it is going to be up the jury to decide whether what you did was fair.

The chances are they will agree.

CHAPTER 25

Pressure Points

The doctor had been beautifully prepared for his deposition. He was an experienced witness who had testified in a number of trials and had his deposition taken more times than he could remember. He knew that only if he recognized a book or article as authoritative in its field could it be used to impeach his testimony at trial. There would be no problem; he was not going to recognize any writing as authoritative.

Or so he thought. After just twenty minutes, the doctor was volunteering a long list of books and articles that he said were reliable, authoritative sources in the area. His lawyer, who knew it was too early to ask for a break to go to the bathroom, had given up trying to signal the doctor to stop talking and had buried his head in his hands.

What happened?

The lawyer who was taking the deposition had pushed the right pressure point.

Pressure point?

The term is used by Cleveland lawyer Eric Kennedy. And just as in the first-aid manuals, pressure points are the right places to push. Only instead of stopping the flow of blood, pushing on a pressure point makes a witness do what you want.

Here is how it worked with the doctor.

> Q. Well, after four years of college, another four years in medical school, one year of internship, and three years of a residency, you had a total of twelve years of education

after high school to prepare you for your profession, correct?
A. Yes, that's right.
Q. And then you took a series of comprehensive examinations, both written and oral, in your specialty?
A. That's right.
Q. After all that, you are probably delighted to have finally finished studying?
A. *(Suddenly wary)* What do you mean?
Q. Well, you're finished with academic work, aren't you? You don't have to study anymore. Now you can do it instead of just reading about it.
A. I'm afraid you don't understand the practice of medicine. It is a constantly changing field. New discoveries are being made every day, and you have to keep current if you are going to be a responsible practitioner.
Q. What does a responsible practitioner do to keep current, Doctor?
A. Read books, articles, attend lectures and workshops. Professional education is never finished.
Q. Could you tell me some of the books or articles you have read—say in the last two years—to keep you current in your field?

Then came the list. After that, the final questions on the subject were almost anti-climactic.

Q. You read these articles and consulted these books to keep current on recent developments in your field of medicine?
A. That's right.
Q. So they are what you consider reliable and authoritative works?
A. Of course.

One note before we go on. It probably occurred to you that you do not have to get the opposing expert to recognize a learned treatise as authoritative if you are under the Federal Rules of Evidence. Under Rule 803(18) you can also establish that the treatise is authoritative through the testimony of another expert, or even by judicial notice.

Still, it is worth getting the witness you are going to attack to agree that a learned treatise is authoritative. Then, when the article or book disputes the witness's testimony, it seems more like a prior inconsistent statement than just another expert who happens to have a different point of view.

Obviously, the right pressure point can be effective. The question is how do you find it? One good guide is the witness's sense of self-protection. It is demonstrated by a variation of what happened in *State v. Oswald*, 381 P.2d 617 (1963).

Oswald was charged with robbing a bank in Seattle on July 14. But Oswald claimed he could not have robbed the Seattle bank because he was in Portland, Oregon, on July 14. To prove his alibi, he called the owner of a Portland restaurant. The restaurant owner said that throughout June and July, Oswald was courting one of his waitresses. According to the restaurant owner, Oswald made such a pest of himself that he was in the restaurant every day during that period, including July 14.

When it was time to cross-examine the restaurant owner about Oswald's alibi, the prosecutor had very little to work with. He had nothing on the restaurant owner: no prior inconsistent statements, no arrests, no convictions, no prior bad acts, no one who had a bad word about his reputation for truth. But he did have one fact: An FBI agent saw Oswald in Seattle on June 20. That was nearly a month before the robbery, but it was also during the time that Oswald was supposedly making a pest of himself at the restaurant.

The prosecutor wanted the restaurant owner to say that Oswald was at his restaurant on both June 20 and July 14. If those two dates could be tied together, the prosecutor would have a better chance to put the FBI agent on the stand to testify that Oswald was in Seattle on June 20. What pressure point would help encourage the restaurant owner to link June 20 to July 14?

Self-protection.

Q. Mr. Ardiss, you say Mr. Oswald was in your restaurant on July 14?
A. That's right.
Q. He was courting one of your waitresses?
A. Yes. Alice.
Q. And coming to see her every day throughout June and July?
A. That's right.
Q. Mr. Ardiss, you don't have a business relationship with Mr. Oswald, do you?
A. *(Concerned)* What do you mean, business relationship?

Q. He doesn't own any part of your restaurant, does he?
A. No, no. Just me and my wife, we own the restaurant.
Q. And you don't participate in his business?
A. No.
Q. Mr. Ardiss, you didn't have any reason to know that the First National Bank of Seattle was going to be robbed on July 14, did you?
A. Of course not.
Q. Or that Mr. Oswald would be charged with that crime?
A. Absolutely not.
Q. And I gather that he did not tell you to mark your calendar for July 14?
A. No.
Q. Or tell you to remember that he was in your restaurant on July 14?
A. No.
Q. So as far as you were concerned, July 14 was not a special day?
A. Not really.
Q. You say he was in your restaurant on July 14 because he was there every day during June and July?
A. Yes, that's right.
Q. Just as he would have been there July 1 or June 20?
A. That's right.
Q. So as far as you are concerned, then, there was no reason to pay any more attention to the 14th of July than the 20th of June?
A. That's right.
Q. He was in your restaurant on both of those days?
A. Yes. He was there every day.

Now think how pertinent the FBI agent's testimony will seem.

Once you start thinking about pressure points, you will see opportunities to use them everywhere you look.

Take a simple medical malpractice case. A patient who was hospitalized for a routine operation suddenly took a turn for the worse. The attending nurse called the patient's doctor and reached her at home. Based on what the nurse told her, the doctor prescribed a medication. The trouble is, the patient was allergic to the drug—which was noted on the patient's medical chart. The results were catastrophic, and both the hospital and the doctor were sued.

To keep the doctor from protecting the nurse, who looked as if she had slipped up, the plaintiff's lawyer shrewdly pushed the doctor's pressure point.

At the doctor's deposition, he told her lawyer that it was important to find out just what had been said over the phone. If the doctor had been told about the patient's allergy, then she was obviously in big trouble.

The results at the deposition were gratifying. The doctor explained how she had to rely on what the nurse told her over the telephone, and how failing to mention an allergy to a medication was a serious breach of the nurse's professional duty. The right pressure point made the co-defendant one of the best witnesses for the plaintiff.

CHAPTER 26

Careful Cross-Examination

Dick Mudger and Flash Magruder were holding forth on cross-examination, and Angus was trying not to listen.

"It doesn't really matter what you do on cross-examination," said Flash, "it's how you do it. It's theater. The value of cross is the emotional impression it conveys, not its actual content."

Angus snorted, but kept on reading the paper.

"Wrong," said Mudger. "Anybody who thinks that the jury doesn't hear what the witnesses say hasn't ever talked to a jury after the trial. Cross-examination is an opportunity, and you're a fool not to take advantage of it. Every witness has some vulnerable spot, some weakness, some soft underbelly waiting to be slashed open. The point of cross-examination is not just to create some kind of mood—the point of cross is to draw blood."

Angus put down his paper and looked up. "What if there isn't any blood?" he said.

"What do you mean?" asked Mudger.

"Maybe you've both overstated your positions a little," said Angus.

"Oh, come on," said Flash. "You're not going to give us that Wigmore line about cross being 'the greatest engine for the discovery of truth,' are you?"

"Nope," Angus said. "Wigmore could exaggerate, too. I just think there is a lot more to cross-examination than creating a mood on one hand or drawing blood on the other. And I also think there are times when trying to create a mood or draw some blood can get you into a lot of trouble."

Angus was at it again, so I got a pad and started writing. Here are my notes.

Control Yourself

All of the popular media—books, newspapers, radio, television, videotapes, audiotapes, and live theater—contribute to the poisonous notion that cross-examination is a time for all-out war.

And we rise to the occasion.

Convinced that any witness on the other side must necessarily be a vicious liar, we rarely pass up an opportunity to make an attack.

Armed with all the modern weapons—supersonic sarcasm, laser-guided anger, heat-seeking argumentative questions (were you lying then or are you lying now?)—we do what the Army Field Artillery calls "firing for effect." We keep lobbing in shells, hoping to obliterate the target.

It is almost always a mistake.

Self-control is even more important than witness control. Cross-examination does not mean angry examination. The last thing you want to do is seethe and fulminate, hurling wild accusations of mendacity. A good cross-examination does not tell the jury the witness is a liar—it shows them (if it has to do it at all).

Only If You Must

Even when you exercise superb self-control, it is a mistake to challenge a witness on cross-examination unless you have both the means and the need.

The two ingredients are absolutely essential to any destructive cross-examination: The attack must help your theory of the case, and you must have something with which you can work.

Even then it can be the wrong thing to do.

Momma takes the stand to tell the jury that her son, Lefty (she calls him Sonny), was at her house on the night of August 19, and so therefore he could not possibly have committed any robbery.

Forget it.

People don't identify with the lawyer, they identify with the witness. They expect Momma to stand up for her son, no matter how badly things are going for him. They are ready to forgive her for her loyalty—and discount what she says—unless you hammer her with questions like, "You love your son, don't you?" and

"You'd do anything to keep him out of jail, wouldn't you?" Not that you must never cross-examine Momma. Sometimes you must, but you need to know the cost.

A respected local minister testifies truthfully in a land dispute. His testimony has only hurt your case a little, but you can humiliate him with a bit of embarrassing bias from his personal life.

Don't touch it.

Attacking testimony you think is the truth is usually a disaster. To be sure, the rules of evidence permit it, and we will leave the interesting ethical questions for another time. But please understand. When you make the attack, your very cross-examination says two important things to the jury: first, that something on direct-examination was untrue—perhaps deliberately untrue. Second, it says that revealing this personal information is justified because it is essential to a fair trial.

But now suppose one of your own witnesses agrees with the minister's testimony, or you concede the point in your final argument.

The jury will feel you have cheated them and will resent the way you sacrificed other people to do it.

None of this means you should shy from the task of taking on a witness if you must. But do not assume it is the right thing to do, especially because you have other options.

Constructive Cross-Examination

For the most part, the law deals with destructive cross-examination. We regulate how to impeach a witness with a prior inconsistent statement. We have rules about what kind of convictions can be used to attack credibility and whether you can inquire about other bad acts that have not resulted in convictions. We limit the use of character evidence and have varying rules about whether a witness must first be confronted with bias before permitting independent proof.

And then we seem to assume that because the law regulates destructive cross-examination, it is the most important thing we can do.

That does not follow.

Sometimes a constructive cross-examination is more valuable than any attack.

A constructive cross-examination is when you use the witness to develop facts favorable to you rather than trying to undercut what he has said on direct-examination.

Say you represent a plaintiff who received a serious head injury in an automobile accident. Six months after the crash he developed Jacksonian seizures—a form of epilepsy. In his case, his left arm and leg suddenly and uncontrollably start twitching and shaking. His spells come sporadically and without any warning; medication has not been much help.

Your expert witness says the problem was caused by the trauma in the crash. The defense expert says it is a congenital condition.

Forget about destructive cross-examination of the defendant's doctor for the moment. Look at the opportunities for a constructive cross. Here is some information you have from his deposition:

The plaintiff's condition is real. It shows up on an electroencephalogram as random abnormal brain waves, and once the plaintiff even had a seizure while an EEG was being performed.

The cause of his condition is an abnormality—such as a scar—on the part of the brain that controls the movement of his arms and legs.

There is no cure. No medicine will make the scar go away or stop the seizures. There is no operation that can remove the abnormal tissue in the brain without doing even more damage.

There is more, but that ought to be enough to start you thinking about how you could use this witness to support your case on injury, whether or not you attack his testimony on causation.

Two important points before we go on. First, it is possible to do both a constructive and a destructive examination in the same cross—but it is not easy. You have to take pains to get the constructive material first, before you make any attack. Even so, you may confuse the jury. After all, you are asking them to accept part of what the witness says and reject the other part.

Second, a constructive cross-examination does not mean you should surrender witness control or ask open-ended questions. You should do the testifying with your leading questions and have the witness agree with what you say. When you ask the witness for information, you are sending the signal that he is a trustworthy source—a message you may not want to transmit.

Phantom Cross-Examination

A phantom cross is different. It sounds like a cross-examination. It can have all the emotional charge of a cross-examination. But it is a low-risk procedure because it does not deal with facts that are really at issue in the case.

One of the simplest ways to do a phantom cross-examination is to show what the witness does not know. For example, you can go through his deposition, picking out the questions he was unable to answer because of lack of information. Then the cross-examination is a laundry list of what the witness cannot say. And if he suddenly claims to know the answers, you have the deposition with which to impeach him.

Another kind of phantom cross-examination makes the points the witness must agree with but that are not really in contention. That does not mean the phantom cross deals with things that are irrelevant or even unimportant to the case. Sometimes setting out what is not in contention is one of the best ways to limit the scope of what the case is all about.

No Questions

There are times when even a phantom cross-examination is too dangerous. The direct examiner forgets to make one of his most important points before turning the witness over for cross-examination.

When that happens, a warning strobe should start flashing inside your head. You are being mouse-trapped. No matter what questions you ask on cross-examination, the witness is going to try to slip in the damning information that was left out of direct examination—so it will have even more impact. And if for some reason the witness can find no place to blurt it out on cross, your opponent will be ready to ask about it on re-direct.

Unless you are willing to help your opponent make his case, now is when you should tell the judge you see no need to cross-examine.

CHAPTER 27

An Impeachment Checklist

"It's hard to decide how to attack a witness when you don't know what your options are."

—*Angus*

The hardest way to learn the law of impeachment is to read the Federal Rules of Evidence. Even at their best, the rules are a legislative pincushion, with unconnected provisions sticking out here and there, while the guiding points and basic principles are usually hidden under the surface.

If you think that sounds unfair, look through Article VI, Witnesses—Rules 601 through 615—and try to find the rule that covers how you impeach a witness with bias, or the one that says whether you can impeach a witness on a collateral matter.

You will find no rule on bias, although you will see the word used in the article on relevance.

You will see no rule about impeaching witnesses on collateral matters, even though Rule 608(b) is an unspoken example of the general idea.

Worse than that, the Federal Rules of Evidence never even mention what has to happen before you can impeach any witness.

So to understand impeachment, we take the basic ideas from the common law and then weave in the Federal Rules of Evidence as they fit in the overall scheme.

The starting point is what opens the door to impeachment—testimony. As soon as any witness takes the stand and testifies, his credibility is at issue.

Timing is critical. Pre-emptive strikes and anticipatory defenses are not allowed. No attack before testimony, and (with only a few exceptions) no support before attack. The purpose of the rule is to keep us from needless diversions. Why should we worry about the credibility of someone who never testifies, or rehabilitating someone who is never attacked? There is enough clutter in trials without speculative attacks or defenses.

The rule against attacking a witness before he testifies is virtually absolute (although you can probably find a federal district judge somewhere who says the court's power to control the mode and order of interrogation under Rule 611 of the Federal Rules of Evidence implies the right to permit attack before testimony).

You would figure that the rule against supporting a witness before he was attacked would be just as strict, but it is not. Victims of sex crimes may be supported with evidence of a fresh complaint even if their credibility is never attacked. And under Rule 803(18) of the Federal Rules of Evidence, an expert witness may be supported with a learned treatise while he is still on direct examination.

There is an area that is more custom than established rule. Most judges let the defendant in a criminal case explain his prior convictions before the prosecution cross-examines the defendant with his criminal record. And some judges even permit witnesses in civil cases to explain apparent admissions and prior inconsistent statements before attack, although others insist it is wrong.

There it is—testimony puts the credibility of the witness at issue. When you think about it, that explains what impeachment is all about. Impeachment is not just a pointed bit of cross-examination that exposes some mistake or unjustified assumption. Impeachment undercuts testimony by impugning the source. It attacks the witness, not just what he says. Here is the list of what you can use to do that.

Bias

Showing the witness has a motive to lie is powerful medicine, which is why it has to be used carefully. Most lawyers keep pouring long after the tablespoon is already overflowing, with predictable results—the jury resents it. Better to use a light touch than to get an adverse reaction.

Bias is never collateral. That means that not only can you deal with it on cross-examination, you are not "bound by the witness's answer." If the witness denies the bias on cross-examination, you can prove it with "extrinsic evidence"—documents and other witnesses.

Do you have to give the witness a chance to explain or deny the facts that show bias before you can use extrinsic proof? Many states say yes except for instances where the bias is indisputable, such as an interest in the outcome of the case.

The real artistry in using bias is in linking. Bias is a general attack. And the point of linking is to tie the facts that suggest the witness is taking sides to the testimony you most want to attack. When you do that, remember the powerful medicine rule. It is better to put things together so the jurors feel they have figured it out for themselves than to try to pour the idea down their throats.

Prior Convictions

The common-law rule about impeachment with convictions was straightforward and harsh. Any felony or any misdemeanor of "moral turpitude" could be used. The probative value of the conviction was not weighed against the risk of unfair prejudice, and there was no time limit for stale convictions. When a witness took the stand, his criminal record was fair game.

Not under Rule 609 of the Federal Rules of Evidence. Now there is a ten-year time limit from conviction or release from confinement, unless the cross-examiner gives notice that he wants to use the conviction and the court finds that the probative value "substantially outweighs its prejudicial effect."

And under the amendment to Rule 609 that went into effect in December of 1990, there are three different situations in which a witness may be impeached.

First, any witness may be impeached with a crime of dishonesty—whether it is a misdemeanor or felony. There is no weighing and the court has no discretion; crimes of dishonesty may be used to impeach. Misdemeanors that are not crimes of dishonesty may not be used in any situation.

Second, when the witness is not the accused in a criminal case, felonies may be used unless the prejudicial effect of the evidence substantially outweighs the risk of unfair prejudice—the general relevance test that is used under Rule 403. In other words, the bias is in favor of admissibility.

Third, when the witness is the accused in a criminal case, felonies that are not crimes of dishonesty may only be used if their probative value outweighs their prejudicial effect to the accused. Then the bias is against admissibility.

Prior convictions are not collateral, and if the witness denies the conviction it may be proved with a public record.

The customary time to deal with convictions is on cross-examination of the witness. That used to be required by Rule 609, but was quietly dropped in the December 1990 amendment. That is an unfortunate change that may lead some lawyers to try to sandbag the witness by waiting until after he has left the stand before bringing out his criminal record.

Be careful using convictions in civil cases. What is standard fare in a criminal trial can easily look like a deliberate attempt to smear the witness in another setting.

Prior Bad Acts

A dishonest act itself has just as much probative value as a conviction for that act.

But a mere act is easier to allege (and a lot harder to prove) than a conviction. And that accounts for the differences between cross-examining about a witness's misdeeds under Rule 608(b) and his convictions under Rule 609:

First, there is no right to cross-examine about bad acts. The court has discretion to permit the cross-examination if the acts are probative of truthfulness. And while Rule 608(b) says nothing about it, you should expect that the court will be more cautious with the cross-examination of the accused in a criminal case, when the jury is more likely to misuse the evidence.

Second, you are stuck with the witness's answer. When the witness denies committing the act, you cannot prove it with extrinsic evidence.

And here is an important tip. If the bad act shows bias, you can prove it with extrinsic evidence. Remember? Bias is never collateral. And the acts that prove bias are not inadmissible just because they are also bad acts.

Bad Reputation

At common law you could attack any witness with a "reputation witness," who would testify that the witness being attacked (call him the principal witness) had a bad reputation for honesty.

The process was only changed a little by Rule 608(a). Now "reputation witnesses" can also give their personal opinions about the honesty of the principal witness—which is what they were really doing all along. The underlying idea is still the same. We do not want reputation or opinion witnesses testifying to specific instances of conduct. That would take too long.

But because specific instances of conduct are the most efficient way to pop the reputation (or opinion) bubble, they may be asked about on cross-examination. And as you would expect, the cross-examiner is bound by the witness's answer, and may not use extrinsic evidence to prove the specific conduct.

No Firsthand Knowledge

Lack of personal knowledge goes to the basic competency of a witness. If a fact witness literally does not know what he is talking about, his testimony is inadmissible.

So the scholars think of firsthand knowledge as a competency test that can keep a witness off the stand—not as a basis for impeachment.

But in actual practice, witnesses rarely concede that they do not know the facts. And the lack of firsthand knowledge is a proper subject for both cross-examination and extrinsic evidence, since it attacks the very foundation of the witness's testimony.

Mental Defect

Having a psychiatrist attack a witness for being a "psychopath with a tendency toward making false accusations" seems like powerful testimony, indeed. And that is exactly what Dr. Carl Binger said about the prosecution witness, Whitaker Chambers, in the famous trial of Alger Hiss in 1950.

Did it work? Or did Dr. Binger bite off too much? According to the late Irving Younger, who did a special presentation on the trial of Hiss, when the prosecution was through cross-examining Dr. Binger, "there was nothing left."

And there it is—potentially powerful, dangerous, and seldom used.

Contradiction

When one witness contradicts another, it does not seem like impeachment, but rather simple disagreement. And precisely because it does not have much persuasive force to attack the general credibility of the witness, the common law developed an important limitation on contradiction:

You cannot impeach a witness on a collateral matter. And that means you cannot call one witness to contradict another on something that is not an issue in the trial. While credibility is important, so is saving time. It is simply not worth pursuing a witness about testimony that does not matter to the case.

Inconsistent Statements

The impact is felt by everyone. The witness is contradicted out of his own mouth.

But the legal theory behind it is attractive only to lawyers. The prior inconsistent statement is not admissible to prove its truth, but only to cast doubt on the credibility of the witness—or at least that is what everybody assumes.

But under Rule 801 of the Federal Rules of Evidence, prior inconsistent statements are admissible for their truth whenever the witness is subject to cross-examination about the statement and it was given under oath subject to the penalty of perjury at a trial, hearing, or other proceeding, or in a deposition.

In other words, most prior inconsistent statements are admissible for their truth.

Finally, a word of warning about impeaching any witness. There is a seductive logical fallacy that takes years to learn to resist. Just because the law permits something does not mean it is a good idea. If the body blow to the integrity of the witness is not both justified by the facts and necessary to your case, let it go.

CHAPTER 28

Prior Inconsistent Statements

Ernest Droner was back in court and was having trouble. One of his key witnesses got turned around about the color of the traffic light, and Droner tried to straighten him out.

First, Droner was surprised to learn at sidebar that under Rule 607 of the Federal Rules of Evidence, he was permitted to impeach his own witness without having to pretend he was "surprised" by the witness's testimony. The way was clear to impeach him with his deposition.

Which is what he did.

Later, in The Brief Bag, Droner had a lot of reasons why he lost the case. "But even though I made some mistakes," he said, "I am proud of that impeachment. Just like we learned in Evidence, that statement went right to his credibility. By the time I was through with him, the jury didn't know whether the light was red or green."

That is when Angus finally stirred. "Droner," he said, "you *are* saying that just to rattle my cage, aren't you?"

But Ernest Droner was serious. "What do you mean, Angus?" he asked.

"Three things," said Angus. "First, you've got some important reading to do in the Federal Rules of Evidence. Second, the way you attacked that witness's credibility probably didn't help your case, even though you liked the way it went. And third, it's not all your fault."

"Hey, come on, Angus," said Flash Magruder. "Aren't you being just a little blunt?"

"I can handle it," said Droner. "What are you talking about, Angus? Get specific."

"All right," said Angus. "First come the rules of evidence. You're not in court every day, so you haven't picked up some of the points that some lawyers seem to just absorb through their skin. But that doesn't let you off the hook. It means you've got to do a little extra work every time you have a trial."

"Like what?" asked Droner.

"Like reading Rule 607," Angus said, and Droner looked a little sheepish. "But Rule 801 is a lot more important than that."

"Rule 801? That's a hearsay rule, isn't it? What does that have to do with anything?" asked Droner.

Angus did not answer. Instead, he took out his wallet and said, "I've got five dollars that says if I asked you to write the common law theory of what prior inconsistent statements are admissible to prove, you would get the answer absolutely right."

"I'm not going to take that bet, because you're right—I know the answer," said Droner. "At common law, a prior inconsistent statement was admissible only to attack the credibility of the witness, not to prove its truth—unless, of course, the witness is a party. Then the prior inconsistent statement is an admission."

"Bravo," said Angus. "In other words, a prior inconsistent statement was hearsay at common law, right?"

"Right," said Droner.

"Which is where Rule 801 comes in," said Angus. "And Rule 801 of the Federal Rules says that prior inconsistent statements are admissible for their truth when the statement was given under oath, subject to the penalty of perjury, at a trial, hearing, or other proceeding, or in a deposition. The deposition doesn't even have to be from the same case. Any time you impeach a witness with his deposition, it comes in for its truth."

"Angus," Droner said, "don't think I don't appreciate your knowledge of the rules and all that, but so what? Who cares about the technical theory of admissibility? The only difference it makes is what the judge tells the jury, which they don't even begin to understand."

A lot of us thought Angus might bite off Droner's head with some remark like, "It's easy to claim that the rules are irrelevant when you don't know what they are," but he didn't.

Instead, he smiled and said, "Droner, you might be a lawyer yet. Tell you what. I've got another five dollars that says I can reproduce your impeachment of that witness—almost verbatim—even though I wasn't there and no one told me what you said. All I need is his name, what he said on the stand, and what was in the deposition. And of course, you've got to let me make up little details like the page number in the deposition and the date it was taken."

"Angus," said Droner, "get ready to lose five dollars. I've got to win *something* today. The witness's name was Willson. On the witness stand he said the traffic on Commerce Street had the red light when the collision took place, and at his deposition he said the Commerce Street traffic had the green light."

"One more thing, just to be sure," said Angus. "You win the case if the light was green, you lose if the light was red, right?"

"You got it," said Droner, smiling. "Now let's hear my impeachment."

Angus started, and in a few seconds Droner's smile started to fade.

> Q. Mr. Willson, a few minutes ago, you testified that the light for the traffic on Commerce Street was red at the time of the collision, is that correct?
> A. Yes, that's right.
> Q. Are you sure it was red at that time, Mr. Willson?
> A. Let me think. Yes, I'm quite sure.
> Q. Commerce Street was the northbound traffic?
> A. Yes.
> Q. And they had the red light?
> A. That's right.
> Q. Now, Mr. Willson, you recall that on the 12th of November we had occasion to take your deposition?
> A. Somewhere around that time, yes.
> Q. At lawyer Mudger's office?
> A. Yes.
> Q. Do you recall that I asked you about the color of the light for the traffic on Commerce Street?
> A. Yes, I guess so.
> Q. And at that time did I ask you these questions, and did you give these answers? Page 147, Counsel:
>
>> "Question: Were you able to see the traffic signal for the traffic on Commerce Street?

Answer: Yes.
Question: What was the color of the light for the traffic on Commerce Street at the time of the collision?
Answer: The Commerce traffic had the greet light."

Q. Mr. Willson, did I ask you those questions and did you give those answers on that occasion?
A. Yes, I guess so.

"You probably didn't ask him if he was lying then or lying now, did you?" Angus asked Droner. "You probably asked him which was correct, his testimony on the witness stand, or his testimony in the deposition—right?"

Droner was angry—probably because it was his second loss for the day. "What is this, Angus, some kind of parlor trick? You've been talking to the court reporter or somebody who was at the trial, and I don't think it's very funny."

"Ernie," Angus said, "calm down. What you did is what 90 percent of all lawyers do, which is why I was able to replicate it. And it's also the reason why it's not your fault that it doesn't work very well.

"The point is," Angus continued, "that the theory of admissibility of the prior inconsistent statement is one of those lessons that everybody learns too well. Our mind-sets are poisoned by the legal theory. Instead of trying to sell the notion that the deposition proves the light was green, lawyers are showing that the witness has said two different things, so neither one should be believed.

"Of course," Angus said, "it is an approach we were never required to take. Like you said, the legal theory really only controls how the judge instructs the jury.

"Sometimes it makes a difference whether you survive a motion for a directed verdict, but not often.

"But the amazing thing is, we still just attack credibility even though the law changed twenty years ago, when the Federal Rules of Evidence were adopted.

"For example, you kept repeating that the light was 'red' when you were talking to Willson. You were setting up 'red' because you wanted to knock it down with 'green.' So what the jury heard was 'red,' 'red,' 'red,' and then one 'green.' Think of the impression that makes. If you had been concentrating on 'green,' it would have been the other way around.

"Once you free yourself from the notion that you are only attacking credibility, you will focus on what really counts. For example, you want to convince the jury that the deposition was correct. So you build it up. You emphasize that it was taken months or years ago, when everything was fresh in the witness's mind. And the jury doesn't know what a deposition is. So you explain it to them, just a bit, with questions about how the witness took the same oath as he did today and how he tried to tell the truth.

"Finally, you can get away from those awful phrases like, 'Did you have occasion to give your deposition?' and 'Do you recall that I asked you questions concerning the color of the traffic light?'

"As far as the jury is concerned, an 'occasion' is when you rent a hall. And it seems unfair to ask a witness whether he remembers something that you can look at and he can't.

"But the worst is, 'Are those the questions I asked and the answers you gave?' No rule requires that convoluted formulation. Besides, like James W. Jeans of the University of Missouri at Kansas City says, it is an open invitation for the witness to claim that you didn't ask that question or that the court reporter got his answer wrong."

"So what should I do instead?" asked Droner.

"Show him his deposition while *you* do the reading," said Angus. "That way you can be sure it will be read loud and clear, so everyone understands what he said in the deposition. Besides, you know that when you ask, 'Did I read that correctly?' it is the one question he has to answer 'yes.' "

CHAPTER 29

Phantom Impeachment

Ben Matlock does it all the time on television. The witness on the stand is the real killer, and only Matlock knows it. Matlock says on cross-examination:

> Q. You know what I think? I think you put the bottle of poison inside the marble elephant and then called the florist to cancel the order for the dozen long-stemmed roses.

(That is when you say, "I knew those roses were part of it," and then, "No judge I know would ever let me ask a question like that." But never mind that now.)

Then the witness says:

> A. You're wrong. I couldn't have done that because I didn't even know there was a marble elephant.

And then comes Matlock's crushing blow.

> Q. Oh, yes? See that man over there? (And a man in a green leisure suit stands up in the back of the courtroom.) He's the cotton-candy salesman who works out in front of the aquarium, and he's prepared to testify that he saw you walk out of the aquarium with that marble elephant in your hand on Tuesday morning—three days before the killing. You not only knew there was a marble elephant—you bought it, didn't you?

That's when the witness, visibly shaken, says:

A. I want to talk to my lawyer.

There it is, the Phantom Impeachment. The witness is impeached—contradicted on key testimony—by someone who never takes the stand and who never says a word in court. It only happens on television, right?

Sorry. Before you laugh it off, you should understand that real lawyers try the Phantom Impeachment all the time—not that it makes it right—and not that they do it well. And the main difference is that real lawyers are usually not as effective with it as Ben Matlock is. They tend to do it this way:

Q. So you say the light was green?
A. That's right.
Q. Well, if Sergeant Robertson were to testify that the light was red, would he be lying?

Time out for a minute. Is that a proper question? We start with some basic rules.

First, under Rule 607 of the Federal Rules of Evidence, any party may attack the credibility of any witness. That is also the trend in an increasing number of states (although some states still say you must be genuinely surprised and actually injured by the testimony before you can attack your own witness). The point is, you can go after the believability of this witness even if you are the one who put him on the stand, so that is not the problem.

Second, look at the list of ways in which you can attack the credibility of a witness:

- Bias
- Prior inconsistent statement
- Bad reputation for honesty
- Prior convictions
- Prior bad acts that relate to honesty
- Lack of firsthand knowledge
- Mental defect
- Contradiction

Notice that contradiction is one of the ways that you can attack the credibility of a witness. But what was that business you learned in law school about being bound by the witness's answer?

As long as the evidence is relevant to the issues in the case, you are not "bound" by the testimony of anybody. Just because one witness says "red" does not mean you cannot call another who says "green." If the color of the light goes to an issue in the case, you can have as many witnesses as you like tell what color they thought it was.

Of course, there are times when you are stuck with someone's answer. If you cross-examine a witness about some act of dishonesty that is not part of the case, then you will not be able to contradict him with another witness. That is an example of the general rule that you cannot contradict a witness on a collateral matter.

Apply that to a question about the color of the light and whether Sergeant Robertson would be lying if he said it was red. Say that the color of the light has nothing to do with the issues in the case. You want to call Sergeant Robertson so you can attack the credibility of the witness who said "green."

You can't do that.

We do not want the lawsuit trailing off into arguments about facts that do not bear directly on the case. We have enough trouble figuring out who hit whom without dealing with an irrelevant traffic light.

But the Phantom Impeachment usually relates to something that is at the center of the case, so we cannot dismiss it by calling it collateral. You can put Sergeant Robertson on the stand to tell the jury that the light was green. And the fact that his testimony would also tend to attack the credibility of the witness who said "red" would not make it improper.

But that is not how the Phantom Impeachment goes. Instead, Sergeant Robertson stays home; nobody calls him as a witness. And now the question predicts what he would say if he were here (which he isn't).

What's wrong with that?

It assumes facts that are not in evidence. That means two things in this situation: First, the witness is being asked to assume something that has not been (and may never be) established. Robertson may never come to court, and if he does, he may say the light was green, he may say he has forgotten what color it was, or he may say he never saw it.

Second, there is a hearsay aspect to the question that says, "The light was red—Sergeant Robertson says so." Not only does the question smack of hearsay, the lawyer is doing the testifying.

All right, you say, we'll fix it. We call Sergeant Robertson to the stand. He says the light was red. And now the other witness gets on the stand and insists the light was green. We try to rub his nose in Robertson's testimony like this:

> Q. You say the light was green?
> A. That's right.
> Q. Well, Sergeant Robertson was on the witness stand earlier today, and he testified that the light was red. Are you telling us that he was lying?

Now what? You can't complain that it assumes facts not in evidence. And if there were a hearsay aspect before, it is not a practical problem now.

But the question also does something else. The witness was asked, "Are you telling us that he was lying?"

That asks the witness to speculate about the mental process of another person. A lie is a deliberate misstatement. Even if the sergeant were wrong, how would the witness know whether it was intentional or a mistake?

So the question violates Rule 602 of the Federal Rules of Evidence. It says a "witness may not testify to a matter unless evidence is introduced sufficient to support a finding that the witness has personal knowledge of the matter."

The Phantom Impeachment has another problem. The real purpose of the question was not to get information about Sergeant Robertson's thinking—or any information at all, for that matter. It was argumentative. It was saying to the jury in the middle of the trial, "This witness is lying like a dog. Remember Sergeant Robertson? He said the light was red, and he obviously had no motive to lie"—which the lawyer is welcome to say in final argument, but not now.

And why risk an adverse ruling that will interrupt the flow of your cross-examination when you can do it the right way in the first place?

Say the witness is the defendant in a criminal case, and you are cross-examining him. Just this morning Sergeant Robertson got on the stand and said the light was red, and you want to make something out of it.

> Q. You were here this morning when Sergeant Robertson took the witness stand?
> A. Yes.

Cross-Examination

Q. You saw him raise his hand and swear to tell the truth?
A. That's right.
Q. He testified that the light was red, didn't he?
A. I guess so.
Q. I don't want you to guess. You were seated at that table, next to your lawyer?
A. Yes.
Q. Sergeant Robertson was on the witness stand—where you are now?
A. Yes.
Q. You heard what he said?
A. Yes.
Q. I asked him about the light?
A. Yes.
Q. And he said the light was red, didn't he?
A. Yes.
Q. That was the truth, wasn't it?

Wait a second, you say, isn't that improperly argumentative? Sorry.

The question invites the witness to change his testimony, and gives him a good reason for doing it. There is nothing in the evidence rules that says you cannot hope.

CHAPTER 30

Refreshing Recollection

> *Special Prosecutor Dan Webb: Do you recall . . . that it covered all other intelligence agencies? Do you remember that?*
>
> *Lt. Col. Oliver North: No.*

The trial of John Poindexter for lying to Congress—the most successful of all the Iran-Contra prosecutions—was a difficult business. Dan Webb, borrowed by the government from Winston & Strawn in Chicago, had a solid paper case.

But he knew that the key to the prosecution of Admiral Poindexter—the national security adviser to President Reagan—would be the testimony of Poindexter's military assistant, Marine Lt. Col. Oliver North.

Would North be a difficult witness? Webb knew the answer to that one. North had already sent Webb two messages explaining how he felt about testifying against his old boss. First, he made a pre-trial motion that he not be called as a witness (which was denied). Second, he refused even to talk to Webb before trial.

Webb would have to examine North as a hostile witness—as if on cross-examination. And he would have to examine him cold, without any of the usual pre-trial witness preparation.

Should you even call a witness like that to the stand?

Webb decided to make North his very first witness, to use him to lay out the basic story to the jury, to have North paint the picture of governmental dishonesty and deliberate cover-up.

But the "hero" of the Iran-Contra hearings did not recall details as well as he had before Congress or before the jury in his own trial. He became hazy, forgetful, uncertain. At one point Judge Greene asked him, "You couldn't have forgotten since Friday, could you, Colonel North?"

How can you prove a case with a witness like that? Webb did it by knowing every fact better than the witness, by having a reference in support of every question at his fingertips.

And he did it by being a master of "refreshing recollection." When North "forgot," Webb asked questions like this:

"Does that refresh your recollection, Colonel, that you knew when you went before Congress that day on August 6, before you lied to them—you knew, when you went in there, that John Poindexter had generally instructed you to conceal facts from Congress?"

And when the defense objected to how Webb "refreshed" North, Judge Greene replied, "[E]very time a question is asked of him—almost every time—he says he doesn't remember. It's like pulling teeth. So his recollection has to be refreshed in this manner. I am going to give the government the greatest latitude doing that."

And that takes us to the rules. The problem is basic. Witnesses forget because everyone forgets, and there have to be ways for dealing with lapses.

First, when a witness seems to forget an important fact, the real problem is often in the question instead of the answer.

Lawyers who ask stilted, convoluted questions deserve the confused, incomplete answers they sometimes get. If the answer does not seem to mesh with the question, do not blame the witness. Take the blame yourself. Accept responsibility for making things clear, and restate the question.

Then if the witness still leaves something out, it is time to go to work. Just asking the witness whether there is "anything else" is usually not very productive. It is time to ask a question that points the witness in the right direction without telling him what to say: "How were the road conditions?" "What was the weather like?" "Can you tell us how long it took?"

If "pointing questions" do not work, the next notch up is to ask leading questions. Under Rule 611(c) of the Federal Rules of Evidence, "Leading questions should not be used on the direct examination of a witness except as may be necessary to develop the witness's testimony," which means the judge has the discretion to let you lead a witness who has difficulty recalling something.

But leading is a step you may choose to skip. The implication of any leading question is that the lawyer has to tell the witness what to say—a message you may not want to send on direct examination.

Refreshing a witness's recollection—especially with a letter or a memorandum—is different. A writing that was made to preserve details is serving its purpose when it nudges a witness's balky memory. The written word seems less partisan than the lawyer who looks like he is coaching the witness with leading questions.

That sense of accuracy is a good introduction to the idea behind refreshing a witness's recollection. Whatever impression it gives, the witness's testimony is the evidence—not the thing that jogs his memory. Say the witness forgets some important facts, and you bring them back with a letter that the witness received during the business negotiations that are part of the lawsuit. Even though the letter played an important part in the trial, the testimony—not the letter—is the evidence in the case.

Of course, if the letter is admissible for other reasons (say as a business record or an admission), it still comes into evidence. It is not disqualified because it also helped a witness remember.

Because whatever is used to stir the witness's memory is not evidence, it can be virtually anything. As Judge Moylan said in *Baker v. State*, 35 Md. App. 593, 371 A.2d 699 (1977), "It may be a line from Kipling or the dolorous refrain of 'The Tennessee Waltz'; a whiff of hickory smoke; the running of the fingers across a swatch of corduroy; the sweet carbonation of a chocolate soda; the sight of a faded snapshot in a long-neglected album.

"All that is required is that it may trigger the Proustian moment. It may be anything which produces the desired testimonial prelude, 'It all comes back to me now.' "

That makes an important point. While you can't use another person's statement to impeach a witness, you can use anybody's statement to refresh his recollection.

And that leads to the thin line between impeachment and refreshing recollection. It is a practical problem that bedevils lawyers and judges, and which is not discussed in most of the books.

First, thousands of trial judges are hypnotized with the empty formalism of the witness's words. They say that witnesses who remember wrongly cannot be refreshed, they can only be impeached.

On the other hand, they say that difficult witnesses who "forget" cannot be impeached, they can only be refreshed.

So what, you say. All you have to do is use the right buzzwords and then you can do whatever fits the situation.

Wrong.

If the witness remembers incorrectly—and all you have to impeach him with is another witness's statement—you are stuck. You cannot use it to impeach.

And if the witness "forgets"—and the judge makes you let the witness read the "refreshing material" silently to himself—you are stuck again. You are not impeaching, you are just refreshing—which is useless unless the witness "remembers."

Rule 607 of the Federal Rules of Evidence helps a little. It says, "The credibility of a witness may be attacked by any party, including the party calling the witness." That means you don't have to pretend you are refreshing when you are really impeaching.

But probably the most important thing is for the trial judge to realize—like Judge Greene in the *Poindexter* case—that lawyers need some latitude in examining troublesome witnesses. The simple truth is, the formal words of the witness are not necessarily a good guide to what is happening. One way to forget is to remember incorrectly, and one way to lie is to "forget."

And how do you go about refreshing the witness?

If you have something you want the witness to look at, have it marked as an exhibit. It is good housekeeping, which lets the court and the reporter keep track of everything in the case, even if it is not received in evidence.

If you are using a writing, can you read it out load to the witness so the judge and jury hear it too?

If the writing is admissible in evidence, the problem is only a technical one. But suppose you are trying to refresh one policeman's memory with another policeman's notes, which are not admissible in evidence.

The argument in favor of letting you read them out loud is that the jury is the judge of the credibility of the witness, and the jurors should be able to hear what does (and what does not) spur the witness's memory.

But the argument against it is hearsay, even though the statement is not formally admitted in evidence. Reading from the document not only gives the jurors inadmissible information, it tells them where it came from. Of course, if it makes the witness remember, then there is no real problem. But because the jury might hear something improper, some judges insist that the witness be permitted to read the document silently, to himself.

What do you do then?

If you are on cross-examination or if it is a hostile witness, be like Dan Webb examining Oliver North. Ask leading questions that tell the whole story. Just because the witness says he has forgotten doesn't mean you can't ask the questions that should bring it all back. Then if the witness "forgets" and has to read something to himself, at least the jury has a good idea of what it says.

CHAPTER 31

Nine Ways to Cross-Examine an Expert

It was a Friday evening in The Brief Bag, and Flash Magruder was pontificating about cross-examining expert witnesses.

"There's only one way to cross an expert," Magruder said. "Punch him full of little holes and let all the air leak out."

Everybody laughed—all except Angus.

"Flash, the trouble with that theory is that someone might actually try it."

"Why not?" asked Flash.

"Because," said Angus, "it suggests that it doesn't matter what you do—that the only thing that counts is how you do it."

"And what's wrong with that?" asked Flash. " 'It Ain't Whatcha Do But the Way Hutcha Do It.' "

"Look," said Angus, "I have no quarrel with technique. If you don't do it well, you might as well not do it. But before you ever get to technique, you have to know what your options are, and cross-examining expert witnesses is a perfect example. There are at least nine ways to cross-examine an expert witness—in addition to the approaches you can take with any other witness."

It was obvious that Angus was in rare form, so I got out my pencil. Here are my notes.

Make Him Your Witness

First, do not attack any witness—especially an expert—unless it will help your case. Cross-examination is a lot easier if you and the witness do not disagree. True, you say, but so what?

Simply this. Say you represent the plaintiff in a traumatic brain-injury case. The defendant's doctor has just testified on direct examination that your plaintiff's seizures are not due to trauma, but to a congenital abnormality.

You can take the doctor head-on if you want, but maybe that will not be necessary. The doctor's only adverse testimony is on the cause of the plaintiff's injuries. He admits they are there; he only disputes how they arose.

Note that the defendant's own doctor admits that the plaintiff will be subject to sudden seizures for the rest of his life; that this form of epilepsy can only be treated, not cured; and that the plaintiff's condition puts him out of work as a machinist and means he can never drive a car again.

If you have a strong case on causation, you may decide it is better to make this witness your own on the issue of damages than to try to beat him down on the subject of cause.

Attack His Field

Attack an entire field of expertise? This one is likely to make you snort in derision until you think about it a bit. Just because the court lets a witness testify does not mean you have to dignify the field—which is what a lot of cross-examination does.

Say you are for the defense in an automobile case, and the plaintiff calls an accidentologist to the stand. If you are not going to call an accidentologist yourself, you can go after the whole field.

Q. I'm a little confused here. How do I address you—Doctor, Mister, or what?
Q. Now then, do you have a degree in accidentology from some college or university?
Q. In other words, you have never worked for the police or any other law enforcement officials?

Attack His Qualifications

The range in this option is wonderful. It covers training, experience, accomplishment, and awards. No matter how well-qualified the witness, there is always a higher level he has not reached. Approached subtly, you even can have the witness accredit your own expert's standing.

Of course, it is a mistake to slam a witness gratuitously, but if the witness literally asks for it, then the jury will appreciate what you do.

How do you know if the witness is asking for it? One place to look is his resume. That is what Keith Roberts from Wheaton, Illinois, did in one of the most delightful examples of this method. An orthopedic surgeon actually included a junior-high school citizenship award in his resume.

Q. Doctor, I see here that you attended Thomas Jefferson Junior High?
A. Yes.
Q. And it says here they gave you the Bronze Buffalo Award. Is that right?
A. Yes.
Q. I gather it was a good citizenship award?
A. That's right.
Q. Doctor, I don't suppose there was a Silver Buffalo Award, was there?
A. Well, yes, there was, actually.
Q. But you didn't win it?
A. No.
Q. Tell me, Doctor, was there a Gold Buffalo Award?

Expose His Bias

Of course, any witness can be biased because of friendship or enmity, but experts are special. They can be biased because of money—their fees for testifying. Because bias is never collateral, it is always a proper subject for cross-examination, and if it is denied, it may be proven with other witnesses.

You must have a sense of proportion. Just because a witness gets paid for his time does not suggest his integrity is for sale. But witnesses who spend a disproportionate amount of time in court or who charge large fees are surely vulnerable to attack.

Attack His Facts

An expert witness is an explainer. And while the explainer himself may be unimpeachable, his explanation is no more reliable than the facts he is relying on. Attacking the information (instead of the expert) is particularly suited for the expert witness who has done no factual investigation himself, but relies entirely on the reports of others. It does not have to be hostile to be effective:

Q. Doctor, can we agree that your opinion can be no better than the information on which it is based?
A. Well, yes, I guess so.
Q. If the information you have is not accurate, then the opinion would have to suffer too?
A. Of course.
Q. Which is why you would rather gather the information yourself than have to trust some source you have not worked with before?
A. Absolutely.
Q. But you were not given an opportunity to do that in this case?
A. Well, not exactly. No, I wasn't.

And now a word of warning. Do not be like the hack adventure-story author who has a character leave a gun in his sock drawer in Chapter One and then never does anything with it for the rest of the book. If you point out the possibility of unreliable facts, there better be something you can point to later on, or the jury will feel cheated.

Vary the Hypothetical

Changing the hypothetical is closely related to attacking the facts on which the expert relies. You are permitted to change the facts around to see at what point they alter the expert's opinion—depending on whether the question on direct examination originally was asked as a hypothetical.

You can insert facts you feel were left out on direct, or take out facts you feel should not have been included. But watch out. This does not mean you are free to invent facts like some first-year torts teacher, just to see how the witness responds. You must have a factual basis for all your changes. If the basis for your question is not already in evidence, you must be able to connect it up later.

Impeach with a Treatise

The point is simple. If the expert differs with others in his field, he may be wrong.

One way to attack him is with a learned treatise—a book or article by a recognized authority—that disagrees with what the witness has said on the stand.

Before the Federal Rules of Evidence, the expert had to have relied on the treatise in forming his opinion, or at least recognized it as being authoritative in the field.

Unfortunately, this put the witness in charge of his own impeachment. Properly prepared, few expert witnesses would admit that any works were truly authoritative. So Rule 803(18) of the Federal Rules of Evidence lists three ways to establish that a learned treatise is authoritative: from the testimony of the witness himself, from the testimony of some other witness, or by judicial notice.

Attack Him Head-on

Notice that until now everything has been indirect. The most difficult and dangerous way to cross-examine an expert is by fighting him on his own ground. You can do that in any number of different ways, such as trying to show he erred in his factual investigation, his computation, or his logic.

But be careful. This is a game that is easy to lose, so you should not play it unless you must. It is usually better to base your cross-examination on some combination of the other options.

At that point Angus stood up and paid his bill. "Well," he said, "I've got to get home."

"Wait a minute," said Flash. "You said there were nine ways to cross-examine an expert, but I counted only eight. What's the ninth?"

"Easy," said Angus, putting on his coat. "Punch the witness full of little holes and let all the air leak out."

CHAPTER 32

Blind Cross-Examination

Civil litigators have a horror of blind cross-examination that approaches phobia. Every year we spend millions of dollars on needless depositions of "witnesses" who have little to say and nothing to add about the cases in which they would never be called to testify anyway.

Why? To guard against the unknown bug that could be crawling under the unturned leaf. To learn every possible "fact." To forfend "trial by ambush." To avoid ever having to conduct a blind cross-examination.

The Federal Rules of Civil Procedure are designed to permit complete discovery. And the Federal Rules of Evidence are based on the assumption that complete discovery is what we will all get—one reason why "surprise" was taken from the list of relevance objections in Rule 803. (The logic is impeccable, if a little naive. If everyone knows everything before trial, there is no excuse for ever being surprised by the other side's evidence.)

The "commandments" of cross-examination tell us never to ask a question unless we know the answer. The implication is pretty clear: If we know no answers, we ask no questions.

Blind cross-examination is so unthinkable that most trial advocacy training programs don't even bother teaching how to do it. It's kind of like the FAA's decision that private pilots need no actual practice in getting an airplane out of a spin. If they simply avoid getting the airplane into a spin in the first place, they don't need to know how to get out.

But the truth is, blind cross-examination is everyday stuff. It's the normal situation in criminal cases (which is one of the reasons why the federal government increasingly uses criminal law to enforce basic national policies). It's common in all kinds of administrative hearings. Some states still have limited discovery. And despite everything we do, there are lots of times when we have to do a blind cross-examination, or do no cross-examination at all, in the ordinary civil case.

Litigation is just not a risk-free pastime. It's better to have a strategy for dealing with blind cross-examination than to pretend it will never happen. As more than one private pilot has found out, once your airplane is actually in a spin, it's a little late to start training.

Fight the Problem

Army instructors used to have a saying that was intended to help students do well on standardized army tests: "Don't fight the problem." It meant you should deal with the situation you've got and solve the problem it presents. They didn't want you to challenge the facts and try to solve some other problem the test writers didn't intend to pose.

Cross-examination is not a standardized army test. You don't care what kind of grade the machine would give your answer sheet. So one of the smartest things you can do when approaching a blind cross-examination is to fight the problem. Make it unblind. Get as much information as you can before you ask any questions on cross-examination.

Criminal defense lawyers know about the Jenks Act, 18 U.S.C. § 3500, which gives you the right to see the witness's prior statements before you start your cross-examination. Technically the statute does not require the prosecutor to turn this information over until after direct examination. But because that inevitably produces a request for a recess long enough to study the prior statements, most federal district judges tell prosecutors to turn over the Jenks material before the trial—if the defense asks for it.

Like the Jenks Act, think of Rule 612 of the Federal Rules of Evidence as giving you a little last-minute discovery. If a witness uses a writing to refresh his recollection on the witness stand, Rule 612 lets you see it as a matter of right. And if the witness used a writing to refresh his recollection before trial, the court has discretion to let you see it.

How do you know whether the witness used anything to refresh his recollection before trial? You've got to ask.

Next, if you can't get a deposition of a witness before trial, try doing it in the middle of trial, before he testifies. Sound crazy? Sorry. It's the voir dire examination of the witness outside the presence of the jury, and we do it all the time. It's almost always in the judge's discretion to permit or deny, but there are some things that should influence that discretion.

First, only ask for it when you think you need it. When you ask for a voir dire of every witness, you condition the judge to say no.

Second, keep the voir dire short and tight. It should be directed to the qualifications of the witness or the admissibility of his testimony. Educate yourself quickly while the jury is out of the room. Put the information to use when it returns.

Third, the Federal Rules of Criminal Procedure, Rules 16(a)(1)(E) and 16(b)(1)(C), now require a summary of an expert witness's testimony, describing the opinion, the reasons for the opinion, and the qualifications of the witness. But even if the summary satisfies the letter of the rule, you can still ask for a voir dire of the witness before he testifies.

Use What You've Got

Just because you've never talked to the witness before and don't have a deposition or the witness's own statement doesn't mean you can't cross-examine him. There are lots of other sources of information you can use. Here are some of the more important ones, in a rough order of preference.

A quoting document

The document was written by someone else, it's not admissible in evidence, but it quotes the witness who is on the stand. It's worthless for this cross-examination, right?

Wrong, but you've got to be careful how you use it. The basic rule is that you can't use one person's statement to impeach another person's testimony. But you can use virtually anything—including someone else's statement—to refresh a witness's recollection. And when you have a document that quotes what the witness on the stand said before, you should be able to use it to good effect:

Q. You say Folsom Street had the red light?
A. That's right.

Q. Your name is Max Gaines, isn't it? *(As you pick up the document.)*
A. That's right.
Q. And right after the police got to the scene, do you recall telling Officer Mooney that the Folsom traffic had the green light?
A. No.
Q. You don't remember saying that?
A. No.
Q. Maybe it would help your recollection if you were to look at Officer Mooney's report?

Usually it is a mistake to use the words "recall" and "remember" on cross-examination, precisely because they invite the witness to forget. But when the witness has already said the light was red and all you have is something that might refresh his recollection, "forgetting" is just what you want.

Three more points. First, if the witness corrects his testimony and adopts what's in the document, you just scored a knockout. It's unusual, but it happens. Second, even if he sticks with his story, he can still admit he made the prior statement. And third, remember, the document doesn't have to be the witness's own or even admissible in evidence for you to use it to refresh his recollection.

A quoting witness

The statement doesn't have to be in writing for you to be able to use it on cross-examination. If the witness talked to somebody else before trial and his testimony on the stand disagrees with what he said earlier, you're all set. You can tell the witness about his earlier statement for the purpose of either refreshing his recollection or laying the foundation for a prior inconsistent statement—or both.

Another person's document

Now you've got a document—say, a letter or a memorandum—that contradicts the witness. The trouble is, the letter is not admissible in evidence and it doesn't even quote the witness who is on the stand.

Can you still use it to refresh the witness's recollection?

Of course, but you've got a lot less to work with, because the document isn't tied directly to the witness on the stand.

Another person's statement

Now we have an oral statement that contradicts the witness. It was made by another person who is not going to testify. Too often lawyers try to solve this problem with what's called the "phantom impeachment":

Q. You say that Folsom Street had the red light?
A. That's right.
Q. You're sure it was red?
A. Absolutely.
Q. Well, if another person took the stand and testified that the light was green, would he be lying?

The problem is, the attack is speculative, argumentative, and doesn't work very well. You are often better off just developing the fact that there were other witnesses who saw what happened—which suggests that they may disagree with the witness on the stand.

"Duck facts"

Sometimes you don't have anything to work with except what the witness tells you—and duck facts. You already know what that means: If it looks like a duck and walks like a duck and quacks like a duck, it's a duck. There are some things for which you need no proof. The judge and jury just assume they are true. They are duck facts, and they work as long as you don't push them too hard.

Q. You say Schultze didn't throw the bowling ball at Malone?
A. No way. He just dropped it. It was an accident.
Q. So Schultze just dropped the bowling ball?
A. That's right.
Q. And then it just rolled onto Malone's foot?
A. That's right.
Q. Uphill?

Watch Out for Mousetraps

Any blind cross-examination has risks, but the witness who refused to talk to you before trial is more likely to be part of a mousetrap than anybody else.

The mousetrap always has a piece of cheese—just a little too obviously out in the open. The cheese is some apparent inconsistency, some forgotten detail, some enticing avenue that promises rich rewards for the fearless cross-examiner.

You are just two questions into the subject when the witness lets you have it. The trap snaps shut and you have to listen to his beautifully prepared answer that kills your case, and all you do is twitch while the steel spring holds you tight.

If you manage to evade the trap, the other side will just spring it on redirect. Which tells you what to do if you smell a mousetrap. Don't cross-examine unless you must. That way, there won't be any redirect.

CHAPTER 33

Liar!

It was at the fall meeting of the ABA Section of Litigation in Washington, D.C. Four hundred fifty lawyers were watching Michael Tigar re-create the cross-examination of Jake Jacobson in the trial of John Connolly. It was done the first time by the late Edward Bennett Williams in the early 1970s, with a young Michael Tigar sitting second chair.

It was the criminal case in which the late John Connolly was on trial for his political life. Connolly had been the Secretary of the Treasury under President Nixon. And Connolly was charged—as part of the fallout of Watergate—with having received a $10,000 bribe from the milk producers' lobby to urge President Nixon to increase the level of milk price support.

Now Tigar had returned to Washington to do the cross-examination of the government's principal witness—Jake Jacobson—one more time; not as Williams had done it, but as Tigar might. Tigar's very first question showed he was going to do it his way: "Mr. Jacobson, you're a liar—aren't you, sir?"

All 450 lawyers gasped. They knew they were watching magic. This was no Saturday morning bar association demonstration. This was the dragonslayer returning to take on a very special dragon, and the battle had begun in earnest and at once.

What's more, the dragonslayer seemed to have thrown caution to the wind. He had used the dreaded "L" word out loud, and in his first question. Wasn't that a fatal mistake that would prove to be his undoing?

Certainly the conventional wisdom is to avoid charging a witness with lying. Judges and juries often try to avoid deciding that a witness is a liar. Calling testimony a lie seems to be taking on a needless burden. Why assume the obligation of proving the malice of a lie when it is so easy to argue that someone was mistaken, or had forgotten?

Hesitation to cry out "Lie!" is why we have developed so many circumlocutions that we use instead: *fabrication, whole cloth, story, claim, invention,* and *not a shred of evidence* are some typical examples.

None of this means that lying in court is not a serious problem. The Ninth Commandment says "Neither shall you bear false witness against your neighbor" precisely because it has been one of our recurring sins since the dawn of time.

Liars Are Everywhere

The fact is, we have come to accept an amazing amount of dishonesty as our daily fare, even from clients. I sometimes do a little survey with continuing legal education audiences: "How many of you have never had a client lie to you?"

The responses are dismally predictable. Out of thousands of lawyers, only one never had a client lie to him. The lawyer had just started practice with a large firm and had not yet talked to a client.

Lies and liars come in all types of packages. At some point the difference between an honest witness and a dishonest one is attitude. According to Eric Zagrans of Cleveland, who clerked for the late Federal Judge Roszel Thomsen of the District of Maryland, "Honest witnesses remember the facts the way they must have been; dishonest witnesses remember them the way they should have been."

Thomsen understood that all witnesses rebuild facts they have forgotten—the dishonest ones fashioning the facts to suit the case. Zagrans says lawyers have an obligation to minimize rebuilding the past by telling their witnesses not to guess, and if they don't know or don't remember, to say so.

Faced with a difficult fact they don't want to admit, most witnesses would rather evade than lie—something that good cross-examiners instinctively realize. A witness's reluctance helps establish that what the cross-examiner says is true.

David Weiner of Cleveland says that perjurers are prosecutors' best witnesses, which is one reason why we have seen relatively few perjury prosecutions.

And it makes a difference who is on the witness stand. Michael A. Ficaro, a former state's attorney in Chicago, talks about criminal trials. "Witnesses can lie," Ficaro says, "but defendants can't. A witness will be forgiven for lying. A defendant is expected to lie, but is never forgiven for it. When the jury catches the defendant in a lie, that's it. The case is over."

Be Careful

Look at the law of evidence. Sometimes it seems that half the rules are dedicated to dealing with mendacity. First is the castle of cross-examination and the hearsay moat that protects it. Then there are prior inconsistent statements, bad acts, convictions, and impeachment with bias. Even in business records, the famous case *Palmer v. Hoffman*, 318 U.S. 109 (1943), is concerned with the honesty of records that are made with a view toward litigation.

And remember how tricky some of the rules can get. The saying is, "Bias is never collateral," which means that if the witness denies the facts that show his bias, you can prove them with extrinsic evidence—documentary evidence or other witnesses.

On the other hand, some states won't let you "sandbag" a witness with bias by waiting to attack his credibility until after he has left the witness stand. A number of courts say that, much the same as impeaching a witness with a prior inconsistent statement, you've got to first confront the witness with the bias on cross-examination.

And while most courts will let you cross-examine a witness about prior bad acts that reflect on the witness's honesty, extrinsic evidence is not permitted. If the witness denies committing the bad act, you are stuck with his answer.

Sometimes the law is maddeningly formalistic about what you can do (and how you can do it) in response to mistaken and dishonest answers. Refreshing recollection is typically limited to situations when the witness forgets, not when he remembers incorrectly. And impeaching with a prior inconsistent statement is only supposed to apply to situations when the witness contradicts what he said before, not when he forgets.

But the fact is, "forgetting" is a popular way to lie, and remembering incorrectly is a common way to forget.

All of this means you've got to be careful to plan how you are going to handle dishonesty when you plan your theory of the case. Sometimes you just take it head-on.

Mike Ficaro has the prosecutor's view that lying is a deliberate process that has to be hit hard.

"Liars are like snakes," Ficaro says. "Sooner or later they shed their skin. The cross-examiner's job is to make a few small incisions that will help them do this right in front of the jury. Cross-examination is a process in which you loosen the witness's skin."

Ficaro says Chicago prosecutors attribute the following saying to the local public defenders: "A well-conceived lie, stuck to, is often better than the truth." Of course, there are some defenders who attribute the saying to prosecutors.

This shows that whatever side you are on, finding, exposing, and dealing with the opponent's dishonest acts and statements is one of the most important things you can do. Expect your opponent to do the same.

Contain the Damage

Try to do everything you can to keep your case scrupulously honest—not only out of professional responsibility, but also for the practical reason that you don't want to unnecessarily provide your opponent with any ammunition.

But sometimes the problem is already there. Michael Tigar talks about it in his book *Examining Witnesses* (ABA Section of Litigation 1993), at 81:

> You may find that your witness has made a statement in a deposition or before the grand jury that is demonstrably wrong. You may have striven mightily to keep the prior statement out of evidence until your witness testifies, thus giving you and the witness the first chance to introduce the prior statement and talk about it.
>
> You must meet such a statement head-on. You and the witness lose credibility by trying to twist and reconstrue words to make them say what they did not.

Back to the attack. If the witnesses on the other side lie or misstate facts, you want to expose that as simply and effectively as you can.

Normally you should stay away from any kind of characterization at this point. There will be plenty of opportunity for that in a little while. You can even write the witness's key words on a chalkboard or on a transparency for an overhead projector under the headings "Then" and "Now" as you ask your questions:

Q. Then you said the light was red?
A. Yes.
Q. Now you say it was green?
A. That's right.

Do you go ahead and ask the traditional question, "Were you lying then, or are you lying now?" The answer is, only if it helps your case. Typically you want the jury to believe the first statement, so you are usually better off showing why the witness had some motive for changing his story rather than letting him choose which statement was wrong.

Call It Like It Is

Whether or not you charge the witness with lying, he's likely to say, "I was mistaken." That's when Judah Best of Washington, D.C., has a grand riposte: "Oh, I see, you're not a liar, you're a mistaker."

Now return to Mike Tigar's cross-examination of Jake Jacobson. Remember his first question, "Mr. Jacobson, you're a liar—aren't you, sir?" Was it a mistake?

In *Examining Witnesses*, Tigar says at 164, "You will, in trying cases, come to label many witnesses as liars and should not shrink from this duty when the occasion demands. The occasion demands, however, far less frequently than some people think."

So, did the occasion demand?

Jacobson had lied to the grand jury, lied to the bankruptcy court, and lied to the prosecutors before he testified against John Connolly. There was no way to call his conduct a mistake, a failure of perception, a lapse of memory.

Immediately after his first question, Tigar exposed the lies. One after another, Tigar confronted the witness playing Jacobson with what he had said. Jacobson squirmed and evaded but had to admit that what he had said was untrue.

Then came time for final argument, and Tigar was more eloquent than Edward Bennett Williams.

"The government," said Tigar, "is not what it says, but what it does. And look what it does. These prosecutors put a man they know is a liar on the stand. They know he lied to the grand jury—and they don't care. They know he lied to the bankruptcy court—and they don't care. They know he lied to them—and they don't care."

It was magic.

CHAPTER 34

Breaking the Rules of Cross

Professor Peter Joy, the director of the Kramer Law Clinic at Case Western Reserve University, was critiquing my trial tactics students when he hit on a great truth.

"Lawyers just have to learn to break some of the rules of cross-examination," he said.

"Amen," said Angus, from the back of the room.

To some people that sounds like heresy. Irving Younger's "Ten Commandments of Cross-Examination" have been heard or read (or both) by more lawyers than any other legal education presentation. Thousands have committed every point to memory, almost like a catechism:

1. Be brief.
2. Ask short questions; use plain words.
3. Ask only leading questions.
4. Ask no question to which you don't know the answer.
5. Listen to the answers.
6. Don't quarrel with the witness.
7. Don't let the witness explain.
8. Don't go over direct examination.
9. Don't ask one question too many.
10. Save the explanation for final argument.

"Peter Joy is absolutely right," says Angus. "Irving Younger meant the 'Ten Commandments of Cross-Examination' to be an anchor for beginners and a guideline for journeymen, not the measure of excellence."

Professor Thomas Mauet of the University of Arizona, author of *Fundamentals of Trial Techniques* (3d ed. 1992), says, "The commandments are a nice starting point, but they are just that."

Dan Webb from Chicago says whether you break the rules is strictly a risk/reward decision. "Janis Joplin used to sing, 'Freedom's just another word for nothing left to lose.' When you've got nothing to lose, break the rules and risk the home run."

Professor James W. Jeans of the University of Missouri at Kansas City, author of *Trial Advocacy* (2d ed. 1993), goes even further. He says, "The commandments are painting by the numbers. After that level we need to do more than go outside a line now and then. We need to forget painting by the numbers and get more creative—to break out of stultifying rules.

"The whole thrust of the 'Ten Commandments' is 'Don't make an ass of yourself.' They are strictly defensive. And like the 'prevent defense' in football, they almost guarantee mediocrity."

"Be brief"

Who can disagree with the need for being brief? Excessive brevity is a problem that bedevils almost no one in the legal profession. And yet, says Joy, there are times when you cannot be brief:

"I saw Gerry Messerman of Cleveland cross-examine the major prosecution witness in a case where a lawyer was charged with obstruction of justice. Piece by piece, Messerman took that witness apart—and then put her back together again.

"It left you with the image of a three-dimensional person who had not hurt the defendant. She was real, but she was a very different person from the one the prosecution had presented.

"It took a long time, even though it didn't seem very long," says Joy. "It was credible because it was emotionally satisfying—instead of seeming like a series of quick tricks that would have looked like the cross-examiner was creating a false impression."

"Ask only leading questions"

Mauet says the leading-question rule is not for an experienced cross-examiner. "It produces a series of 'isn't that right' and 'isn't that so' that is tiring."

Joy says the leading-question rule can really hamper a cross-examiner. "If you want to show that the witness is a braggart or is giving carefully rehearsed testimony," Joy says, "leading questions don't let you expose the witness."

Eric Kennedy of Cleveland says violating the leading-question rule can sometimes let you give the right kind of emphasis to some important testimony.

Kennedy was trying a medical malpractice case in which there was devastating brain damage to a newborn child. In his deposition, the defendant doctor was asked who had the duty in the particular hospital to resuscitate a child who wasn't breathing. Was it the doctor, the nurse, the anesthesiologist—who?

The doctor's answer was more helpful than Kennedy could have hoped for: "We really don't have any rules. It's kind of a grab bag."

At trial, Kennedy could have covered the whole thing with one leading question.

Q. Doctor, you really don't have any rules for who is in charge of infant resuscitation. It's kind of a "grab bag," isn't it?
A. I guess so.

But instead he said:

Q. Doctor, explain the hospital's rules about who has the duty to resuscitate a newborn child who is not breathing.

(The doctor tries to sugarcoat it a little.)

A. Well, of course, it's a concern that everybody has, so there is not exactly a precise set of guidelines.
Q. Pardon me, Doctor, but we've talked about this before?
A. Yes.
Q. And that's not what you told me then, is it?
A. No.
Q. What did you tell me then?
A. It's kind of a grab bag.
Q. A "grab bag"?
A. Yes.

Having the doctor repeat his own words—while he was trying to avoid it—created a much stronger impression than, "This is what you said, isn't it?"

"Ask no question to which you do not know the answer"

Bob Habush of Milwaukee says, "If there is a Golden Rule to the Ten Commandments, this is it. And yet there are times to break it. It is an instinctive thing. And if you watch the witness, you will know when you can do it. You can read the fear in his eyes."

Peter Pearlman of Lexington, Kentucky, has a guideline for asking a question when you don't know the answer: Ask it when you don't care what the answer is.

Bob du Puy of Milwaukee says there is an important principle to remember. "It's analogous to 'the fork' in chess—that's when one piece of yours threatens two of your opponent's. He can only save one by sacrificing the other. When you've got the witness in that situation, you don't care what he says. Either way, you're ahead."

Sometimes you have to take a chance. Dan Webb tells about representing a Chicago judge in a bribery case. The witness was a lawyer who had worked undercover to set up the case against the judge. He was in protective custody and had refused to talk to Webb before the trial. Webb didn't know what the witness would say on the stand.

But Webb had "intelligence" from other lawyers in the Chicago bar who told him that if he asked the witness whether he knew or had ever heard of the judge doing anything dishonest in the twenty years before this incident, the witness would say no.

It was a dangerous situation. Were Webb and his client being set up?

First, Webb tested the water—gradually. Then he risked the home-run question:

> Q. In fact, did you ever know or ever hear that the judge had done any act of dishonesty in the twenty years he was on the bench?
> A. I never did.

"Don't let the witness explain"

Young lawyers seem to have a deadly fear of letting witnesses explain anything on cross-examination. So they try to cut them off with loud "thank yous," "you've answer my question," "just answer the question," and "Your Honor, would you instruct the witness to give only responsive answers?"

The judge, by the way, typically says, "The witness may explain his answer."

If you think about it, trying to cut off the witness draws a lot of attention to the answer you do not like—especially if you succeed in cutting it off. It almost guarantees that your opponent will do something like this on redirect: "Mr. Robbins didn't ask you this question, so let me. Why didn't you pull off the road when you heard the siren?"

Ask yourself—would you rather hear the answer on cross-examination when you can deal with it, or on redirect examination when there's nothing you can do? You don't want to invite the witness to explain something, do you?

You might, says Michael E. Tigar, a professor at University of Texas Law School and author of *Examining Witnesses* (1993).

Tigar says, "If you have built a box of the right size and shape to hold the witness, it is laudable to drop him in it and let the jury watch him run around in it. For example, suppose you develop that the witness has been guilty of a series of inconsistencies. Then it may be desirable to ask, 'Why did you change your story?'

"But if the witness is going to say, 'Because your client threatened to kill me,' you shouldn't do it."

Bill Pannill of Houston says it's dangerous to follow the rule that says never let the witness explain.

Pannill says, "The jury roots for the witness, not the lawyer. The jury is looking for a reason to hate you, and the attitudes are worse than you might think.

"Here in Texas, doctors lose about 25 percent of the medical malpractice cases brought against them. But lawyers lose about 65 to 70 percent of the legal malpractice cases brought against them.

"Even though you do a technically perfect cross-examination that follows all of the commandments, you can alienate the jury by reinforcing the lawyer stereotype. The short, leading questions and the refusal to let the witness explain anything can seem terribly unfair.

"We can't afford to act like jerks," says Pannill. "Yet that seems to be the direction in which the profession is headed. We scream, yell, intimidate, show off in front of the jury.

"We've got to convince the jury that we are decent people. We've got to be scrupulously fair and approach people with great courtesy. And you can't fake it. You can't put it on and take it off."

"Save the explanation for final argument"

The idea is a carryover from the days before discovery, when trial by ambush was the rule. The thought was that if your opponent didn't know what you were doing until final argument, he couldn't do anything about it.

But, according to Dan Webb, "Sometimes you just can't wait until final argument to correct a false impression."

Finally, you need to take some risks to put some of yourself in the cross-examination. "A superb cross-examination," says Peter Joy, "is like a soufflé—not Hamburger Helper. If you don't put some of yourself in it, it won't be soufflé."

PART FIVE

Foundations and Objections

Every part of the trial counts. Foundations and objections are important because they shape the case—they determine which of the facts will be taken into account by the judge and the jury in making their decision. But that is not all there is to it. How you lay foundations and make objections has a lot to do with how persuasive you are.

CHAPTER 35
The Evidence Steps

CHAPTER 36
Laying Foundations

CHAPTER 37
Authentication

CHAPTER 38
The Objection List

CHAPTER 39
When to Object

CHAPTER 40
The Art of Objecting

CHAPTER 41
Making the Record

CHAPTER 35

The Evidence Steps

Handling exhibits is not just a matter of following rules of evidence and procedure. It is a series of verbal and physical moves that communicates a lot about you and your legal ability to the jury. Going through the right steps with a picture or letter is serious courtroom choreography; how well you do the evidence steps will have an influence on whether the jury will listen to your witness or pay attention to your arguments.

How you handle yourself as you move through the courtroom is one of the factors in that ineffable sense of presence that makes any audience—including judges and juries—think you are worth watching.

But the trouble is, unless you are in court often enough, the steps can get confusing. So here they are, complete with some comments about where to stand and when to turn. And one other point before we start. If you don't do the steps often enough so your feet remember what to do, you can always tuck this list in your trial notebook and follow the steps as you go. It is a lot better than letting the judge or your opponent take over.

Have the Exhibit Marked

First, know where you are headed. Exhibits are usually marked by the court reporter, but sometimes it is done by the clerk of court, the bailiff or even the judge. Find out before you get to court.

The traditional way to start is to ask the reporter to mark the exhibit for identification. It is usually a mistake to play Perry

Mason or Ben Matlock and tell the reporter which number to use ("Your Honor, I request the reporter mark this defense exhibit six for identification"). It is the reporter's job to keep track of the numbers or letters, and you can easily ask for the wrong one. Of course, if the reporter makes a mistake, call it to her attention.

And it is needless pretension to use a formal litany such as, "Your Honor, the United States requests that the court reporter mark this as a prosecution exhibit for identification, numbered next in order." Just ask the reporter to mark the exhibit for identification.

Give a Copy to Your Opponent

Technically you do not have to show your opponent the exhibit until you offer it in evidence. Then it is his turn to examine it and object if he wants.

But no matter what the rule is, waiting until your offer to show the exhibit to the other side runs the risk of triggering an objection that will suggest you are trying to sneak something past them—"Your Honor, may we see the exhibit that counsel is showing to the witness?"

But on the other hand, giving the exhibit to your opponent right at the start lets him keep you standing there, waiting, while he holds up your exhibit and studies it as if it were a clever forgery of a famous painting. So if it is a photograph or a document, it helps things move more quickly (and gets you some jury points for being courteous) if you have extra copies for the judge and the other lawyer.

If the exhibit is not a photograph or a document, but rather a physical object like a gun or a rope, you can try to guard against an interruption by telling your opponent that this is the exhibit you showed him during the pre-trial conference.

Which leads to another point. Should you say anything when you give your opponent his copy of the exhibit?

It is silly to lard the record with formalities such as, "Your Honor, may the record reflect that at this time I am giving a copy of prosecution exhibit six for identification to counsel for the defense." A simple "Counsel, here is a copy for you" both makes the record as well as tells the jury you are minding your manners.

A quick warning before we go on. Keep the statement to the other lawyer businesslike. Do not let yourself get drawn into bantering with your opponent. Other than a few formal remarks, you are supposed to address all your comments to the judge. The give-

and-take between lawyers can quickly degenerate into an argument that you are better off avoiding. Besides, your opponent is not stopping you in the middle of the dance to make you look more professional.

Give a Copy to the Judge

The judge wants to see the exhibit, too, and would like to look at it while you are laying the foundation. So it might strike you as odd that the rules say you do not have to give the exhibit to the judge until you have finished laying the foundation and offer it into evidence.

The rule was evolved before the photocopy machine. Now that copies are inexpensive and convenient, there is usually no good reason to make the judge wait to look at the exhibit.

Lay the Foundation

Now is the time to turn to your checklist for the elements of your foundation, and use it as you question the witness.

Offer the Exhibit in Evidence

Here is another opportunity to use plain language. Some lawyers fill half a page of transcript with each exhibit by saying something like "Your Honor, the prosecution moves prosecution exhibit number six for identification into evidence as prosecution exhibit number six and requests that the court reporter strike the words 'for identification' from the exhibit."

You do not need to do that. First, court reporters are increasingly using little yellow stickers instead of rubber stamps to mark exhibits. They cannot strike the words "for identification" from the exhibit because those words are not on the little stickers. And since an offer of evidence already *is* a motion, saying that you are making a motion only tends to make it confusing. All you have to say is, "Your Honor, we offer prosecution exhibit six into evidence."

Voir Dire

Now it is the opponent's turn to talk, but first another note on language.

Only lawyers (who defend legalese with the need for linguistic precision) could call jury selection, the preliminary examination of an expert witness on his qualifications, and a cross-examination on the foundation for an exhibit by the same name—voir dire.

Believe it or not, there really is an excuse for using the same term three different ways. "Voir dire"—Old French for "to say the truth"—was part of the oath that both jurors and witnesses took concerning their qualifications.

So it made sense to lawyers who were examining witnesses and jurors on their oath to talk about examining them "on their voir dire."

But now that the bond of language has become an historical oddity, we can update our speech, especially in front of the jury. We can talk about questioning jurors, asking experts about their qualifications, or questioning the witness about the foundation.

Back to the opponent and his objection. He has a decision to make. Should he ask the judge for permission to examine the witness now so as to provide ammunition for an attack on the foundation, or is he better off saving his attack for cross-examination?

It is a good question, and the answer is clear and unequivocal.

It depends.

The way to answer it is to play it out in your mind. If the voir dire examination is going to spell the difference between winning or losing your objection, then the answer seems obvious. Do it.

But before you do, consider. What if the judge says (like they always seem to do) that your objection goes to the weight of the evidence, rather than its admissibility?

The jury is likely to think that the ruling means your objection is without legal merit. Which means that unless there is a good chance you are going to win your objection, you probably ought to hold your fire until cross-examination.

But wait. Aren't two cross-examinations better than one?

Not necessarily.

First, most judges are going to limit you to specific questions about the foundation. Second, if you go back over these points on cross-examination, you will look like a scavenger, picking over something that has already been thrown out.

Objection and Response

How to object and respond to objections is an art in itself. Probably the most important point for now is that buzzwords—labels of conclusion—are not enough. In a sentence or two you have to *show* the judge why the evidence should be excluded, or deserves to be admitted.

Ruling

This is an important step, so do not let the judge forget it. The jury is not permitted to see the exhibit or hear its contents (except to the extent necessary to lay a proper foundation) until it is admitted in evidence.

Show It to the Jury

Ask permission from the judge before you show the exhibit to the jury. How you show it to them makes a difference. Passing the exhibit from one juror to the next takes time, so using a blowup or an overhead projector so everyone can see it at the same time is usually worth the trouble.

CHAPTER 36

Laying Foundations

Everyone was in pain.

Judge Wallop was squirming around on the bench, wondering whether to take over the direct examination or maybe just tell Tucker what he was doing wrong.

Dick Mudger was uncomfortable, too. He was on the other side. He wanted to keep the exhibit out of evidence, but now he was worrying that maybe the jury would start feeling sorry for Tucker.

The jury felt like captives, forced to watch repeated forays of ineptitude into (for Tucker) an unknown territory of evidence law.

But Tucker Phillips felt worse than anyone else. His shirt was sticking to his back, soaking with perspiration, as he started over for the third time, trying to lay a proper foundation for a business record.

"It doesn't need to be that way," said Angus, talking about it later in the Brief Bag. "You do not have to have read all of Wigmore on Evidence, or be able to recite the Federal Rules of Evidence just to lay a simple evidentiary foundation."

"But, Angus," said Beth Golden, "a business record is not a simple evidentiary foundation."

"It is if you do it right," remarked Angus.

"Oh, come on, Angus," said Beth. "I try business cases all the time, and I still have trouble laying a business record foundation as neatly as I'd like."

Angus smiled. "There are some things that can make almost any foundation simple," he said.

I could tell Angus was about to do another one of his lists, so I started writing. Here are my notes.

Lay Foundations Before Trial Whenever Possible

There is nothing like the pressure of trial to make even the best lawyers stumble. So the easiest way to stay out of trouble is to avoid having to lay foundations when the heat is on.

And the pretrial conference is a great place to get rid of things like evidentiary foundations.

But it is not the only way. Take business records, for example. If you frame your document requests the right way, your opponent will be admitting that most of the documents he produces are not only authentic, they also qualify as proper business records.

But be careful. When you do that, make sure you follow up your initial document request with another one for all other documents that relate to the case that may be in your opponent's possession. Unless you do this second sweep, your effort to avoid laying foundations can leave you with only part of the documents in the case.

Then there are Requests for Admissions under Rule 36 of the Federal Rules of Civil Procedure. They are tailor-made for getting rid of foundations. Couple your requests with supplementary interrogatories, which your opponent should answer for each request he denies. That way you will not only know which foundations you will have to lay at trial, you also will know which objections your opponent is likely to make.

Use a Checklist

You would be shocked if a Lear jet pilot tried to land without going through the landing checklist. And the chances are the Lear Jet pilot would be shocked if he saw you try to lay a foundation for a business record without an evidence checklist.

Take the trouble to write out the elements for every foundation you will have to lay in the trial and tuck them in your trial notebook. You will find Edward Imwinkelreid's *Evidentiary Foundations* (Michie, 2d ed., 1989) invaluable in making sure you cover all the bases.

Prove Authentication and Firsthand Knowledge

The common law takes nothing for granted. If you want to introduce a letter written by the defendant, you have to show he wrote it. If you want to introduce past recollection recorded, be ready to establish that the writing was based on the author's firsthand knowledge. And if you want to introduce a business record, you have to show that the document is authentic as well as showing that its contents are based on firsthand knowledge that comes from inside the business chain. (*Johnson v. Lutz*, 170 N.E. 517 [N.Y. 1930].)

The Proponent Picks the Theory

The principle is simple. You get to choose which rules apply. If you offer a bystander's statement as an excited utterance, it does not matter if it fails to pass muster as a declaration against interest. And if your memorandum qualifies as past recollection recorded, it does not make any difference that the opponent says it is inadmissible as a business record.

The principle works most of the time, but not all of the time. Even though you pick the theory of admissibility, that does not save your evidence if it is unfairly prejudicial under Rule 403 of the Federal Rules of Evidence. And in *United States v. Oates* (560 F.2d 45 [2d Cir. 1977]), the court refused to let the prosecutor offer a laboratory report as a business record to get around the protection that the public-record rule gives the accused in a criminal case.

The Rules of Evidence Do Not Have to Apply to Foundations

This one may surprise you, so read the rule for yourself. Rule 104(a) of the Federal Rules of Evidence says that in determining whether a proper foundation has been established, the court "is not bound by the rules of evidence except those with respect to privileges."

This is the rule that lets you ask whether a photograph is a "true and accurate representation" of what it shows, and not get in trouble for leading. It also can let you fill a hole in a chain of custody with hearsay, or use a letter to establish one of the elements of a business record.

But watch out. Rule 104 does not suspend the rules of evidence for foundations. It just gives the judge discretion to consider inadmissible evidence as part of a foundation if he wants. If you want to be sure that the foundation is sufficient, come to court with admissible evidence in support of every element.

The Bias Is in Favor of Admissibility

Even with every part of the foundation firmly established, there is always the chance that your evidence can be excluded in the relevance balance. So any time you lay a foundation, you have to be ready to defend its probative value when it is weighed against the risk of unfair prejudice.

Fortunately, you have some help. Built into Rule 403 of the Federal Rules of Evidence is a bias in favor of admissibility—one which any number of lawyers and judges do not know is there. "Although relevant, evidence may be excluded if its probative value is substantially outweighed by the danger of unfair prejudice...." The rule makes it plain. In a close case, admit the evidence.

Find Out What Is Wrong

You are sure you have gone through every fact you have to establish to get the exhibit admitted. But when you offer it into evidence, your opponent says, "Insufficient foundation," and the judge sustains the objection.

At this point the easiest way to slip into the abyss of failure is to think that just asking some additional questions will cure the problem.

Why?

Because we do not know what is wrong. We do not know the real reason for your opponent's objection or the real reason for the judge's ruling—and they may be very different.

If the judge knew the real reason for the objection, she might well overrule it. And if we knew the real reason for her ruling, at least we would know what holes needed to be filled.

But rather than admit we do not know what the judge and the other lawyer are thinking, we flail around, asking questions that mostly have been asked before, apparently on the theory that even a blind pig can find a chestnut if he roots around long enough.

Instead of doing that, find out what is wrong. Do not ask the judge to explain; put it on your opponent: "Your Honor, we feel we have laid a sufficient foundation. So if counsel would tell us what he thinks is missing, I would be happy to supply it."

Make the Record

Using a foundation checklist not only makes it easy to respond to your opponent's objection, it also makes it easy to tell whether you have made the record of your foundation if his objection is sustained.

And be careful. In addition to making a record of the foundation, be sure that the record shows the contents of what was excluded. When it is an exhibit, that is easy. In most jurisdictions, just marking it and offering it in evidence makes it part of the record. But when testimony is excluded, you have to make sure the transcript shows what the witness would have said if the evidence had been admitted. Do that with an offer of proof—using the actual witness whenever possible instead of just telling the judge what the witness would say if he were permitted to testify.

Get a Ruling

One way judges have to minimize the number of errors in a record is to put off actually admitting any exhibits into evidence until you rest your case—a practice that unfortunately is on the rise.

The problem is the late ruling keeps you from knowing whether the judge thinks you have laid a proper foundation until it is too late to fix it.

Since it is improper to have testimony about the contents of an exhibit (or even show the exhibit to the jury) before it is admitted, you are entitled to a ruling when you make your offer.

You Are Always an Advocate

Finally, it is a mistake to think of foundations as little interludes that are irrelevant to the jury. First, most of the facts in any foundation are an important part of the overall picture you hope will persuade. Just as important, how you execute the craft of trying the case has a profound effect on whether the jury thinks you know what you are talking about.

CHAPTER 37

Authentication

Mike Pirelli came into the Brief Bag and sat down next to Angus and Beth Golden. "What do they have that will fix a wasted afternoon?" asked Mike.

"Nothing that comes in a bottle," said Beth. "What happened?"

"I set aside a whole afternoon to prep some important witnesses who are going to testify next week, and not one of them showed up," said Mike.

"Welcome to the club," said Beth.

"Well, it's got me worried," said Mike. "I've got four witnesses who claim they can authenticate Amos Creake's handwriting, and they are absolutely essential to my case."

"Creake?" asked Angus. "Isn't he the multimillionaire who died last fall?"

"Right," said Mike. "And I've got a contract case against his estate. The first hitch is the Statute of Frauds. I've got to have a writing signed by Creake, otherwise I'm out of court.

"My plaintiff has a letter from Creake that refers to the contract," said Mike. "I think that ought to be enough for the Statute of Frauds. But the second hitch is that I've got to prove the letter's authentic."

"Shouldn't be too hard," said Beth.

"That's where my witnesses come in," said Mike. "They used to work in Creake's household staff a few years ago. They got paid by check, and they say they can recognize Creake's signature."

"Sounds pretty standard to me," said Angus. "What were you going to do to prep them for their testimony?"

"Well, it's been a while since they've seen Creake's signature. So first I was going to make sure they are familiar with his handwriting by showing them a number of exemplars of his signature. Then I was going to see if they could authenticate the letter," said Mike.

"But you haven't done this yet?" said Angus.

"No," said Mike. "I told you that."

"The defendants gave you the known exemplars of Creake's handwriting?" said Angus.

"Right," said Mike, "after I told them what they were for."

"I don't wonder," said Angus.

"Mike," he continued, "buy us all a drink. This is not a wasted afternoon. This is your lucky day."

Mike Pirelli looked suspicious. "How do you figure?" he said.

"You almost prepped those people right off the witness stand," said Angus.

"Here. Take a look at Rule 901(b)(2) of the Federal Rules of Evidence."

Angus pulled his rules out of his briefcase. There it was, just as he said (although how he can remember those numbers is beyond me): A lay witness can give his opinion about the genuineness of handwriting "based on familiarity not acquired for purposes of the litigation."

"You can test your witnesses' ability to identify the handwriting on the letter," said Angus, "but if you try to train them by having them look at a bunch of other exemplars of Creake's writing, it will be hard to convince the judge that their familiarity was not 'acquired for purposes of the litigation.'

"It's a little trap in the rules," said Angus. "What might seem like good witness preparation turns out to torpedo your foundation."

The starting point for discussing authentication is the basic approach of the common law. It's up to you to prove your case. The common law takes almost nothing for granted. That idea applies to all kinds of evidence, but it is most familiar in introducing real evidence (the thing itself), documents, and testimony about telephone conversations. Authentication means you have to prove that your evidence is genuine.

How do you do that? The late Irving Younger used to say, "Any way that makes sense." It is an excellent summary of the law.

Consider documentary evidence. You have a letter typed on Angus' personal stationery. There is a signature, big as life, at the bottom of the page, in real ink, written with a real fountain pen—"Angus." Anybody with any common sense would assume that Angus wrote and signed that letter, unless there was a mighty good reason for thinking otherwise.

After all, it takes a bit of trouble and some serious risk to steal someone else's stationery (or pay for an order of phony stationery) and then forge a signature. People do it, but it isn't common.

But the law doesn't make that same commonsense assumption. So you have to prove the signature is genuine; otherwise, the letter is not coming into evidence. You can authenticate a signature by the testimony of a witness who saw it signed. Or, like Mike Pirelli, you can use a lay witness's opinion that it's the right persons' handwriting.

Or the jury can do the job for you. You can have the jury compare the questioned document with known exemplars and decide whether they were written by the same person. Jury comparison, by the way, is not sufficient evidence (without more proof) to convict someone of forgery in some states.

Next is the questioned-document expert, who may just concentrate on handwriting, or who (in the right circumstances) may also go into word choice and frequency, spelling, grammatical patterns, inks, papers, and other esoterica that can sometimes nail down authenticity.

There is another way to authenticate a document that pays no attention to the signature—the knowledge of the author.

Say you write a letter to Angus, mailed to the proper address. Two weeks later you get a reply—purporting to be from Angus—that was written by someone who had obviously read your letter. Does that guarantee it is genuine?

Of course not. But the extra bit of circumstantial proof is enough to get the letter into evidence.

Next come telephone conversations, or other conversations where the witness did not see the person he was talking with. The starting point is the same. You have to prove your case, and the law does not assume you were talking to the right person.

Voice recognition is the most obvious way to solve the problem. You've talked with Beth Golden before, and her voice has distinctive qualities—easier to recognize than they are to describe.

Next, if the conversation was recorded, it opens the door to an expert witness using spectrographic analysis for voice identification. *United States v. Smith*, 869 F.2d 348 (7th Cir. 1989).

Once again, distinctive knowledge can be used to authenticate. As with a letter, if the person on the other end of the telephone had particular information that was sent only to the right individual, that is an authenticating circumstance.

But do not assume that voice identification is treated entirely the same as handwriting identification. Take a look at Rule 901(b)(5) of the Federal Rules of Evidence. Voice identification is admissible, "whether heard firsthand or through mechanical or electronic transmission or recording, by opinion based upon hearing the voice at any time under circumstances connecting it with the alleged speaker."

Notice there is nothing in the rule that excludes a lay opinion based on familiarity with the voice "acquired for purposes of the litigation." That means you can hear the questioned statement first, and become familiar with the voice later.

So your client gets a call in the middle of the night, threatening his business with extinction if he does not sell some critical machinery to the defendant. Who made the call? Was it the defendant's brother-in-law, or not? As far as Federal Rule 901(b)(5) is concerned, you can have the plaintiff go to the brother-in-law's deposition to see if he recognizes the voice.

There is another way to authenticate a telephone conversation—calling the right number. You look up Mike Pirelli's number in the telephone book and make a note of it. Later on, that's the number you call. (One quick point, before we go any further. Have you ever wondered whether there are hearsay problems with using the telephone book and your note pad? Don't worry. When you lay a foundation, the court is not required to apply the rules of evidence to the foundation facts. Rule 104(a) of the Federal Rules of Evidence.)

Someone answers your call to Pirelli, saying "Law offices." You say you want to speak to Mike Pirelli. The voice says, "May I ask who is calling?" and you give your name. A minute later another voice says, "Mike Pirelli here." Those facts authenticate your telephone call, even though someone might have just been playing a trick on you.

Which raises another point. The law is concerned with the admissibility of your evidence, not whether it is persuasive. When

AUTHENTICATION

your whole case hinges on the admissibility of a central document, like Mike Pirelli's case against the Estate of Amos Creake, then pick the most persuasive ways you can find to authenticate the evidence, not the minimum acceptable way of getting it in.

Finally comes real evidence: the bloody knife, the broken suture, the plastic bag of crack cocaine, the soft lead bullet extracted from the victim's aorta. It is the thing itself, and with it comes the tradition of the chain of custody.

To establish a proper chain, you need to prove:

- From whose custody the evidence is produced.
- Who had custody of the evidence in a continuous chain back to the relevant time.

Is a chain of custody required to get real evidence admitted over the opponent's objection?

Absolutely not. There is nothing magic about the chain of custody (although some judges do not understand that). It is simply circumstantial evidence of two facts:

- Identity. This is the real thing.
- No change. The evidence is in the same condition as when originally received.

Some things are unique. A gun has its own individual serial number. A fountain pen may have a distinctive inscription or a noticeable crack. Evidence like this can be enough to establish identity without a chain of custody.

Some things don't change easily. "This paperweight is in exactly the same condition as when I found it in the dead man's hand two years ago." That is enough to show it hasn't changed.

But without direct eyewitness testimony that "this is it, and it hasn't changed," the chain of custody is the usual way to proceed.

One last point. How carefully the evidence has to be handled to create a proper chain of custody depends on the circumstances. A criminal case usually demands more precision than a civil action. If the object is at the heart of the case, more is required than if it is something at the fringe. Distinctive objects are easier to identify than piles of white powder that can easily get adulterated or exchanged.

When guilt or innocence depends on careful handling and accurate labeling, we are entitled to a high degree of professionalism.

CHAPTER 38

The Objection List

Federal District Judge John M. Manos of Cleveland, Ohio, has a reputation for knowing the rules of evidence and following them. It delights some lawyers, annoys others, and earns the respect of almost everybody. You always know how you are supposed to try a case in Judge Manos's courtroom—the right way.

Years ago, when Manos first started judging on the Court of Common Pleas in Ohio, he suddenly realized he was supposed to make intelligent rulings on evidentiary objections. It is an uneasy feeling that comes to almost all judges at the start of their judicial careers, but most of them don't do anything about it, and after a while the feeling goes away.

But Manos did something. He made a list of the most common evidentiary objections and studied it. Pretty soon he had it committed to memory. Today he gives his list to his clerks and externs to guide them when they attend trials.

I asked Judge Manos for a copy of his list, thinking it might help other lawyers, too. But when it arrived, it was just a list of words—with almost no explanations. So I asked Angus if he would add his commentaries to the entries. Here is their combined effort.

Relevance

Relevance is the puzzle of circumstantial evidence. Direct, eyewitness testimony of a fact in issue never presents a relevance problem. It is circumstantial evidence that makes things difficult. The basic question is whether the evidence advances the inquiry. If it does, it has probative value.

But even if the evidence has probative value, it is excluded if its probative value is substantially outweighed by the risk of unfair prejudice.

Fortunately, not every relevance issue is treated as an original matter. There are a number of questions that keep coming up for which the law has developed answers:

- A person's character is generally not admissible to prove how he acted at a particular time (except when it is used as a defense in a criminal case).
- Subsequent remedial measures are typically not admissible to prove negligence.
- Offers to compromise are not admissible to prove liability.
- Liability insurance is not admissible to prove fault.

Materiality

The common law treated materiality as separate from relevance. Relevance is whether the evidence advances this inquiry. Materiality is whether this inquiry is an issue in the case. The Federal Rules of Evidence have merged the two ideas.

So today relevance is whether the evidence advances an inquiry that is an issue in the case. Even though it is part of relevance, focusing on materiality can be useful.

Privileged Communications

Attorney-client, doctor-patient, husband-wife, and clergy-penitent communications should ring the privilege bell. Trade secrets, attorney work product, political votes, and governmental secrets may also qualify for privileges.

Best Evidence Rule

If you are going to prove the contents of a document, you must produce the original or account for its whereabouts. Under the Federal Rules, photocopies are usually satisfactory unless there is a genuine dispute about the authenticity of the original.

Parol Evidence Rule

The parol evidence rule is actually a rule of contract interpretation expressed in evidence terms: Prior or contemporaneous evidence is not admissible to change a written contract that was meant to be the complete agreement.

Insufficient Foundation

Foundations (called "predicates" in Texas) are the preliminary facts you must prove before you can introduce the evidence you are after.

Hearsay

The test is whether the out-of-court statement (either written or oral) is being offered to prove the truth of what it says.

Leading

Leading questions suggest the answers to them. They are generally not permitted on direct examination except on preliminary matters or to refresh the recollection of the witness.

Narrative

A witness's narrative may let the jury hear inadmissible evidence before the other side has a chance to object. So the judge has discretion to permit a narrative or require traditional questions and answers instead.

Opinion—Calls for a Conclusion

Lay witnesses are supposed to supply basic information, not interpret it. To be admissible, a lay witness opinion has to be both rationally based on the witness's observations and helpful to the finder of fact.

Repetition

The typical objection is "asked and answered." Actually the court has discretion to permit some repetition if it will help reorient everybody.

Cumulative

The power to stop cumulative evidence is the same as the power to stop repetition. So when a second or third witness is called who is simply going to say the same thing as the first witness, the judge can call a halt.

But the objection is seldom made and even more rarely sustained. The concern is the next witness might say something a little bit different.

If the rule were more vigorously enforced, cases with two thousand documents might be tried with only ten or twenty documents with no real loss.

Assumes Facts Not in Evidence

A question that assumes something not in evidence is typically multiple, confusing, and probably tricky, to boot.

When experts are asked questions about facts that are not in evidence, they are being asked to give opinions that are not supported by the proof in the case. The cure is to prove the underlying facts first or promise the court you will "connect up later."

Misstates the Evidence—Misquotes the Witness

Whether it is part of a question or something a lawyer says in final argument, misstating the evidence may mislead the jury as to what the proof actually was. But whenever the objection is made, the judge is likely to dodge making a ruling by saying "the jury is the judge of the evidence." It is judges' code for "I don't remember what the witness actually said."

Improper Characterization

This is like misstating the evidence or misquoting the witness. But now the objection says the lawyer's characterization or summary of the evidence is unfair. The phrase is also used to object to mildly argumentative questions.

Confusing—Misleading—Ambiguous—Over-Broad—Vague—Unintelligible

Poorly framed questions produce all kinds of sins. Testifying is hard enough with good questions. It's almost impossible with bad ones.

Speculative

We have enough guesswork in the judicial process without asking the witnesses for theirs. Questions that call for speculation are improper.

Compound

A compound question asks two or more questions at once. Everyone gets confused and no one knows what the answer means.

Argumentative

Questions are supposed to develop information. When the purpose of a question is not to get a useful answer but rather make a little speech to the jury, it is argumentative.

Nonresponsive

Witnesses are supposed to answer the questions put to them. But some witnesses volunteer extra information or try to answer questions they were not asked.

Technically, only the questioner can object that an answer was nonresponsive and have it stricken for that reason. But lots of lawyers and judges do not know that rule, so in most courts either side can object to a nonresponsive answer. In any event, even if you are not the questioner you can object to a nonresponsive answer for any other reason, such as hearsay or improper opinion. Normally you have to object after the question and before the answer. But with a nonresponsive answer, you don't know there is going to be anything improper until you hear what the witness actually says.

Beyond the Scope of Direct or Cross-Examination

Normally cross-examination is limited to the scope of direct, plus anything that goes to the credibility of the witness. The judge has discretion to permit you to go beyond the scope of direct, but then it is your witness and you can no longer ask leading questions (unless it is a hostile witness or the adverse party).

Most judges are pretty strict in keeping redirect examination limited to the scope of cross. Otherwise some lawyers would just keep on asking questions.

Improper Impeachment

The two most common problems are:

- You can't impeach one witness with another witness's statement.
- You need to confront a witness with a prior inconsistent statement before you can introduce it in evidence. This requirement rule has been relaxed by Rule 613 of the Federal Rules of Evidence, which simply requires that the witness be given an opportunity to explain or deny the statement at some time during the proceedings.

CHAPTER 39

When to Object

Good lessons are supposed to be memorable. On that basis, Judge Wallop's attack on Dick Mudger was a great lesson, because there is no way Mudger will ever forget it.

Mudger was in the middle of trial against Flash Magruder, and he had no real defense, so he was doing what he always does—making life difficult for his opponent. Mudger was intent on interrupting the flow of the case, so he was making every possible objection.

Flash had just asked the witness for a little hearsay, when Mudger heaved himself up and said, "I am sorry, Your Honor, but I *must* object."

That gave Judge Wallop his chance. "No, Counsel," he said, "that's not right. There is no requirement that you make any objection."

Mudger tried to respond. "Well, Your Honor, I only meant that I . . ."

Wallop cut him off. "I haven't finished, Counsel. You have conducted this entire trial as if you were under the erroneous assumption that the law required you to make every conceivable objection whether or not it helped your case.

"But that is not true," Judge Wallop continued. "A trial is not an evidence examination. You get no points for making every possible objection. The law permits you to object, but that is all. Whether you actually do is up to you."

Mudger is one of those lawyers who sometimes thanks the judge for an adverse ruling in the hope that it will make the jury think the ruling was actually in his favor. But this time he had the sense to realize that a "Thank you, Your Honor" probably would bring an additional rebuke. So Mudger took his punishment rather than ask for more.

"Very well, Your Honor," he said.

The question is when to object. And whether or not you think Mudger had it coming—and he probably did—Judge Wallop was right. A trial is not an evidence examination. You are under no duty to protect the judge and jury from proof just because it violates some rule of evidence.

But why not object anyway?

The answer is that you have a limited good-will account with the judge and jury at the start of trial. Everything you do in the trial affects that account. You are always making deposits and withdrawals.

And—you guessed it—an objection looks like you are trying to keep something from the judge and jury, so it usually counts as a withdrawal. That is the justification for the first rule.

Wait for a Reason

Rule One—Do not object unless you have a good reason for it.

A good reason means that it advances your theory of the case.

Knowing that jurors (and judges, for that matter) resent objections, just how cautious do you need to be?

That depends. Jurors expect some objections and come to court with a little built-in latitude. Sometimes they are more forgiving of criminal-defense lawyers than they are of other lawyers. Criminal-defense lawyers are expected to make the prosecution turn square corners.

By the same token, attorneys for the prosecution are expected to do things right. If they can't follow the rules, how can they expect other people to follow the rules?

Most importantly, jurors know that objections are intended to keep things from them—and that very fact will make them curious about the information you want to keep out.

Don't Educate Your Opponent

Rule Two—Do not object when it will help your opponent.

Surely that is obvious, you say. Why is it even worth mentioning? Because there are times when you might not know you are helping your opponent. Two examples will make that clear.

In the first example, the other side is leading a key witness on direct examination. So much time has passed since the central events in the case that the witness is a little fuzzy.

But your opponent is leading much more than necessary. Should you object?

Maybe not. One of the unintended messages sent by a leading question is that the witness cannot be trusted to remember properly—he needs to be told what to say. Your objections may force your opponent to improve the witness's credibility by asking fewer leading questions or by introducing some document that qualifies as past recollection recorded.

In the second example, opposing counsel is fumbling around as he tries to lay the foundation for a business record. Despite all his questions, he still has not established that the record was made in the ordinary course of business.

Should you object? If you do, it may help educate him so he will do a better job with other business records that are much more damaging than this one.

Can It Be Sustained?

Rule Three—Do not object unless your objection deserves to be sustained.

Ordinarily, you will want to win every objection you make. While being sustained means you have succeeded in keeping something from the jury, it also means you know the rules.

Does that matter? Think about it for a second. Say you are lost in a swamp and have two potential guides, each offering to show you the way out. Who are you going to follow—the one who seems to know the territory or the one with the nice shirt?

Next, note that the rule says you should not object unless your objection deserves to be sustained—not that it *will* be sustained. There are times when you simply must make your record, knowing the trial judge will overrule your objection.

Remember the Jury

Rule Four—Object outside the presence of the jury whenever it is possible.

Outside the presence of the jury is different from outside their hearing. Sure, there is a difference, you say, but does it matter?

The answer comes from an Oregon survey done a number of years ago by Judge Robert E. Jones. He wanted to find out what juries liked and disliked. Heading the list of their dislikes was the bench conference.

Why?

From our standpoint, bench conferences keep from poisoning the well with improper information.

But from a jury's standpoint, it appears that we are keeping something from them because we do not trust them.

They particularly resent it because they are captives in the jury box, forced to sit and watch while we whisper secret information.

When you think about it, you may resolve never to have a bench conference when the jury is present. That is not a bad idea, but there will be times when that is impossible. Even so, the damage done by a bench conference suggests that you should make evidence objections with pretrial motions whenever possible or at least when the jury is not in the room.

Be Prompt

Rule Five—Object promptly.

We usually say you must object as soon as the question is asked, otherwise the objection is waived. But the real rule is that you must object as soon as the basis for the objection is reasonably apparent.

It is an important distinction. Suppose the other side asks a perfectly proper question, but the witness answers with hearsay. Under those circumstances, the objection is not waived because it came after the answer instead of after the question.

The reason for requiring prompt objections is obvious. The best time to fix a mistake is when it is on everybody's minds—not later, when they are frying other fish.

The prompt objection rule presents an awkward problem in opening statements and final argument: You have to interrupt your opponent when it is his turn to talk. And that is different from objecting during direct or cross-examination when there already is a back-and-forth exchange taking place.

Nevertheless, the usual rule is that you should object right away or else lose your objection. (*Thomson v. Boles*, 123 F.2d 487 [8th Cir. 1941].) But in *London Guarantee & Accident Co. v. Woelfle*, 83 F.2d 325 (8th Cir. 1936), the court said the objection could be made at the time of the remark or at the close of the argument—which has the advantage of encouraging civility.

You may have an alternative to objecting or biting your tongue—and that is biding your time. The idea comes from C.L. Mike Schmidt in Dallas. When he has a chance to follow his opponent in final argument, he almost never objects. Instead, he waits until it is his turn to talk. Then he deals with it in his argument.

"You remember the defense lawyer said that Jack Williams was going over 50 miles per hour at the time of the crash. You know that is not what the testimony was. All of the evidence was that Jack was going between 30 and 35 miles per hour. No one said he was going any faster than that—except the lawyer for the defense.

"Where did he get that 50 miles per hour? I have no idea. When he said that, the law would have permitted me to jump up and object—right then and there—and interrupt his argument. But I didn't, because I wanted to see just how far he thought you had to go to find in his favor."

A Time to Be Heard

Rule Six—Stand and be counted.

There are times when—no matter what the case or whom you represent—you must object because it is the right thing to do. Suppose the judge makes a prejudicial comment about your opponent because of sex or race. It happened in a Pittsburgh federal district court when the judge ordered a woman lawyer to use her husband's last name.

When it happens—and it will—do not stop to reckon the cost. It does not matter if you think you will benefit from the injustice. There are times to stand and be counted.

CHAPTER 40

The Art of Objecting

Angus was conducting one of those trial advocacy workshops—where the young lawyers go through their paces and then get critiqued by the members of the teaching team. The plaintiff was trying to get a gory picture of the accident victim into evidence. It showed the victim lying dead in the middle of the street, blood everywhere.

After the witness finally said that the photograph was a "fair and accurate representation" of what he had seen, a number of lawyers tried their hand at keeping it out.

"Insufficient foundation," said one.

"Irrelevant," said another.

"Prejudicial," said the next.

"Highly prejudicial," said the fourth.

"Unfairly prejudicial," said the next.

"Here's my ruling," said Angus, who was playing the judge. "The exhibit comes in. The plaintiff laid a proper foundation—although it was pretty mechanical. That means the 'insufficient foundation' objection was wide of the mark. So was 'irrelevant.' The picture tells something about the case. It has probative value. And the way the Federal Rules of Evidence are set up, it is relevant—although it might be kept out for being 'unfairly prejudicial.'

"But it is not technical accuracy that bothers me," he said. "What troubles me is something deeper, and it's not your fault. It comes from the law schools. It is the notion that the way to deal with objections and foundations is to call out a series of buzzwords—almost like magic incantations. The idea is, if you just say the right words, you have done your job and made your record. The evidence will be admitted or excluded, and you can get on with the trial.

"Wrong.

"It is not enough just to be technically accurate when you make an objection. Remember this. It's important. The time to win the objection is when it counts—at trial.

"There are a lot of lawyers and judges who have things turned upside down. They look at trials as if they were just preliminary appeals, and all the mistakes will be fixed later.

"But that's wrong, especially when it comes to evidence rulings. Unless they are outrageously unfair—or reach constitutional levels—you will not get the case reversed on appeal for the trial judge's evidence mistakes. Evidence rulings shape the whole case, and the time to win your objection is at trial.

"That means your task is to persuade the judge—and buzzwords like 'highly prejudicial' don't do the job. They may orient the judge to the problem, but they don't show him which way to go."

Angus is right. The point is to persuade the trial judge. But the problem is, how do you do that? The best trial lawyers understand there is an art to making objections. And not surprisingly, they all have a slightly different approach.

For Jim Jeans of the University of Missouri at Kansas City, you have to understand what motivates judges. One of the factors is they don't like to be reversed on appeal. So a good advocate—a zealous advocate who knows the rules—has an advantage.

Jeans says, "When judges make important rulings that could go either way, in part they are picking an advocate they can count on to defend their rulings on appeal."

Randi McGinn of Albuquerque, New Mexico, agrees. "Confidence counts," she says. "And it helps to know the rules. If you know the number of the rule, cite it to the court. It sends the message that you know what you are doing. Making objections is a gut test. Your guts tell you something is wrong, and you have to have the guts to do something about it. You've got to sound confident, even if that's not how you feel. When in doubt, the judge tends to go with the lawyer who sounds most confident."

Partly because of this factor, some lawyers like to make the first objection in the trial and make it stick. They want to foster the impression that they know the rules and are going to do what they can to enforce them. But being the first to object can also be the ticket to disaster. When you make silly, annoying objections, you undercut your authority with the court.

Ron Williams of Wichita, Kansas, says, "Judges like patience. They don't like to blow the whistle. They don't like to sustain objections. They expect you to take a few shots, and experience will show how much you should take before you react:

"'Well, they continue to do this, Your Honor, and we're not going to waive it anymore.'"

There are times, says Williams, when you have to stand in front of the court and take the blame to get the judge to rule in your favor.

It happened in an airplane crash case. The plaintiff said that air got in the fuel-line system and killed the engine. Williams represented the defendant, who said an air lock simply could not happen if there was enough gas in the tanks.

So Williams had a mock-up of the plane built to test the plaintiff's theory. It worked like a champ. No matter what they did, Williams's experts could not make the fuel system fail. So Williams started ragging the plaintiff's lawyer. "Of course you are welcome to test our exhibit. We will even make it case dispositive if you like. If you can make it fail, you win."

The plaintiff, of course, turned down Williams's offer. But the plaintiff's experts tested the exhibit. On the very first run, the fuel system failed.

And now Williams had to face the judge and argue that his offer should not be admissible. Buzzwords would not be enough.

"Your Honor," said Williams (whose nickname is Tiny), "it takes a big man to admit his mistakes. It takes an even bigger one to laugh at them. And as the biggest man in the courtroom, I want to tell the court what Peter Ustinov said: 'If the world should blow itself up, the last audible voice would be that of an expert saying it can't be done.'

"This case, Your Honor, should be decided on the facts and not on what I was foolish enough to say about the exhibit."

It worked.

For Tom Demetrio of Chicago, the lawyer's credibility is key. "You've got to maintain credibility with the court. If you lose credibility with the judge, the jury will know it.

"So I am very discriminatory about making objections. My attitude is, 'Let's hear all the facts.' Because I make very few objections, when I do object, the court knows, first, I am serious, and, second, I am right.

"Your credibility with the court is such a serious issue, if you discover you have led the judge into making an error, you've got to take responsibility for fixing it."

Mike Tigar of the University of Texas says, "Let the law do your talking. If you are facing resistance from the trial court, then appellate decisions that have reversed trial judges are very important.

"Mini-memos, three pages long, are the best. The judge doesn't have the time to read an eighty-page brief, but the mini-memo has the power to persuade. They should be instructive but not disrespectful. When the judge is more oriented in your direction, then talk about discretion, fairness, and door-opening. But when the judge seems to lean the other way, use the law to persuade."

For Cyril McIlhargie of Chicago, persuading the trial judge starts with knowing whom you are talking to. "You must know the judge's sense of fairness. The way you object has to touch the judge's felt sense of making a difference—not by being partisan, but by being fair.

"Judges are used to hearing hyperbole—overblown adjectives and exaggerated injuries that will come from minor rulings. They have no value. Judges have an outer membrane to protect themselves from the routine, mundane, indifferent sorts of objections like these.

"The only thing that has value is to show the judge there is something wrong—like a thorn of unfairness—that he wants to remove from the trial. You have to shape your argument so that it pierces the judge's outer membrane and makes him want to right that wrong. Put it this way: You have to communicate in fundamentally human terms the impact of what is being objected to."

McIlhargie's understanding of the dynamics of persuasion sounds right on target. But you probably are asking, "How do you do that in the middle of trial?"

JoAnn Harris of New York City has an approach that leads to exactly what McIlhargie is talking about. Harris says you should not just tell the judge the evidence is unfair, you have to show it is unfair. You have to paint the picture so he can see it himself.

"Your Honor," she says, "this is how the evidence is going to come back to haunt us." And then she does a minisummation for the other side, showing how they could take unfair advantage of the evidence.

It forces the opponent to make a choice. Either they have to admit that's what they had in mind, or they have to promise not to use it that way.

One last point about objections. Somebody always loses. And when you lose, you have to be ready to go on as if nothing happened.

CHAPTER 41

Making the Record

Michael was reporting to Angus on how his first jury trial had gone. "You can't believe what a stupid mistake Judge Feckler made," Michael said.

"What did he do?" said Angus.

"He wouldn't let my stipulations go to the jury room with the other exhibits. But that's okay. I figure it's like an insurance policy. If the verdict goes the wrong way, it's bound to be reversible error," Michael said.

"You had already read the stipulations to the jury during your case in chief?" Angus asked.

"No," said Michael, "I didn't want to take the time."

"But you offered them in evidence?" asked Angus.

"Why should I offer them in evidence?" Michael said. "They are stipulations. The whole point of stipulations is to avoid messing around with the rules of evidence."

Angus just looked at Michael for a minute and then he said, "Suppose you list a witness in a case and then do not call him to testify. Can you talk to the jury in final argument about what the witness would have said if he had taken the stand?"

"Of course not," said Michael. "It's not on the record."

"Exactly," said Angus. "Same thing with a stipulation. It is not enough that you and your opponent agree that something is true. You've got to put your agreement in evidence.

"It's part of a more fundamental point. You've got to make your record for every part of the trial. It's something you have to do yourself. There is nothing automatic about it, and no one is going to do it for you. So unless Judge Feckler lets you reopen the case and you offer those stipulations into evidence, it's not his mistake that the jury doesn't know about them—it's yours."

Angus is right. Making the record is important. Interestingly, nearly all of the rules (except those that deal with specific objections and how to make offers of proof) are not in the Federal Rules of Evidence. They are part of the common law of trials. Most of them fit comfortably into three groups:

- Help the reporter.
- Be eyes for the appellate court.
- Get it on the transcript.

Each one is worth looking at up close.

Help the Reporter

Every time you go to trial, make a list of all the lawyers on your side as well as all the witnesses you intend to call and give it to the court reporter. Helping the reporter spell everyone's name properly is the kind of gesture that will earn genuine gratitude.

If there are difficult words that you and your witnesses must use, make a glossary for the reporter. But watch out. You are probably better off spending the time thinking of easier words to use. But when only the proper word will do, the glossary will help the reporter.

Any time you read anything to the jury—no matter what it is—have a copy for the court reporter. It turns a difficult time into an easy one for the reporter.

Next, don't talk too fast. Listen to television newscasters. They typically have found a pace that is easy for others to understand. You should do that, too. And vary the pace. Use pauses to let ideas sink in and to let the court reporter catch up.

Be careful with numbers. There is a lot of difference between 225 and 2.25, but it will not be in the transcript unless you say "point" in the proper place.

Keep your eye on the reporter. If he raises his hand and asks the witness to speak up (or you to slow down), you should be the first to help.

Lots of court reporters, by the way, are good sources of information about what is going on in the courthouse as well as good critics for the way you conduct your case. Only beginners are too proud to listen to reporters and bailiffs.

Be the Appellate Court's Eyes

Like a child who cannot see over the fence, an appellate court depends on what it can figure out by looking through the knotholes—the transcript.

Whether those knotholes afford enough information to correct judicial mistakes (or even deliberate misconduct) depends on you. Caught in the middle of what is going on, you have to take time out to look at the fence and see whether the knotholes are big enough to see through.

Put It in Words

Read all nonverbal gestures into the record. "Let the record show that the witness nodded his head 'yes' " (or "shook his head 'no' "). Then tell the witness to answer out loud. The law, by the way, does not require that you say something long, redundant, and incomprehensible such as, "Your Honor, may the record reflect that the witness has nodded his head in the affirmative, indicating a positive response?"

Translate

Translate grunts, humms, uh-huhs, uh-uhs, and nuh-uhs into yesses and nos. Once again, keep it simple. "That means 'yes'?"

Describe

Describe gestures and other physical actions for those on the other side of the fence. "Let the record show the witness has held his hands approximately five to six inches apart."

(Another aside. Should you say "Let the record show," or are you better off asking something like, "Your Honor, may the record show?" Good question. For those who treasure independence, "Let the record show" says you are in charge. On the other hand, "Your Honor, may the record show?" forces the judge to agree that what you have said is right.)

Include Misconduct

Read improper conduct—opposing counsel's or the judge's gestures, faces, grimaces, groans, pencil throwing, paper crinkling, and book dropping—into the record. You do not have to be confrontational about it (it can be done at sidebar or in the judge's chambers), but you should do it.

Get It on the Transcript

Depending on the jurisdiction, a lot of what happens in a trial is not in the transcript: oral pretrial motions and rulings, jury voir dire, opening statements, sidebar conferences, motions in chambers and requests for instructions, final arguments, instructions, verdict, polling the jury.

In other words, about the only things you can count on being in the transcript are the questions, answers, objections, and rulings that take place in open court. (Even then, be careful. Sometimes the judge will say something is off the record, and there will be nothing on the transcript to show what happened.)

Throughout the trial you have to think about the people on the other side of the fence and whether they have a good enough view of what is going on.

Opening and Closing

It is a good idea to get a transcript of opening statements and closing arguments if that is not customary in your jurisdiction. It is almost always worth the extra cost.

Written Motions

If it is worth making a motion, it is worth putting it in writing. It does not have to be long. Often a single page will do. The point is a written motion will be taken more seriously by the judge, in part because it is part of the record.

Objections

Make sure your objections—and the court's rulings—are on the record. Some courts try to discourage objections by requiring the lawyers to approach the bench just to state the grounds for the objection. If you forget to ask the court reporter to come to the bench with you, the entire transaction will be off the record.

Include the Grounds

If the court rules against your objection, be sure to read the specific grounds for the objection into the record—the judge will not do it for you. While Rule 103(a)(1) of the Federal Rules of Evidence says specific grounds are not required if they are "apparent from the context," do not rely on context to do your work for you; context is an unreliable ally.

Offer of Proof

If the court sustains your opponent's objection and excludes your testimony, make an offer of proof. The point is to put in the transcript what has been excluded by the judge's ruling. Once again, do not count on context to do the job for you.

Unless the court (or local practice) requires that you make the offer with questions and answers, you are free to do it by simply making a statement for the record. But while a lawyer's statement is quick and easy, formal testimony makes a more impressive record—one that is more likely to tell the trial judge that the appellate court has a good view through the fence.

Make a Note

Some courts delay ruling on exhibits until the end of each party's case in chief, or until the end of the entire trial. Like the rule against objections in open court, the real purpose of this rule is to discourage objections. The point is simple. If you have an important objection, make a note of it so you will not just let it slide when you are starting to think about instructions and final argument.

Put It on the Record

If the court makes an adverse ruling that is off the record, you should make a respectful statement describing that ruling for the record.

What if the judge will not even let you do that?

It happens more often than it should, and it is wrong. The power of the court to control the order of trial under Rule 611(a) of the Federal Rules of Evidence is not the power to keep you from showing what happened at trial. If the trial court will not let you make your record, you surely have the right to attach your affidavit to your brief on appeal, explaining why some of the judge's rulings are missing.

PART SIX

Evidence

Facts win trials. Juries make a conscious effort to ignore the apparent skill of counsel and concentrate on the proof. This means that what you introduce into evidence makes a tremendous difference, and the lawyer who knows the rules of evidence has a real advantage.

CHAPTER 42
The Real Witness

CHAPTER 43
It's Not for Its Truth

CHAPTER 44
The Big Four

CHAPTER 45
Hidden Rules

CHAPTER 46
The Best Evidence

CHAPTER 47
Limited Admissibility

CHAPTER 48
Using the Wrong Deposition

CHAPTER 49
Understanding Character Evidence

CHAPTER 50
The Catch in Character Evidence

CHAPTER 51
One Size Fits All

CHAPTER 52
Publishing the Exhibit

CHAPTER 42

The Real Witness

By all rights the young lawyer should have been elated. He had won his first trial and the results were better than anyone had hoped for. But he was stung by a remark made by one of the litigation partners from his firm who had watched the trial: "You missed every hearsay objection in the entire case—and some of them were important."

The partner was right. Despite weeks of study in law school, days of review for the bar examination, and hours of continuing legal education lectures, hearsay was still a mystery. The young lawyer could recite the definitions without hesitation. But when it came to applying them in the middle of the trial, he couldn't recognize hearsay when it was gnawing on his leg.

Worse, the young lawyer thought he was alone. He was convinced his incapacity was the result of some deep-seated inadequacy. He did not know his ailment was a simple problem shared by thousands of lawyers. He thought he was defective.

And all because no one had ever told him about the real witness rule.

The what?

The real witness rule.

It is a way of looking at hearsay.

The problem is the ordinary hearsay rules are too cumbersome to use at trial. Take, for example, the scholarly definition: "Hearsay is evidence that depends for its probative value on the veracity of an out-of-court declarant." By the time you determine whether you have an out-of-court declarant, the opportunity to object may well

227

have passed—long before you have thought about whether this evidence "depends for its probative value on the out-of-court declarant's veracity," much less figured out what "probative value" and "veracity" actually mean.

Then there is the other definition—the one that is supposed to be easy to understand: "Hearsay is an out-of-court statement offered to prove the truth of the matter asserted." It is supposed to be easy to understand because it breaks down into two parts:

1. An out-of-court statement.
2. Offered to prove the truth of the matter asserted.

But no matter how often it is described as simple, "offered to prove the truth of the matter asserted" is an awkward phrase that describes a difficult idea. Even if you trim it down to "offered to prove its truth," it still takes too much time to apply in the middle of a witness's testimony.

The traditional hearsay definitions simply do not work very well as initial screening devices in trial. That should be no surprise because they were not meant for that. They are fine for arguing about whether some contested evidence is, in fact, hearsay once an objection has been made. But they are nearly useless for sifting through what goes streaming by when a witness testifies.

What is needed is a way to spot hearsay quickly and accurately in the middle of trial.

Enter the real witness rule. It works by taking advantage of your litigation instincts. Instead of simply being a mechanical tool, it can actually help you do a better job of framing your hearsay objections. The real witness rule is based on the purpose behind the hearsay rule. It explains why some statements that look like hearsay and sound like hearsay are not hearsay. Best of all, it uncovers hearsay when it is hardest to find—in the middle of trial.

Start with a simple auto crash case. You represent the defense, and the plaintiff calls an eyewitness to tell what he saw when the two cars collided.

Hearsay?

Absolutely not. And now the question that establishes whether there is hearsay. When the other side is through with this witness's direct examination, who will you want to cross-examine? The witness who is on the stand. (If you think that is an odd question, wait just a moment.)

Now the witness is asked what he was told by other people at the accident scene. The witness says that a bystander told him the

The Real Witness

defendant had been speeding right before the collision. That evidence is offered to show the defendant was at fault.

Hearsay?

Without a doubt. In traditional terms it is an out-of-court statement that is offered to prove the truth of the matter asserted.

What does that have to do with the real witness rule?

To answer that question, remember the question we asked before. Whom do you want to cross-examine?

The answer is, not only the witness who is on the stand, but also the bystander whose story the witness repeated.

Why?

As soon as the witness started telling what the bystander told him, he was no longer the real witness. You want to cross-examine the bystander. Your client wants to look the bystander in the eye as he takes the stand. The judge and jury want to watch and listen to the bystander as he talks about the speed of the cars. Someone else is now the real witness, and your trial instinct—whom do you want to cross-examine?—is the test that shows who he is.

Asking who is the real witness shows why we have a hearsay rule. Its purpose is to protect the rights of confrontation and cross-examination, as well as the evaluation of the witness by the judge and jury. They are rights that only have meaning when the real witness is on the stand. So when the real witness is not on the stand, we have hearsay.

Wait a minute, you say. This is all too simple. Of course the hearsay rule was designed to protect the rights of confrontation and cross-examination. Obviously, asking who is the real witness can spot out-of-court statements. But there is no trick to that. The hard part is figuring out whether the out-of-court statement is offered to prove its truth. How can the real witness rule do that?

Easy. The real-witness test asks the question, whom do you want to cross-examine: the witness on the stand, or the one who spoke out of court? The answer to that question depends on whether it matters that the out-of-court statement is true. Wait another minute, you say. Put that way it sounds like the question is whether the statement is offered for its truth.

Isn't that the traditional hearsay test?

Exactly. The real-witness test—whom do you want to cross-examine—is also a simple way to ask whether the evidence is offered to prove the truth of what it asserts.

Suppose another case. The witness on the stand says he heard a mechanic warn a pilot that the ailerons on his airplane were sticking. It is offered to show that the pilot knew his airplane had a dangerous condition. Whom do you want to cross-examine? Isn't the mechanic the real witness?

No. If we were concerned with proving whether there was actually anything wrong with the airplane, then the mechanic would be the one we want to talk to. But the witness on the stand can tell us what the mechanic said and whether the pilot apparently heard it. In other words, the person who spoke out of court is only the real witness when what he said is offered to prove its truth.

One last case will show that the real witness test can make some difficult-looking hearsay problems simple. Say you want to prove the terms of an oral contract, and you call a bystander who heard both the offer and acceptance. Is his testimony hearsay?

No. You want to prove what was said, and the bystander is the real witness for that.

Now look at that problem from the standpoint of the traditional hearsay test.

Are there out-of-court statements?

Of course.

Are they offered to prove their truth? Doesn't it seem that way? When the seller offered to deliver goods on August 21, wasn't that statement offered to prove that he was to deliver the goods on August 21? If that is so, then this must be hearsay, right?

Wrong.

An oral contract is made by what people say—not whether they secretly intend to keep their promises. So when the witness testifies that the offeror promised to deliver goods on August 21, that statements is not offered to prove that the witness actually meant what he said—only that he said it.

This means that even under the traditional test the words that form a contract are not hearsay. But see how easy it is to get tangled in the words of the traditional test and come up with the wrong answer.

Finally, notice that the real witness test is not the *only* witness test. It does not mean you may not want to cross-examine someone else as well as the one on the stand. It simply determines whether this witness is the one you want to question about this statement. For the hearsay rule, that is what counts.

CHAPTER 43

It's Not for Its Truth

Barbara Swanson (who has been trying cases longer than I have) stopped in the Brief Bag for lunch on Friday, and ran into Tucker Phillips.

"Tucker," she said, " I saw you this morning in Judge Feckler's courtroom, and it looked like you were getting all kinds of outrageous hearsay into evidence from the policeman you had on the stand. What was going on?"

"Just a personal injury case," said Tucker. "My plaintiff was injured when an elevator cable failed and the emergency brake didn't work. The cop is the guy who got my client out of the elevator car."

"I gathered that from what I heard," said Barbara. "But what I want to know is why you wanted to get all that hearsay into evidence?"

"Well, in the first place," said Tucker, "it's great hearsay. The cop is a much better witness than the people whose statements he's repeating. Second, it saves me the trouble of calling all those other witnesses. And third, Judge Feckler lets me do it.

"You see," said Tucker, "I've found out something important about Judge Feckler. He doesn't understand hearsay."

Barbara looked over her half-glasses at Tucker.

"Oh, he can recite the magic words as well as any other judge," said Tucker, "but that doesn't mean he really understands them. If the other side objects to your evidence as hearsay, all you have to say is, 'It's not for its truth, Your Honor,' and Judge Feckler will overrule the objection. It works every time."

Barbara slid her half-glasses farther down her nose and looked at him again. "Tucker," she said, "that's outrageous. It would never occur to me to make a response that I knew was incorrect for the purpose of getting some testimony into evidence—no matter how I thought the judge was going to rule."

"Who said my response was incorrect?" asked Tucker. "In Judge Feckler's room it's the right response. It's what you need to say to get the objection overruled. Believe me, nothing else works nearly as well."

"But it's not the law," said Barbara.

"Sure it is," said Tucker. "It's the law in Judge Feckler's court."

"But it's not the law on appeal," said Barbara. "And besides, even if your policeman is a good witness, that doesn't mean the jury is going to like his hearsay. Juries are suspicious of hearsay for the same reason we are. They don't trust rumors. They want to hear testimony from the real witness."

That's when Tucker Phillips started looking for help from someone else. "Angus," he said, "explain it to her, would you?"

"Sorry," said Angus, "I'm on Barbara's side, and the problem is a serious one. Like Judge Feckler, there are thousands of lawyers and judges for whom the rules of evidence are a series of buzzwords—kind of like magic incantations. And 'It's not for its truth' is a perfect example.

"Everybody knows there are two requirements for hearsay. First is an out-of-court statement. Usually that's easy. If the declarant—the one making the statement—did not say it in this court, as a witness during this trial, then it is an out-of-court statement.

"But the second requirement can seem a little more difficult, largely because of language. In the words of the Federal Rules of Evidence, the out-of-court statement has to be offered to prove 'the truth of the matter asserted.' Those words are awkward because they were written by law professors who were unconcerned with ease of comprehension.

"But the idea is really a simple one. A slander suit is the best example. Suppose Jimmy says, 'Angus, you're a lying, thieving, no good s.o.b. who would steal anything not nailed down, and sell his grandmother's bones for a nickel to buy flowers for a harlot.' When I sue him for defamation and Barbara testifies to what Jimmy said, it is not hearsay because I am not trying to prove that what he said is true. On the contrary, I am simply proving that he said it.

"And now you see why 'the truth of the matter asserted' is awkward. The question is whether you are trying to prove the truth of what was said. That idea comes across much more quickly with the simple words, 'its truth.'

"So hearsay is:
1. An out-of-court statement that is
2. Offered to prove its truth.

"The key is relevance. When the out-of-court statement is relevant for any purpose other than proving its truth, it is not hearsay. And in theory, at least, the other possibilities are endless.

"That thicket of endless possibilities is what makes the buzzwords, 'not for its truth' so attractive. Some lawyers figure they can lose the judge and the other lawyer in the bushes, wondering what the evidence really proves.

"And it's amazing how often it works. Caught in the tangle of awkward phrases and endless possibilities, some lawyers and judges would rather pretend that they, too, like the way the emperor is dressed, instead of confessing they don't see what he's got on. It is a trap for the intellectually insecure who don't want to appear as if they don't understand."

That's when Frank Logan said, "Wait a second. Suppose you're on the receiving end of this. How do you get the judge out of the trap so he will rule in your favor?"

"You've got to make the judge understand that just because the other side says the evidence is not offered for its truth doesn't make it so," said Angus.

"Absolutely," said Barbara Swanson. "I like to say, 'Judge, if this evidence is no good for its truth, then what is it good for? The plaintiff has got to tell us why he is offering it.'"

"And there is something else that will help," said Angus. "While theoretically there are endless possibilities for why a statement might be relevant for something besides its truth, in real life there is only a handful worth knowing:
1. A verbal act
2. A verbal part of an act
3. Knowledge
4. State of mind.

Verbal Act

"Remember what Jimmy said about me buying flowers?" said Angus. "That was a verbal act. Speaking (or writing) the words of defamation is an act that causes injury, just as much as hitting someone over the head with a baseball bat.

"It is the same with an offer or acceptance. Say you offer to sell me your car for $5,000, and I accept. Those are verbal acts. In a lawsuit based on our contract, the offer is admissible in evidence because the words were spoken—not because they were true. We don't care that you secretly intended to keep your car. Your liability is based on what you said.

"Fraud is even easier to understand. Like the words of defamation, fraudulent representations are obviously not offered to prove their truth, but rather to show they were spoken."

Verbal Part of an Act

"There are lots of situations where a physical act would be impossible to understand without the words that went with it. A man hands a policeman twenty dollars. Is it a bribe? Repaying a loan? Buying tickets for a hospital benefit? The words that go with the act and give it meaning are part of the act, and are not hearsay."

Knowledge

"It works two ways—both coming and going. Suppose Tucker Phillips hears your auto mechanic tell you that your brake pads are worn out. Tucker's testimony is not admissible to prove your brakes are bad—but it is admissible to show that you were on notice about a possible defect in your brakes.

"Now suppose you tell Barbara Swanson that you've got bad brakes. If we are trying to prove the condition of your brakes, it's hearsay—but if the question is whether you knew something was wrong with them, it's not hearsay."

State of Mind

"Of course there is a state-of-mind exception to the hearsay rule. But you only need it when the out-of-court statement says, in effect, 'This is my state of mind.' Most of the time what people say is simply circumstantial evidence of their state of mind.

"If that sounds tough, don't worry. A simple example will make it clear. A woman leaves everything to her nephew, John, cutting off the rest of her relatives. Whether she really meant to favor him is the heart of the case. Now suppose she said, 'I care more for John than any of my other relatives.' That is hearsay because it is an out-of-court statement that is offered to prove its truth. And it's admissible through the state-of-mind exception.

"But now suppose she said, 'That Johnny is a clever rascal. He's the finest relative I have.' John's good qualities are not at issue. You don't need the state-of-mind exception to the hearsay rule. Her statement is admissible because it is circumstantial evidence of how she feels about him."

Then Tucker Phillips stood up and said, "But why does any of this mean I shouldn't simply tell Judge Feckler that the evidence isn't offered for its truth?"

"Well, you know how you've limited your case, don't you?" asked Angus.

"What do you mean by that?" said Tucker.

"It is a truism," said Angus. "You got that evidence in by saying it was not offered for its truth. That means it cannot be used to prove its truth. If the only proof you have of some essential fact is that 'non-hearsay' evidence, you're in trouble. If the defendant's liability depends on the truth of some of those statements, then Judge Feckler should grant the defendant's motion for a directed verdict.

"And it also limits your final argument. Telling the jury that the out-of-court statements proved the truth of what they said would be absolutely improper."

That's when Tucker Phillips left. "I've got to call some witnesses," he said.

CHAPTER 44

The Big Four

He was billing the time as trial preparation, but he was just sitting there, thinking about the hearsay rule and what he would have to go through to introduce all that business correspondence into evidence. And it was starting to bother him.

After all, it seemed like such an undisciplined jumble; countless rules and exceptions to be applied to hundreds of letters, memoranda, and telephone calls—and each one was different. Whoever had said that a trial is not an evidence examination could not have been thinking about business litigation.

There is no question, all business letters and conversations—whether on the telephone or in person—involve out-of-court statements. And that means they virtually invite hearsay objections. But don't let that upset you. There are four responses that take care of more than 90 percent of all the hearsay problems presented by business correspondence:

- Not Hearsay.
- Admission.
- Business Record.
- Past Recollection Recorded.

Understanding them will not guarantee that you will stay out of trouble, but it will surely reduce the risk.

Not Hearsay

Start with whether the correspondence is even hearsay. What does that mean? There are two essential ingredients to all hearsay: first, an out-of-court statement; second, that is offered to prove its truth. Because the business correspondence automatically supplies the out-of-court statement, the question is whether the statement is offered to prove its truth.

Take an offer as an example. A letter from the seller offers a computer system to the buyer for $75,000. The buyer accepts, but the seller never delivers. When the buyer goes about proving the contract, why isn't the letter hearsay? Doesn't it prove the truth of what it says?

No.

This letter is not offered to show that the seller had a computer system or that if he did he would sell it for $75,000. It is only offered to show that he made a promise—not that he was going to keep it. That promise was an offer. It was an act done with words, and so it is not hearsay. (See Section 249, *McCormick on Evidence*, West Pub. Co., 3d ed. 1984.)

So verbal acts (whether written or oral) such as offers and acceptances, or instructions to an agent, are not subject to the hearsay rule, and need no exception to make them admissible in evidence.

A similar rule applies to words that accompany conduct and give it meaning. For example, a woman hands a man a check and says, "This is to repay the money you loaned me last month." Her words are not considered hearsay.

Notice is another kind of verbal act. A telephone call to the plaintiff tells him how the market conditions have changed. Later it becomes important to show that the plaintiff was given this information. Evidence of the message is not hearsay because it is not offered to prove what the market conditions actually were, but rather what the plaintiff was told.

The unifying factor is simple enough. If the point of the evidence is to show that an out-of-court statement is true, it is hearsay. But if it is offered to show that the words were said or that they were heard, then it is not hearsay.

Admissions

Next come admissions. Anything said or done by the other party that is inconsistent with the position it now takes at trial is an admission. So any of the other side's letters or telephone conversations that do not get admitted as nonhearsay should be admissions if they are inconsistent with the party's position in the case.

Notice that the communications do not need to have been directed to your client to be admissions. Letters or telephone calls to other parties or even internal memoranda can qualify. The question is not to whom the communications were directed, but whether they are relevant to this case.

At common law there was a limitation on admissions that presented a serious problem with business communications. A statement made by an employee was not admissible unless it was in the scope of the employee's duties to make the statement. If it was not the employee's job to make the statement, it might qualify for some other hearsay exception, but it was not an admission.

The Federal Rules of Evidence have changed that. Now a statement of an agent or servant is admissible if it concerns a matter within the scope of his employment and is made during the existence of the relationship. Rule 801(d)(2)(D), Federal Rules of Evidence. This makes it a lot harder to keep employees' communications out of evidence.

Before we go on, there is an important point that makes life easier for the party offering evidence. The proponent of the evidence picks the theory of admissibility.

So what, you ask.

Just this. If the evidence is admissible under the proponent's theory, then it does not matter if it is inadmissible under the opponent's theory (unless, of course, the evidence is unfairly prejudicial or violates some privilege). So if a telephone conversation does not pass muster as an admission, it might still be admissible, say, for the nonhearsay purpose of notice.

Business Records

Next come business records. And now an important warning. Unless you have total recall, always use a checklist when laying the foundation for a business record. It is simply too easy to leave out an essential element and wonder what is missing when an objection is sustained. Here is such a list, drawn from Rule 803(6) of the Federal Rules of Evidence:

- A record of acts, events, conditions, opinions, or diagnoses
- Made at or near the time
- By, or from information transmitted by, a person with knowledge

- Kept in the course of a regularly conducted business activity
- It is the regular practice of the business activity to make the record
- It is admissible unless the source of information or method or circumstances of preparation indicate a lack of trustworthiness
- All the elements of the foundation can be shown by the custodian or other qualified witness

Remember that our subject is business correspondence. Can a letter qualify as a record? Yes. Business records are not limited to formal daybooks, logs, or ledgers. Under Rule 803(6) of the Federal Rules of Evidence, a record can be a "memorandum, report, record, or data compilation, in any form." So business letters can be business records, but not automatically. They need to meet all the requirements.

A regular monthly letter reporting on sales and expenses, for example, should be admissible. But be careful. Just because a copy of a letter was kept in the files does not mean that it was a "regular practice of that business activity" to make a record of the information it contains.

While the business records exception is a creature of the legislature, courts have added two important doctrines to it. The first comes from *Johnson v. Lutz*, 170 N.E. 517 (N.Y. 1930). In that case, a police report of an automobile accident that contained statements from bystanders was inadmissible to prove the truth of what the bystanders said. The court reasoned that since the bystanders had no "business duty" to report what they had seen, their statements lacked the extra reliability necessary to qualify as an exception to the hearsay rule.

The other judicial addition to the business record exception comes from *Palmer v. Hoffman*, 318 U.S. 109 (1943), which held that a business record that was made with a view toward litigation was inadmissible.

Past Recollection Recorded

Past recollection recorded is the last item on our list. It is one of the few exceptions to the hearsay rule—perhaps the only one—that you should commit to memory. You should memorize it because you never know when you will suddenly need it. And in a case loaded with business documents there is a good chance you will need it. Here are the elements of the common-law rule:

- A writing (or some other kind of recording)
- Made at or near the event
- By someone who has firsthand knowledge
- Who has no present recollection of the event
- But who can vouch that the writing was accurate when made.

There are two important differences between the common law rule and Rule 803(5) of the Federal Rules of Evidence. First, under 803(5), the writing does not need to be made at or near the event—just "made or adopted by the witness when the matter was fresh in his memory. . . ." Second, under 803(5), the witness does not have to have a total lapse of memory concerning the event to make the statement admissible. He only has to have "insufficient recollection to enable him to testify fully and accurately."

Finally, an advantage of past recollection recorded is that the doctrine of *Palmer v. Hoffman* does not apply to it. Past recollection recorded is not excluded because it was made with a view toward litigation. That means that there will be times when a business letter or memorandum will be admitted as past recollection recorded even though it could not qualify as a business record.

Of course you will need other exceptions to the hearsay rule in dealing with business correspondence, such as declarations against interest or even commercial publications. But if you try the big four first, it makes the rest of it a lot easier.

CHAPTER 45

Hidden Rules

Francis Logan was in Judge Wallop's court, arguing that something the defendant had authorized was an admission, when the judge asked, "Where is that in the rules, Counsel?"

Logan is not in court every day, but he has been trying cases for a long time, so when he couldn't find the exact rule immediately, he was not upset. "If I can have a moment, Your Honor," he said.

But after a few minutes, Logan started to worry. Not only was he unable to locate authorized statements, he couldn't even find admissions. The third time through the hearsay exceptions, Rules 803 and 804, he began to panic. He was seriously thinking that the drafters of the rules of evidence had left out admissions altogether, when he stumbled on Rule 801.

Later on, in the Brief Bag, just around the corner from Judge Wallop's court, Logan told Angus about his brush with humiliation.

"It doesn't make any sense, Angus. Here it is, the most important exception to the hearsay rule, and instead of being with the other exceptions, it is stuck off with the definitions in Rule 801. What in the world is it doing there?"

"Hiding," said Angus.

"Hey, I'm serious," said Francis, giving Angus a dark look.

"So am I," said Angus. "When New York considered an evidence code based on the Federal Rules, it took admissions out of Rule 801 and put them with the other hearsay exceptions precisely because a lot of lawyers thought they were in the wrong place.

"And that's not all," Angus said. "The Federal Rules of Evidence are loaded with hidden rules. They're like one of those cartoons where you're supposed to find the twenty-five missing monkeys—only it's not much fun in the middle of trial."

Angus is right. Although you can defend the way the rules are organized, they are harder to work with than they should be.

Take Rule 801, for instance. It is not just a definition of hearsay. It also includes (depending on how you count them) either four or eight separate exceptions to the hearsay rule, including one that should also be listed in Article Six, Witnesses.

So go ahead and ask Logan's question. Why would the drafters do that?

The answer is a bit of twisted legal theory.

Start with one of the scholarly definitions of hearsay. Hearsay is evidence that depends for its probative value on the veracity of an out-of-court declarant. Using that definition, there is some justification for saying admissions are not hearsay.

Wait a minute, you say. How does that figure?

The scholarly definition focuses on whose credibility is at issue. If your own statement is being used against you, you can hardly complain that you have been denied the right to cross-examine yourself. You have the whole trial to explain what you meant by your statement. So scholars have argued that under their definition of hearsay, admissions do not need to be exceptions to the hearsay rule because they are not even hearsay in the first place.

But you already know that the Federal Rules did not adopt the scholar's definition of hearsay. They went with the trial lawyer's version—one that is easier to use.

It has two parts. Hearsay is (1) an out-of-court statement (2) that is offered to prove the truth of the matter asserted.

Under that definition, admissions are obviously hearsay. They are out-of-court statements, and they are offered to prove the truth of what they say. So if they are hearsay, they need a hearsay exception to be admissible in evidence, right?

Not according to the drafters of the Federal Rules. Even though they started with the trial lawyer's definition of hearsay, they switched to the scholar's definition when it came to listing hearsay exceptions. The result is a whole series of out-of-court statements that are admissible to prove their truth, but are labeled "nonhearsay." Small wonder some lawyers get confused and others cannot even find the right rule.

Here are the different admissions that are called nonhearsay by Rule 801:

- Admissions—the party's own statements.
- Adoptive admissions—someone else's statements that the party has adopted as his own.
- Admissions by authorized agents.
- Admissions by an agent or servant about the scope of his employment. (Notice these do not have to be authorized statements. This is an important change from the common law.)
- Admissions—statements by co-conspirators during the course and in furtherance of the conspiracy.

And there are other statements that are admissible under Rule 801. Prior statements are admissible as nonhearsay if the declarant testifies at the trial or hearing, is subject to cross-examination about the statement, and it is a:

- Prior inconsistent statement given under oath, subject to the penalty of perjury at a trial, hearing, other proceeding (such as a grand jury session), or deposition. In other words, some (but, by no means, all) prior inconsistent statements are admissible for their truth. That is a change from the common law, where prior inconsistent statements were only admissible to attack the credibility of the witness.
- Prior consistent statement offered to rebut an express or implied charge against the declarant of recent fabrication or improper influence or motive. This is another change from the common law, where prior consistent statements also were only admissible on the issue of the credibility of the witness.
- Prior identification of a person made after perceiving him. This, too, is a change from the common law. The earlier rule was that a prior identification of someone was only admissible to corroborate an in-court identification.

  That meant two things: First, there had to be an in-court identification. Without it, evidence of the out-of-court identification was simply not admissible. Second, the out-of-court identification only went to the credibility of the witness. But now it is admissible for its truth, and the rule does not require an in-court identification.

Stop just a minute before we go any further.

Notice that in each one of the last three kinds of "nonhearsay," the declarant—the one whose earlier statement is offered into evidence—must testify and be subject to cross-examination about the statement.

Why does that matter?

The thought is if you can cross-examine the declarant now, you cannot complain that you were unable to cross-examine him at the time he made the statement. Whether you agree with that idea or not, it is the reason for making these statements admissible for their truth.

And another thing. Being able to cross-examine a witness about his earlier statement is why these three categories are not hearsay according to the scholar's definition. How can they depend for their probative value on the veracity of out-of-court declarants if those declarants are in court, subject to cross-examination about what they said?

The trouble is, under the trial lawyer's definition, they are still out-of-court statements offered to prove their truth.

So there you have it. Rule 801 has a total of three different prior statements and five different kinds of admissions, all admissible for their truth. And if you think that is a lot of operative rules to put in a definition, you are not alone.

One last point before we leave Rule 801. The mechanics for dealing with prior inconsistent statements are right where they belong—in Rule 613, the article that deals with witnesses. But the mechanics for dealing with prior consistent statements are in Rule 801.

Do not think Rule 801 is the only culprit. There are other hiding places in the Federal Rules.

The rules dealing with expert opinions are in Article Seven—Opinions and Expert Testimony. But the rules for how to impeach or support an expert with a learned treatise are in Rule 803(18), which is in the middle of an exception to the hearsay rule.

The familiar Rule of Completeness got renamed "Remainder of or Related Writing or Recorded Statements." And it is tucked away under Rule 106, General Provisions, instead of in Article Four under Relevance, where it belongs.

When the accused in a criminal case testifies to a preliminary matter, that does not open the door to cross-examination about other issues in the case. That is in Rule 104(d), General Provisions, not under Relevance in Article Four, or under Witnesses in Article Six.

And look out. Rule 104(d) is really a trap. Even though testifying to a preliminary matter does not open the door to cross-examination about "other issues in the case," it does open the door to cross-examination about prior convictions and uncharged misconduct, Rule 104(e).

Other rules are hidden because the drafters avoided some of the traditional language of evidence:

- The Best Evidence Rule is not found under "Best Evidence." It is in a series of rules, including Rule 1002, Requirement of Original.
- The requirement for hypothetical questions is abolished in Rules 703 and 705 without ever using the words "hypothetical question."
- Rule 103 adopts the doctrine of harmless error without ever calling it "harmless error."

Maybe you are more concerned with what is left out from the Federal Rules (a topic in itself) than you are with what is simply hard to find. Still, it is worth doing what Angus did—annotate, translate, and highlight your set of the rules so you can find what you want when you need it.

CHAPTER 46

The Best Evidence

Flash Magruder was having a hard time getting some demonstrative material into evidence.

The exhibit was a drawing prepared by a medical illustrator. It showed the plaintiff—Mike Sanders—with a portion of his cheek and nose cut away so the jury could see his underlying injury. Sanders had been putting his money in the fare box of a bus just as the bus pulled away from the curb and ran into the rear of a cement truck that had suddenly stopped in front of it. In the crash Sanders's nose was broken and shoved up into his head, and the medical illustration showed how the ragged edges of the broken bones had cut through some important nerves.

It was an impressive bit of medical art, designed to make it easy to understand what had happened to Sanders. Almost like a photograph, it showed him so true to life that even old friends who had not seen him for years would recognize him. And like a medical illustration, the cutaway showed shattered bones and severed nerves colored so they would be easy to identify. It looked nothing like the subtle shadows on the typical X ray that only radiologists seem to understand.

Magruder knew that the typical foundation for a photograph would never do for this illustration. A photograph—say, of an accident scene—has to be a fair and accurate representation of the way the scene looked at the time of the accident.

But no matter how recognizable Sanders was, the illustration was not fair and accurate in the usual sense. Sanders had never gone around with part of his face and nose cut away so you could

The Best Evidence

see his broken bones and torn nerves. And besides, there was no reason for thinking he had color-coded bones, muscles, tendons, arteries, veins, and nerves.

So Magruder asked around and decided that the proper foundation for the illustration was that it would help an expert witness—Sanders's doctor—explain his testimony to the jury. Magruder also thought that while the illustration did not show Sanders's actual appearance, it was a fair and accurate representation of his medical condition right after the collision.

Maybe that is how Magruder got in trouble. He decided that because the medical illustration was so much more effective than the X rays and doctor's notes in showing what happened to Sanders, he would not use those other exhibits.

That played right into the defendant's hands. First Magruder used the doctor to lay the foundation. The doctor said the illustration accurately showed Sanders's medical condition, and would help him explain his testimony to the jury. Then the defense lawyer examined the doctor on voir dire. The doctor explained that the illustration was based in part on the X rays that were taken when Sanders went into the hospital and in part on notes that the doctor took when he first examined Sanders. That is when the defense objected that the illustration was not the best evidence.

Magruder exploded. "That's ridiculous, Your Honor. The best evidence rule applies to documents. This illustration is based on X rays, and X rays aren't documents."

"Yes they are," the defense lawyer said. "It's right here. Rule 1002 of the Federal Rules says the original is required '[t]o prove the contents of a writing, recording or photograph.' And Rule 1001 says an X ray is a photograph."

Then Magruder had (for him) an unusual spark of insight. "But Your Honor, we are not offering this to prove the contents of the X ray, even if it is a document. We are offering this only as an aid to the doctor's testimony."

The court was about to rule in Magruder's favor when the defense lawyer said, "Well, if this illustration is not supposed to show the plaintiff's condition, then it isn't relevant to the case. And besides, since the doctor's testimony is also based on those X rays that aren't in evidence, it violates the best evidence rule, too."

So who is right, Magruder or his opponent? The starting place for answering the question is the best evidence rule itself: To prove the contents of a document, you must introduce the original or account for its whereabouts. It is a rule that has its roots in a time before word processors, copier machines, typewriters, or even carbon paper. Handmade copies might have deliberate changes or at least contain mistakes. And oral testimony about what some document said is even more suspect.

But even though modern copying machines are more accurate than scriveners hunched over their work, we have kept the best evidence rule—partly out of habit and partly because it continues to serve some purpose.

There are some important things to understand about the rule. First, from the common law. The best evidence rule only applies to situations in which you are actually proving the contents of the document. And to prove the contents of a document, the information you are introducing in evidence has to come from the document. Just because the information happens to be in a document does not mean you are proving its contents.

Wait a minute, you say. Does that make any sense? It actually does, and a simple example will make it clear. Suppose you want to prove what the weather was like in Chicago on April 23, 1994. You call a witness who was standing outside the Daley Center at 12:00 noon on April 23. You ask him whether it was raining.

Now suppose your opponent jumps up and objects. "Not the best evidence, Your Honor. There is an official U.S. weather report for Chicago. If they want to prove what the weather was, let them introduce the report."

The objection is wrong. The witness knows what the weather was. He saw it himself. Just because the information also happens to be in a document does not mean it comes from the document.

Now recall that the medical illustrator did the cutaway of Mike Sanders based in part on X rays and the doctor's notes. Does this mean that the illustration is not admissible unless the X rays and notes are introduced first?

Not necessarily, although it obviously would have solved a lot of problems if the notes and X rays had been introduced into evidence. That is because the best evidence rule does not prohibit secondary evidence. It only prohibits secondary evidence when it is being used to prove the contents of a document. When the original is already in evidence, the purpose of the rule is satisfied.

But the X rays and notes were not introduced into evidence. So doesn't the exhibit violate the best evidence rule?

Like I said, not necessarily.

It does not matter where the artist got her information; it only matters what the exhibit is being used for. Under the circumstances, it was a mistake for Magruder to have the doctor testify that the illustration was a fair and accurate representation of Mike Sanders's medical condition. That was proving the contents of the X ray.

But then Magruder backed off from that foundation and said the illustration was offered to aid the witness in explaining his testimony. Didn't that solve the best evidence problem?

Not completely.

Why not?

Let us go back to the weather in Chicago on April 23. The witness knows what the weather was like, so the best evidence rule does not require introducing the official weather report. Now let us assume that a commercial artist prepares a chart that shows the weather in Chicago on that day. The chart, we assume, will help our witness explain what he saw.

Should the chart be admitted?

Certainly.

Will it matter that the artist got his information about the weather from the official U.S. weather report?

Certainly not.

The same idea applies to Flash Magruder and Mike Sanders's doctor. But unlike the witness who saw the weather, the doctor got some of his information about Sanders from another source—the X rays. So even if the exhibit is only used to aid the doctor in explaining his testimony, the testimony itself violates the best evidence rule. See *Sirico v. Cotto*, 324 N.Y.S.2d 483 (1971).

The lesson is be prepared to offer the original documents in evidence.

Finally, there are a few things worth knowing about the best evidence rule as it appears in the Federal Rules.

First, "duplicates" are just as admissible as the original unless there is a genuine question as to the authenticity of the original or under the circumstances it would be unfair to admit the duplicate. Rule 1003. "Duplicates" include carbon copies, photocopies, or equivalent techniques that accurately reproduce the original. Rule 1001(4). So for practical purposes, a photocopy is an original, which makes a lot of sense.

Second, the original is not required when the document is not closely related to a controlling issue. Rule 1004(4). In other words, if the document is collateral, the best evidence rule does not even apply.

Third, like the common law, the federal best evidence rule does not require the original if you are able to account for its whereabouts. So if you can show that the original was lost or destroyed, cannot be obtained by judicial process, or is in the hands of your opponent (and you requested he produce it), then the best evidence rule has been satisfied.

It means that so long as your client is not guilty of destroying the original because of the impending litigation, you can deal with the best evidence rule.

If you think of it in time.

CHAPTER 47

Limited Admissibility

"Limited admissibility," said Mike Pirelli, slamming down his briefcase, "is unlimited fraud. It's doctrinal hypocrisy. It says one thing and does another. If there is anything about the law that encourages disrespect, it is this phony idea that evidence that is absolutely inadmissible for one thing is admissible to prove something else, and the judge can fix the problem by telling the jury the right way to use the evidence."

"It sounds like you just lost a motion," said Angus.

"You got that right," Pirelli said. "Judge Mudrock's court. Criminal case. He said the defendant's prior convictions for assault would be admissible on the issue of intent.

"The defendant is charged with assault," said Pirelli. "His prior convictions are not supposed to be admissible to prove he is the kind of person who would commit the crime he is charged with. Yet here come his three prior convictions.

"And if the judge tells the jury to limit the convictions to the issue of intent, there is no way it will help," said Pirelli. "It will just underline something they shouldn't hear in the first place. There ought to be other ways for dealing with limited admissibility besides giving a limiting instruction."

"You're right," responded Angus, "and there are. But they all have problems."

Angus was at it again. I got out a legal pad and started writing. Here are my notes.

The main point of the law of evidence is to shape the case that goes to the jury. It works fine as long as each piece of evidence proves only one point or applies to only one party. But in nearly every case there is some evidence that goes to prove two or more points, or applies to two or more parties, but is admissible against only one.

The evidence is admissible for one point but not another. So what do you do about it?

The common law came up with three strategies for dealing with the situation. Rule 105 of the Federal Rules of Evidence deals with only one of the three: "When evidence which is admissible as to one party or for one purpose but not admissible as to another party or for another purpose is admitted, the court, upon request, shall restrict the evidence to its proper scope and instruct the jury accordingly."

So the approach under Rule 105 is to let the evidence in and tell the jury to only use it the right way. The second solution is to keep the evidence out because it has too much unfair prejudice. The third is to split the trial so the evidence can't cross over from one part to the other.

Each answer has its own set of problems.

- Limited admissibility often guarantees that the jury will use the evidence improperly. Say the truck driver's bad driving record is inadmissible to show he was driving carelessly but is admissible to show that his employer was negligent in entrusting him with a dangerous instrumentality. Put in traditional legal trappings, the limiting instruction is merely hard to understand. Put in real English, it becomes absurd. "Ladies and gentlemen of the jury, the truck driver's bad driving record does not show he was driving carelessly. It only shows that his employer was careless for hiring such a bad driver."
- Excluding the evidence eliminates proof that is perfectly good for the point to which it goes. In the right circumstances, keeping the evidence out can change the result in the case.
- Bifurcating the trial can keep the jury from using proof of liability to increase damages, or the confession of one defendant from poisoning the trial of the other—but often at the cost of longer, more complicated hearings.

There are a number of reasons why judges would rather admit the evidence and give a limiting instruction than do anything else.

First, it is hard to reverse a trial court because of an evidentiary mistake. Unless the question rises to constitutional dimensions, the appellate court is likely to call it harmless error. When a judge lets evidence in for a limited purpose, it is even harder to get him reversed. To the appellate court, it looks like the trial judge already made a reasonable effort to deal with the problem.

Second, there is a bias in favor of admissibility. Under Rule 403 of the Federal Rules of Evidence, relevant evidence is admissible unless its probative value is "substantially outweighed by the danger of unfair prejudice, confusion of the issues, or misleading the jury, or by considerations of undue delay, waste of time, or needless presentation of cumulative evidence." In other words, relevant evidence comes in unless it is clearly inadmissible.

Third, admitting the evidence avoids the hassle of separate trials or bifurcated hearings.

All of this means that the evidence is going to be admitted unless the judge really doesn't like it. And that means that you have to be familiar with the rules of limited admissibility.

First, the proponent—the one offering the evidence—picks the theory of admissibility. If a document is offered and is admissible as past recollection recorded, then it doesn't matter that it doesn't qualify as a business record. It is dealer's call, and if the dealer says the game is five-card draw, that is it—not seven-card stud.

When you have a choice of how to offer the evidence, the best one is usually the rule that makes the evidence admissible for all purposes and against all parties.

For example, suppose a truck crashes into the back of a car stopped at a red light. The driver jumps out of the truck and runs up to the driver of the car he hit. "I'm sorry," he says, "it's all my fault."

Before the Federal Rules of Evidence, the truck driver's statement was an admission—but only against him, not against his employer. Why not? Because the truck driver was hired to drive, not to talk. It was outside the scope of the driver's employment, and therefore inadmissible against the employer.

That is still the law in a number of jurisdictions. In those states, the typical strategy would be to include the truck driver as a defendant. That way the jury hears his admission and the judge gives a limiting instruction.

But if the truck driver's statement qualifies as an excited utterance, then it is admissible against the trucking company, whether or not the driver is a party in the case. Then the plaintiff keeps the theory of admission as a backup argument for admissibility.

That whole game got a lot simpler under the Federal Rules of Evidence. That's because admissions of an employee are admissible against the employer so long as they relate to the scope of employment and are made during the existence of the relationship. Rule 801(d)(2)(D).

Second, either side has to be ready to ask the court for limited admissibility. Look at how it works. A mechanic warns a pilot that the carburetor heat on the airplane does not work properly. The mechanic is not available to testify, but a bystander who heard his warning can repeat what he said.

Offered with intent to prove that the plane was defective, the bystander's testimony is hearsay. It is an out-of-court statement that is offered to prove its truth. But offered against the pilot to show he was on notice of a defective condition, the statement is admissible.

Now suppose that the bystander testifies to what the mechanic said. The airplane manufacturer objects, claiming that the testimony is hearsay. The plaintiff responds that the testimony is admissible to prove notice. The court rules that the evidence is admissible.

Take another look at Rule 105. There is no limitation on the use of the evidence unless the manufacturer asks for it. So the opponent has to be ready to ask for limited admissibility. This time, switch it around. The plaintiff offers the bystander's testimony, and the manufacturer objects that it is hearsay. The court agrees. Unless the plaintiff makes a limited offer—explains to the court why it is admissible—the judge should sustain the objection. So the proponent has to be ready to ask for limited admissibility, too.

That may seem like a pretty complicated game to play to get an instruction that won't be understood or may actually hurt.

But there is more to it than that. Limiting the use of evidence may determine whether or not you are entitled to a directed verdict. If the only evidence of a defect in that airplane was the bystander's testimony, then failing to ask for a limiting instruction would be a serious mistake.

And that's not all. The law of limited admissibility is also the law of final argument. If evidence is admitted for a limited purpose, it is absolutely improper to ask the jury to use it the wrong way.

Remember that. It is one of those points that is easy to forget in the heat of battle.

One last point. Limiting evidence to its proper purpose does not cure any unfair prejudice. Remember Mike Pirelli's case? No matter what Judge Mudrock says, the jury is probably going to use the evidence of the defendant's prior convictions to conclude that he's the kind of person who would commit assault.

In other words, Rule 105 does not change the relevance balance in Rule 403. Excluding evidence that is unfairly prejudicial is a general principle that cuts across all the other rules of evidence. When the jury is going to use the evidence the wrong way, that's unfair prejudice.

CHAPTER 48

Using the Wrong Deposition

Beth Golden came into the Brief Bag. "Angus," she said, "I need help."

"Beth," said Angus. "What's the problem?"

"Evidence," she said, her eyes glazed. "Hearsay . . . depositions . . . former testimony . . . Judge Feckler."

"Sounds like a lethal combination," said Angus. "Tell me about it."

"I'm right in the middle of cross-examining a witness in Judge Feckler's court," Beth said, "and we just quit for the day. Frankly, I'm glad, because now I'll have a chance to see if there is some way I can use that deposition."

"Deposition?" said Angus.

"I'm sorry," said Beth. "It's actually pretty simple. It's just the rules of evidence that make it seem tangled.

"I'm representing the defendant in a fight over an option to buy a shopping center. Three months ago I was about to take the deposition of a possible witness for the plaintiffs when they took him off their witness list.

"Since they weren't going to have him testify, I decided I didn't need to take his deposition a second time. See, I had already taken his deposition about the same transaction for an earlier case."

"Let me get it straight," said Angus. "Two separate trials?"

"That's right," said Beth.

"You represented the same defendant each time?" said Angus.

"Right," said Beth.

"But the plaintiffs are different?"

"Exactly," said Beth.

"And you took the witness's deposition in case one, but not in case two?" said Angus.

"Because the plaintiffs in case two said they weren't going to call him to testify," said Beth.

"Let me guess what happened next," said Angus. "Right in the middle of the trial in case two, the plaintiffs did an about-face and called this witness to the stand. You objected because he wasn't on their witness list. But they came up with some excuse, and the judge let him testify anyway. Right?"

"How did you know?" said Beth.

"You said you were in Judge Feckler's court, didn't you?" said Angus. "Go ahead. Then what?"

"Just what you might expect," said Beth. "The witness remembered everything favorable to the plaintiff, but couldn't remember anything that helped me. And the only thing I had to work with was the witness's deposition from case number one. So first I tried to impeach him with it, but Judge Feckler said I couldn't do that because the deposition did not contradict the witness's testimony.

"It was maddening. Feckler said that just because the witness used to remember something doesn't mean he can't forget later, and forgetting is not an inconsistency that can be impeached.

"I told Judge Feckler that was ridiculous formalism," said Beth, "but I don't think he appreciated my comment."

"I agree with you, Beth," said Angus, "but Feckler's position is the common understanding on the point."

"I know," said Beth, "but I thought it was worth a try. Anyway, then I had my brilliant insight, which also didn't work. I offered the deposition not to impeach, but as substantive evidence. Since the witness couldn't remember the facts I wanted, I figured he was 'unavailable' under the rules of evidence. So I offered the deposition as former testimony."

"And Judge Feckler sustained the plaintiffs' objection?" said Angus.

"Right," said Beth. "He said it wasn't offered against the same party or a successor in interest, so it couldn't work."

"I hate to tell you, Beth," said Angus, "but Judge Feckler's right again."

"I was afraid you'd say that," said Beth. "Anyway, next I thought of past recollection recorded, but the plaintiffs argued that because it wasn't fair to let the deposition in as former testimony, it wouldn't be fair as past recollection recorded—and Feckler bought it."

"Now you've got something," said Angus. "Judge Feckler may have been right about what is inconsistent, and right about the former testimony rule. But when he said you couldn't use that deposition as past recollection recorded because it didn't qualify as former testimony, he blew it. He violated the Spinach Principle."

"Angus," said Beth, "I'm sorry. What did you say? It sounded like you said Feckler violated the 'Spinach Principle.' "

"Exactly," said Angus. "It comes from an old cartoon I saw years ago. It had a profound insight on the value of categories in analyzing problems. The cartoon showed a mother who was trying to get her child to eat his dinner. 'Eat your broccoli, dear,' she said. And the kid said, 'I say it's spinach, and I say the hell with it.' "

"Pardon me," said Beth, "but what does that have to do with the law of evidence?"

"Simple," said Angus. "The proponent—the one who offers the evidence—gets to pick which rules apply. Say the proponent offers a statement that qualifies as a declaration against interest. It doesn't make any difference that it fails the test for a dying declaration, business record, or an ancient gravestone marker. Under the Spinach Principle the opponent is not permitted to say that what qualifies as an excited utterance is no good as medical history. He is not permitted to say, 'I say it's spinach, and I say the hell with it.' "

"Any exceptions?" said Beth.

"Of course," said Angus. "It's a principle of evidence, so it's virtually required to have exceptions—but none that apply here. So let's lake a look at past recollection recorded, and see if it fits the deposition. According to the common law, you need:

- A writing
- At or near the event
- By someone with firsthand knowledge
- Who has no present recollection
- But who can testify that the writing was accurate.

"First comes the writing. It can actually be any kind of recording system—handwriting, typewriting, computer printout, video- or audio-tape—anything that preserves information accurately. A telephone number on the back of a matchbook cover can qualify just as well as a formal inventory of the contents of a warehouse.

"Second is timeliness. The common law said the writing had to be made 'at or near' the event, and that meant right away. Under that rule a deposition would hardly ever qualify as past recollection recorded, so it is natural that you never connected depositions with past recollection recorded.

"But Rule 803(5) of the Federal Rules of Evidence and the more recent cases do not require that the writing be made 'at or near the event'—only while 'the matter was fresh in the witness's memory.'

"And it makes a difference. Back in 1963, for example, Connecticut said six weeks between the event and the writing was too long. *Gigliotti v. United Illuminating Co.*, 151 Ct. 114, 193 A.2d 718 (1963). But by 1975 the 7th Circuit held that admitting a statement made after a three-year delay was not plain error. *United States v. Senak*, 527 F.2d 129 (7th Cir. 1975).

"Next comes firsthand knowledge. Past recollection recorded only admits what the witness would be able to testify to if he remembered. And just as the firsthand knowledge rule applies to what the witness remembers on the witness stand, it also applies to what he once wrote down but now can't remember.

"Of course, if what he wrote down qualifies as an exception to the hearsay rule—such as a declaration against interest made to him by some third person—that would be admissible under Rule 805 of the Federal Rules of Evidence. Hearsay inside of hearsay is admissible if you have an exception for each part.

"Then comes the failure of recollection. One of the keys to the foundation for past recollection recorded is that the witness actually has a failure of recollection. We have a strong preference for the live testimony of the actual witness. As David Binder says in his 'Hearsay Handbook' (2nd. ed. 1983), we do not want trials to be like congressional hearings where the witnesses read prepared statements and then are cross-examined. We admit past recollection recorded, but only if we have to.

"So one of the typical common law requirements—which is not mentioned in the Federal Rules but which most judges still require—is that you use the writing to try to refresh the recollection of the witness.

"On the other hand, the Federal Rules and the modern cases take a more relaxed approach about how much the witness has to forget before past recollection is admissible. According to Rule 803(5), it is just enough to prevent the witness from testifying 'fully and accurately.'

"Being more relaxed about how much the witness has to forget does not really give away too much. Unless it is offered by the opponent, past recollection recorded is read to the jury but not received as an exhibit. We don't want witnesses to 'forget' so the jury will be able to go over one witness's statement again and again in the jury room while the rest of the testimony starts to fade in their memories.

"Finally comes the voucher that the statement was accurate when it was made. And believe it or not, this may cause you a problem with the deposition. While the deposition says that the witness was under oath, that's not all there is to it. If you waived the reading and signing of the deposition by the witness, then you may have to call the court reporter to establish that it is an accurate transcription—because the witness won't know. On the other hand, Judge Feckler really ought to accept the court reporter's affidavit in the deposition on that point."

Beth stood up. "Thanks, Angus," she said. "That's terrific."

"But wait," said Angus. "We're only half done. We still have to figure out how to get Judge Feckler to let you reopen the argument."

"No problem," said Beth. "I've already got it figured. All I do is tell him he's violated the Spinach Principle. He'll know who I've been talking to."

CHAPTER 49

Understanding Character Evidence

Judge Wallop stormed into the Brief Bag. "The problem," he said, "is character evidence. Lawyers don't understand it. Appellate courts don't understand it. I don't understand it. And there's a reason for that. It doesn't make sense."

"Amen," said Beth Golden. "When you read the Federal Rules that apply to character evidence, everything looks simple and reasonable—until you try to apply them to a given set of facts. Then what looks simple becomes incomprehensible."

"That's right," said Judge Wallop. "If there ever was a self-contradictory mass of picky trivialities, it is the law of character evidence."

Angus looked up. "Okay, you two," he said. "I'll bite. You're entitled to it. You've been working on me since you came in. You may not agree with the law of character evidence, but it actually does make sense if you approach it from the right direction."

Angus was at it again and I was already taking notes. After all, I have to get my material somewhere.

There are four basic ideas that explain the law of character and impeachment. If you remember these, everything else falls in place.

- When character is an issue in the case, almost any kind of character evidence is admissible.
- Character is generally not admissible to prove conduct.
- But character can be used as a defense in criminal cases.
- Character is admissible to attack or to support the credibility of a witness.

Let's look at these ideas one at a time.

Character in issue

Everybody knows the ordinary rule that character is not admissible to prove conduct. In other words, we normally don't permit character to be used as circumstantial evidence of what somebody did.

But there are times when the law makes character itself an issue in the case. And when this happens, the rules are totally different. For example, suppose it is a child custody case and the question is who is the better guardian for the minor child, mama or papa.

When character is an issue in the case, the inquiry is wide open. Under Rule 405(a) and (b) of the Federal Rules of Evidence, reputation, opinion, and specific instances of conduct are all admissible. Not only can people who know papa testify to his reputation for violent behavior, they also can give their personal opinions about his fitness to be the custodian and tell about specific things he did that show what kind of person he is.

Character as circumstantial evidence

When the law makes character the issue, we obviously have to admit character evidence. But we don't trust it very much when it's used to prove what someone did. The rule that character is not admissible to prove conduct applies most of the time.

Not that character evidence has no probative value. It's loaded with it, and that's just the trouble. We are afraid that juries will give it too much weight or use it the wrong way altogether. The risk of misuse is at its highest in criminal cases where a jury may reason that someone who committed arson in the past probably did it again—or worse, belongs behind bars whether or not he committed the crime he is charged with now.

Like other areas of the law, once we find a principle in the rules of evidence, we tend to stick to it, even when the reasons for it fade. So character is also not admissible to prove conduct in civil cases. The defendant's bad driving record is not admissible to show that he was careless this time too.

And now for a quick reminder: When character is an issue in the case, evidence of that character is admissible. "I know that," you say. "Why are you bringing that up again?"

Because a driver's character can be an issue in the case. Suppose the suit is for negligent entrustment of a dangerous instrumentality, a large piece of earthmoving equipment. The construction company let a man with a terrible driving record take that machine on the highway, where he was involved in a wreck. His record is not admissible to show he was driving carelessly, but it is admissible to show that his employer should have known what kind of driver it was putting behind the wheel of its equipment.

So far, so good. Character is not admissible to prove conduct, but you've got to be alert for when character is actually an issue in the case.

Then, somewhere beyond the ragged edge of character, lies habit and custom. Under Rule 406 of the Federal Rules, "Evidence of the habit of a person or of the routine practice of an organization, whether corroborated or not and regardless of the presence of eyewitnesses, is relevant to prove that the conduct of the person or organization on a particular occasion was in conformity with the habit or routine practice."

So far the courts have been pretty good in not confusing character with habit, which means you have to prove a routine, specific response to a particular stimulus to get habit into evidence.

Character as a defense

The big exception to the rule that character does not prove conduct is in criminal cases. We let the defendant do what the prosecutor is forbidden to do—open the door to character.

The defendant can introduce evidence of his good character for the specific purpose of proving that he is not the kind of person who would commit the crime charged.

Lots of people talk about this as "putting character in issue," but it is not. It is simply circumstantial evidence of conduct.

"So what?" you say. "What difference does it make? Why bother to make a big deal out of what they call it?"

Because if character were actually an issue in the case, then the defendant could use all kinds of specific conduct to prove what a good person he is. But he can't do that. All he can do is put an opinion or reputation witness on the stand to testify that the defendant has a character that is inconsistent with the crime charged.

"But wait," you say, "the prosecutor can ask about specific bad acts on cross-examination. Doesn't that mean character *is* in issue?"

Nope. The prosecutor can ask character witnesses about specific acts because that is an efficient way to cross-examine.

But if the witness denies the defendant committed the acts or says he doesn't know anything about them, that is an end to it. Independent proof of the specific acts is not admissible.

On the other hand, the prosecutor can call his own character witnesses who can testify to their opinions of the defendant's character. It is one of the prices the defendant is charged for opening the door.

Character and credibility

Any time any witness takes the stand, his credibility becomes an issue. Timing is critical. You cannot attack a witness's credibility before he testifies, and you cannot support his credibility before it has been attacked.

Look at what you have in your arsenal to attack the credibility of any witness:

- Bias, prejudice, and corruption
- Prior inconsistent statements
- Prior convictions
- Prior bad acts
- Credibility witnesses

Notice that character plays a part in all of these weapons.

Bias, prejudice, and corruption are never collateral. You can ask about them on cross-examination, and if they are denied you can prove them independently with extrinsic evidence. What do they go to prove? The credibility of the witness.

Prior inconsistent statements require confrontation on cross-examination (or at least a chance to explain or deny the statement under Rule 613 of the Federal Rules of Evidence). Confrontation is not required if the witness is a party; then his statement is an admission.

What do prior inconsistent statements prove? At common law it was just the credibility of the witness. Today, many prior inconsistent statements are admissible for their truth. Rule 801(d)(1) of the Federal Rules of Evidence.

Prior convictions and bad acts can be relevant to credibility, but we are increasingly cautious about letting them be used on cross-examination. If the witness denies the prior conviction you can prove it with a certified copy of the conviction, but if he denies the bad act, you are stuck with his answer.

Why the difference? Ease of proof.

Finally come the credibility witnesses. They testify to the reputation of (or their opinion of) the credibility of the witness under attack, Rule 608(a) of the Federal Rules of Evidence. And like other character witnesses, they can be cross-examined with specific instances of conduct and contradicted by other credibility witnesses.

"Angus," declared Judge Wallop, "when you explain it, it seems so simple. And yet, I'm not sure it will stay with me."

Angus smiled. "Just remember the four main ideas," he said. "The rest is easy."

"The four main ideas," said Wallop, "are what I think I forgot."

CHAPTER 50

The Catch in Character Evidence

"Whatever else you may think about the United States Supreme Court," said Angus, "they don't know very much about trying cases."

"Amen," said Judge Wallop.

"Wait a minute," I said. "I know some people who might take offense at that."

"I'm serious," said Angus. "And my attack is very narrow. I am not talking about how the Court handles the big issues of national policy or how they manage the federal judiciary. I'm talking about how they sometimes throw monkey wrenches into the law of evidence and procedure because they don't really understand what's involved in trying a case."

"Why do I have the feeling that you have a particular problem in mind?" I said.

Angus smiled. "How about this one," he said. "What's the single most important decision a defendant has to make in a criminal case?"

"Assuming he's going to trial and not going to plead?" I asked.

"Right," said Angus.

"That's easy," said Judge Wallop. "The most important decision for the criminal defendant is whether to take the stand and testify on his own behalf."

"I agree," I said.

"Not bad for a judge and a teacher," said Angus. "Now what's the single most important factor in making that decision?" he asked.

"There are lots of considerations, but I think the most important one is whether the judge is going to let the prosecutor cross-examine the defendant with his prior convictions," I said.

"The judge agrees with the professor," Judge Wallop said.

"And so any sensible lawyer who is representing a defendant in a criminal case makes a motion in limine to keep out that prior record," said Angus.

"I gather this is a real case," I said, "and you are the sensible lawyer who made the right motion. Who is the judge?"

"Judge Gunn," said Angus. "Federal court. I was appointed to represent an indigent who is charged with bank robbery. And he has one prior conviction—an eight-year-old robbery charge in state court."

"So how did Gunn rule on your motion?" Judge Wallop asked.

"Denied it," Angus said. "Just half an hour ago."

"Well at least your defendant knows what he'll be cross-examined about if he takes the stand," I said.

"I don't think he's going to take the stand," said Angus. "And that's the rub. I disagree with Judge Gunn's ruling. I think the jury is much more likely to use an eight-year-old robbery conviction to conclude that the defendant is a robber than to use it to gauge his credibility as a witness.

"And that misuse of the evidence is exactly what is meant by 'prejudicial effect to the accused,' " said Angus.

"You argued the new Rule 609 that's going into effect on December 1?" I asked.

"I did," said Angus. "But it doesn't make any difference in this case. Both the old rule and the new rule have the same bias against admitting prior convictions that are merely felonies and not crimes of dishonesty or false statement. The rule says the probative value—which means the relevance of the evidence to the credibility of the defendant as a witness—must outweigh the prejudicial effect to him. And the essential thing to remember is that the defendant is both witness and the accused.

"It's the opposite of Rule 403 of the Federal Rules," said Angus. "There the bias is in favor of admissibility. Here it is against."

"So Gunn is wrong," said Wallop. "If your man gets convicted, take him up on appeal."

"That's the second rub," said Angus. "*Luce v. United States*, 469 U.S. 38 (1984). The Supreme Court held that when the trial court denied the defendant's motion in limine to keep the prosecution from cross-examining him with a prior conviction, the defendant had to take the stand and get impeached. Otherwise, they said, he did not preserve error for appeal."

"But that's wrong as a matter of principal," said Judge Wallop. "The defendant is just as hurt if he does not testify out of fear of improper impeachment as he is by the impeachment itself—maybe more so."

"It is truly ironic," said Angus, "that you are entitled to a ruling on whether the defendant can be impeached with a prior conviction, but you are not entitled to a correct ruling."

"Not so fast," I said. "That's not quite right. You are not entitled to a motion in limine. In fact, that was one of Chief Justice Burger's points in *Luce v. United States*. The motion in limine is a discretionary ruling. The 'in limine' does not mean 'to limit,' it means 'at the threshold'—before the trial starts. And because of that, it is really an advisory sort of opinion that is not binding on the trial judge. It says, 'This is how things look from here, but that is no guarantee things will look the same when they come up at trial.' And since it is just advisory, it is discretionary. If the court does not want to predict how things will go at trial, it can refuse to even consider the motion.

"That means you should never rely on a motion in limine to preserve an evidentiary error for appeal. You should always renew your objection when the issue comes up in trial, just to be safe. Two 8th Circuit cases prove the point of uncertainty. In *Sprynczynatyk v. General Motors Corp.*, 771 F.2d 112 (8th Cir. 1985), an objection at trial was not necessary when the court had been fully briefed and the matter was thoroughly argued before the hearing. But in *Hale v. Firestone Tire and Rubber Co.*, 756 F.2d 1322 (8th Cir. 1985), the court said you had to renew your objection at trial to preserve it.

"And don't think you are free to ignore the court's preliminary ruling if you are on the receiving end. Before you violate the ruling, you had better go to sidebar and explain why you think you are justified in asking the question or offering the evidence that was ruled improper."

"Wait a minute," said Angus. "What you're saying sounds right, but I am positive that the defendant has a right to a ruling on the admissibility of evidence before he testifies."

"Absolutely," I said. "But the ruling you are entitled to is in the middle of trial, when the defendant actually takes the stand. Rule 104(c) of the Federal Rules of Evidence says 'Hearings on the ad-

The Catch in Character Evidence

missibility of confessions shall in all cases be conducted out of the hearing of the jury. Hearings on other preliminary matters shall be so conducted when the interests of justice require, or when an accused is a witness and so requests.' That's the ruling you have as a matter of right—not the one before trial."

"Then it's simple," said Judge Wallop. "All you have to do is renew your objection at the right point in the trial. Then the court has to give you the right ruling."

"It's not that easy," said Angus. "Chief Justice Burger said the trial judge needed to hear Luce's actual testimony before he could rule on the admissibility of Luce's prior conviction for possession of narcotics. He said '[F]or example, the court was prepared to hold that the prior conviction would be excluded if petitioner limited his testimony to explaining his attempt to flee from the arresting officers. However, if petitioner took the stand and denied any prior involvement with drugs, he could then be impeached by the 1974 conviction.'"

"Angus," I said, "I'm afraid that tends to prove your point about the Supreme Court and the law of evidence. The only question was whether Luce's credibility could be attacked with a prior conviction for possession of narcotics. If it was wrong to use it to attack his credibility, then Luce's testimony that he never had anything to do with drugs wouldn't change that."

"Jimmy," said Judge Wallop, "you're full of beans. Testifying that he had nothing to do with drugs would absolutely open the door to that prior conviction."

"Of course it would, Judge," I said. "But it would go to prove Luce's character. If he says he is not the kind of person that would commit the crime, then he has put his character in evidence. He doesn't need to call another witness to do that. He can do that himself. And when he does, the prosecution can rebut that testimony with evidence of his conviction."

"So it's admissible for one purpose but not another. What's the difference? The jury still gets to hear about the conviction," Judge Wallop said.

"The point is," said Angus, picking up the argument, "that the only example the Supreme Court could think of to justify waiting until the defendant has testified has nothing to do with his credibility. And that means it has nothing to do with his pre-trial motion under Rule 609. It has to do with opening the door to character evidence.

"So when you think about it," said Angus, "it shows there was no good reason for not ruling on Luce's motion in limine. The trial court did not need to wait to hear what he had to say. Luce's credibility would become an issue as soon as he testified before the jury. Nothing in the content of his testimony would change that. The Court was simply wrong."

"But what about Burger's point that defense lawyers will tell their clients not to testify just to create reversible error?" I said.

"Absolutely silly," said Angus. "The defendant is just as entitled to a good ruling about the admissibility of his prior convictions as he is to the prior statements of the prosecution witnesses or the right to confront his accusers. But thanks for bringing it up. It gives me an idea."

Two days later I dropped in on Judge Gunn's courtroom. I saw Angus put his defendant on the stand, outside of the presence of the jury. The defendant took the oath and said he wanted to testify to his innocence, but was not going to do that because of the court's pre-trial ruling.

That's when Angus renewed his motion, and Judge Gunn changed his mind. He decided the defendant should not be cross-examined with the eight-year-old conviction. As he said from the bench, his pre-trial ruling was just advisory anyway.

CHAPTER 51

One Size Fits All

Mike Roper was cross-examining one of the chief prosecution witnesses in a murder trial. The witness was one of two young men who had broken into the defendant's tavern in the early morning hours, looking for money and liquor.

The defendant and his family lived upstairs from the tavern, and they heard the break-in. The defendant got his deer rifle and went downstairs to investigate. There he found two men, Larry Watson and Bernard Fowler, coming through the window.

In what followed, the defendant shot both Watson and Fowler. Fowler was killed and Watson was shot through the spine, making him a paraplegic. The defendant claimed he had acted in self-defense, since it looked to him as if one of the intruders had a gun, while the other was carrying a huge jungle machete.

But the only weapons the police found were a small pry-bar Watson and Fowler had used to break in, and an Oriental throwing-star that was in Fowler's shirt pocket.

So when Watson said the defendant held him and Fowler at bay for more than ten minutes and then deliberately shot them both as they stood there defenseless, the defendant was charged with murder.

Larry Watson took the witness stand for the prosecution. And Mike Roper wanted to cross-examine Watson about his record for auto theft and possessing drugs. But as soon as Roper got anywhere near Watson's past, the state's attorney objected, and they went to the bench.

Prosecution: We object, Your Honor. Improper cross-examination.

Defense: Your Honor, we want to bring out the witness's conviction for possessing drugs, and also that he was facing charges for auto theft when this incident occurred.

Prosecution: We know what they want, Your Honor, and it's wrong.

The Court: Why do you think this is admissible, Counsel?

Defense: It goes to credibility, Your Honor.

Prosecution: Your Honor, the conviction for possessing narcotics is certainly remote to the issue of credibility, and it is highly prejudicial. Second, there is only the charge of auto theft. There isn't even a conviction.

Defense: We don't see why there's any prejudice, Your Honor.

The Court: It seems to me that these two offenses are remarkably similar to what is in the defendant's past. You did make a motion in limine about the defendant's record, didn't you?

Defense: Yes, Your Honor.

The Court: And you did say that admitting the defendant's past acts would be prejudicial to your case?

Defense: Of course, but that's different, Your Honor.

The Court: And I did grant your motion, didn't I?

Defense: Yes, Your Honor, but this witness is not on trial.

The Court: Counsel, what's sauce for the goose is sauce for the gander. I don't think it sits well to offer the same kind of evidence that you objected to from the prosecution. (There is no notation on the record, but at this point the state's attorney smirked.) The prosecution's objection is sustained.

Defense: But Your Honor, ...

The Court: Your offer is already noted on the record, Counsel. Proceed to something else.

Later Mike Roper was in the Brief Bag, talking to Angus about what happened.

"One size fits all," said Angus. "It is one of the most common fallacies in the law. You can find it any area, but it seems to have a special spot in the law of evidence. It is the notion that a rule that is right in one situation will be right in another.

"Take expert witnesses, for example. Under Rule 703 of the Federal Rules of Evidence, the factual basis for an expert's opinion doesn't need to be admitted in evidence for the opinion itself to come in. In fact, the basis doesn't even need to be admissible so long as it is 'reasonably relied upon' by other experts in the field. And under Rule 705 the expert does not even have to say what the factual basis is before giving his opinion unless the judge specifically requires it.

"Notice how that reverses the protection provided by the common law against improper opinions: First, the facts that an opinion explains do not ever have be admitted into evidence. And second, the expert does not even have to tell what facts he is explaining until the jury has already heard the opinion.

"It is a system that only can work when there is the right to complete pre-trial discovery. Otherwise all kinds of improper opinions could come into evidence and never be discovered until it was too late to do anything about them.

"The situation is difficult enough in civil cases. But as Professor Linda S. Eads points out in *Adjudication by Ambush: Federal Prosecutors' Use of Nonscientific Experts in a System of Limited Criminal Discovery*, 67 N. Car. L. Rev. 577 (1989), we have turned around and are using these same rules for admitting expert testimony in criminal cases where there is no pre-trial discovery.

"And if you are concerned about the kind of strange expert opinions courts are admitting these days, how about having to deal with an IRS accounting expert who testifies that in his opinion the defendant is guilty of tax fraud—when you didn't even know the witness was going to be called to the stand, much less know what he was going to say?"

"Good grief," said Roper, "I had no idea this was going on."

"The idea behind it is nothing new," said Angus. "And the idea that one size fits all works both ways—it can throw out useful information or admit evidence that ought to be excluded.

"Take prior acts of dishonesty. Watson—the witness in your case who was facing a charge of auto theft—is a good example. Most people feel that theft is an act of dishonesty. So it is relevant to the credibility of a witness. But if he were on trial for auto theft and you cross-examined him about some other car he had stolen (not the one for which he is on trial), there would be a serious problem of unfair prejudice. The jury might well decide that the defendant is a thief because he has stolen before, not because they are convinced he committed the crime he is charged with now.

"But now Watson is testifying for the prosecution. And the reason for protecting him from the jury using the evidence the wrong way is no longer there. The only purpose to which they can put his criminal record is the right one—his credibility as a witness.

"But as far as Rule 608(b) is concerned, the two situations are the same—one size fits all. Even though there is discretion whether to permit the cross-examination about other bad acts, the rule gives no guidance how to exercise that discretion. Even the Advisory Committee Notes to Rule 608(b) only mention the problem of the accused who testifies when they discuss the right to plead the Fifth Amendment in response to particular questions."

Angus kept on. "And they did virtually the same thing with prior convictions—Rule 609. With only one cryptic remark about weighing the probative value of a conviction against its 'prejudicial effect to the defendant' (whether or not he was a witness), for fifteen years the rule assumed that one size fits all.

"But not anymore.

"Rule 609 has been amended, effective December 1, 1990. Now it recognizes three different situations when a witness may be impeached with a prior conviction.

"First, any witness—whether or not he is an accused who takes the stand in his own defense—may be impeached with a conviction of a crime of dishonesty or false statement. And just like the old Rule 609, when crimes or dishonesty are used to attack the witness, they are automatically admissible. The court has no discretion to keep them out, whether they are misdemeanors or felonies.

"The second category is felonies that are not crimes of dishonesty and are used to impeach any witness other than the accused in a criminal case. But unlike crimes of dishonesty, the court has discretion whether to permit the impeachment. The court is supposed to weigh the probative value of the conviction against the prejudicial effect of the evidence—if there is any.

"And notice that because the second category deals with witnesses who are not the accused, the chances of serious unfair prejudice are reduced, but not eliminated. The witness could be a party in a civil case, or simply a disinterested witness in any sort of trial.

"The new Rule 609 takes this into account. The court is supposed to do the kind of balancing of unfair prejudice against probative value that it does under the general relevance principal—Rule 403.

"There is a bias in favor of admissibility, and the evidence will come in unless its probative value is 'substantially outweighed by the danger of unfair prejudice.'

"The third category in the new Rule 609 is felonies used to impeach the testimony of the accused in a criminal case. But now there is a bias against admissibility. The impeachment is only permitted when the court determines that the probative value of the evidence 'outweighs its prejudicial effect to the accused.' "

"That's amazing," said Roper. "I don't know how you remember all those rules. And I sure wish you were the judge in my murder case."

"I don't think you would be any happier with me," said Angus.

"Why not?" said Roper. "You would have let me cross-examine Watson with his criminal record."

"Sure," said Angus, "but I might well have let the prosecutor cross-examine your defendant with his own record. Since nothing he has done relates to violence, it's pretty hard to argue that the jury would use the evidence the wrong way. Sometimes one size does fit all."

CHAPTER 52

Publishing the Exhibit

Angus got a letter from a lawyer in Connecticut who has a common difficulty. He asked me to answer it for him. Here's the correspondence.

Dear Angus:
I have a problem to which I have not seen an answer. When documents are introduced in a jury trial, how do you get the jury to look at them or know what's important about them before they hear the summation or take them to the jury room?

When I try to question the witness about a document (its date, how the document relates to other events, what paragraph three says, what she understood it to mean), my opponent successfully squelches my questions by objecting that "the document speaks for itself." When I do the same, my opponent is usually allowed to cross-examine the witness about the document.

Can I pass the documents around to the jury? Give each juror a copy? How?

I have the same question about using written admissions. Do I read them to the jury? Pass them around? Describe them to the jury? What is the protocol?

Confused in Connecticut

Dear Confused:
You—like thousands of other lawyers—are the victim of a bogus objection. There is no rule of evidence that says a document speaks for itself.

The problem is that most judges and lawyers don't know that "the document speaks for itself" isn't the law—so for them, it *is* the law. That means your first job is your toughest. You've got to educate your judge in the fifteen to twenty seconds you'll have before you get cut off.

And the time to win your point is at trial. Merely making your record won't do you much good. Since the jury eventually gets to see your evidence and hear your argument, the chances that an appellate court will sympathize with you for not getting to present your evidence exactly how and when you wanted are pretty slim.

From the court's standpoint, the limitation on how you got to put on your evidence is likely to be considered "harmless error" at best, even though how you present your proof is actually just as important as what you present.

That takes us to the first point. What's wrong with "the document speaks for itself"?

It's a misunderstanding of the old "Best Evidence Rule." Even though the drafters of the Federal Rules of Evidence tried to change its name to "Requirement of Original," everyone still calls it the Best Evidence Rule. (It takes more than an act of Congress to change the profession's linguistic habits.)

And even though the drafters spread it out over eight different rules in Article 10 of the Federal Rules, the common-law understanding will suit our purposes just fine:

"To prove the contents of a document you must introduce the original or account for its whereabouts."

So when you ask a witness to tell the jury what was said in a letter that isn't in evidence, you are violating the Best Evidence Rule. You are trying to prove the contents of a document without introducing the original or accounting for its whereabouts.

But instead of saying, "Objection, Your Honor, this testimony violates the Best Evidence Rule," your opponent typically says, "Objection, Your Honor, the document speaks for itself."

In that situation, the objection is proper. The law would rather have the letter itself than some witness's recollection of what it said—when you are proving the contents of the letter.

But thousands of judges and lawyers who hear the objection, "The document speaks for itself," don't connect it with the Best Evidence Rule. They figure it means it's improper for a witness to talk about the contents of a document, even when it has already been admitted into evidence.

That's not the law.

The court has discretion under the common law (and under Rule 611(a) of the Federal Rules of Evidence) to permit documents to be read or shown to the jury at nearly any point of the proceedings after they have been admitted into evidence.

So how do you respond to this bogus objection? Work out whatever suits your style. Angus usually says:

"This doesn't violate the Best Evidence Rule, Your Honor. We satisfied the rule when we introduced the document into evidence. So Your Honor has the absolute discretion to permit the document to be read or shown to the jury in any way." (Angus figures judges tend to rule with lawyers who tell them they've got the power to do something, particularly when it's true.)

There is one more possible justification for saying "the document speaks for itself." The Parol Evidence Rule—which is actually a rule of contract interpretation—works by excluding prior or contemporaneous written or oral evidence that is offered to change an "integrated" written contract.

But the Parol Evidence Rule has nothing to do with whether you can read a document out loud or show it to the jury. It applies to situations where you are trying to modify the written agreement.

On the other hand, "explaining what the contract means" is typically permitted. So when the other side says that a contract "speaks for itself," David Schaefer of Cleveland likes to respond with, "Your Honor, if the contract spoke for itself, we wouldn't be in court."

So the law lets you present your documents to the jury before the end of the trial. The question is, how do you do it?

The answer is simple. Use the most effective way you can. But before you dim the lights and turn on your state-of-the-art magic lantern, some protocol.

Because the court has discretion to let you show the jury some bit of evidence in the middle of trial, it also has the discretion to say "not now." So the first thing you've got to do is get the court's permission. The customary buzzwords that they teach in the trial training programs are typically, "Your Honor, we request permission to publish plaintiff's exhibit five at this time."

If using the customary language is going to increase the chances of your judge granting permission, then go ahead and use it. But I have a problem with the word "publish." It has a baroque ring to it. Even if you ask for permission to "publish plaintiff's exhibit five *to the jury,*" someone on the jury is likely to wonder if you are going to take it out in the hall and give it to a newspaper reporter during the next recess. So I prefer asking permission to *show* the exhibit to the jury or to *give* them their own copies of the exhibit.

Next comes timing. Most lawyers like to show the exhibit to the jury as soon as it has been admitted in evidence. Psychologically there is a good reason for this. You have just finished laying the foundation for the exhibit, usually in front of the jury. They've heard about its qualifications, your opponent tried to keep them from seeing and hearing it by objecting to its admission, and the judge overruled his objection. The jury is probably more interested in the exhibit right now than they will be at any other time in the trial.

Yet some lawyers (typically the kind who hang around the criminal courts in the morning to see if they can pick up a good DUI case and then bet their fee on the horses at the racetrack that afternoon) wait until the end of the witness's examination to show the exhibit to the jury.

Why? They have the idea that if they give the jury the exhibit at the end of their direct, it will distract the jury's attention during the opponent's cross-examination.

The problem is, that kind of polyester tactic easily backfires. The jury is just as likely to ignore the exhibit and concentrate on the cross-examination.

One more point about when you show the jury the exhibit: There are times when the witness who lays the foundation may not be the one who is going to talk about the exhibit. The perfect example is the business record. Often, the "custodian or other qualified witness" under Rule 803(6) of the Federal Rules of Evidence knows how the records are made and kept but doesn't know anything about the issues in the case. Then you're better off telling the judge (so the jury can hear) that you are going to show the records to the jury when the proper witness is on the stand to explain what they mean.

Next, there is a problem with having only one copy of the exhibit. Whenever you give it to the jury, it goes from one person to the next, just like a "wave" going through the bleachers at a football game. One by one, everyone's attention is divided as they look at the exhibit at the same time they are trying to listen to what your witness is saying.

Angus has a personal rule for solving this problem. Either have a copy for everybody—you, the judge, the witness, the court reporter, the lawyer on the other side, as well as every member of the jury—or blow up the exhibit so that it's big enough for everyone to see at the same time.

Evidence books for all the jurors, with all the exhibits in them, are useful for cases with lots of documents. It's a technique that works best when the judge has you pre-mark and pre-admit every document before trial.

But you don't have to use paper. Photographic blowups mounted on plastic foam board and put on an easel in front of the jury can have a powerful impact.

The overhead projector is another way to let everyone look at the exhibit at the same time. You can make a plastic transparency of the document with most office copiers. Just make sure yours is the right kind before you try it. You don't want to gum up your machine with melted plastic.

The overhead projector has a lot of advantages. You don't have to dim the lights for everyone to see the image on the screen (or even on the wall). You can stand behind the projector and see the document right side up on the machine.

In addition, while the projector is on, you can use your pencil as a pointer and even circle or highlight important language with different-colored markers—while you examine the witness. And you don't have to worry whether you are mutilating an exhibit, since the transparency is a "demonstrative aid," not the exhibit itself.

Just because you give copies of the exhibits to the jurors doesn't mean you (or the witness) can't read the exhibit out loud in the middle of the trial. Typically the judge will let you do it when your purpose is to save time by cutting through the verbiage and pointing out the important language to the jury.

You have the same flexibility when you present written admissions. As long as it's your turn to put on evidence, you can ask the court for permission to read an admission to the jury. That means you should do it when it will have the most impact. Most courts will even let you read an admission during the cross-examination of the other side's witness—if it's relevant to your cross-examination.

Just don't try to "explain" the admission until final argument. You're the lawyer, not the witness.

PART SEVEN

Lawyers, Judges, and Ethics

Judges are not like other people—they have power. But they also are human and put their clothes on like you and I do. There are some sensible rules for talking to judges, trying cases to judges, and understanding what they are doing when they make rulings. Then comes ethics, and some basic rules for staying out of trouble.

CHAPTER 53
Talking to Judges

CHAPTER 54
Judge Trials

CHAPTER 55
Games Judges Play

CHAPTER 56
Staying Out of Jail

CHAPTER 53

Talking to Judges

One of the prices of being on the rubber-chicken circuit is you have to sit at the head table. It goes with the job. You get a call from a local judge who tells you she has a First Amendment problem. "I guess the basic question," she says, "is whether you believe in free speech."

"Of course," you say, expecting to be appointed counsel to brief the court on an intricate question of conflicting constitutional principles.

"Good," she says, "I've got you scheduled to give one to the litigation section of the local bar association next Tuesday afternoon."

"Give one what?" you ask.

"Free speech," she says.

Trapped at the head table again.

But there can be rewards—like the time I was sitting at the head table with all the federal judges in the district save one.

The topic of conversation at the table was fascinating. I guess they figured that because I am a teacher it was all right to talk in front of me. And they did. They talked about lawyers: who they could trust and who they could not; who was prepared and who was not; who knew the law and who did not.

I just sat there, pretending to go over the notes for my talk, and I learned some important lessons:

> Even in big cities, the judge club is a small one.
> The judges talk about the lawyers who appear before them.
> Like jurors, judges seem to notice everything you do.

It makes a difference how you talk to the judge.
And that is a good place to start our discussion.

Know Who You Are Talking to

Trial judges are not all alike. Some have a scholarly bent and like learned briefs and arguments. Others enjoy the factual intricacies of business litigation or the complexities of medicine presented in a malpractice case. Some are intent on climbing to the appellate level and want to publish legal opinions. Others are keen on developing whole systems of jurisprudence, new ways to administer justice, or trying the latest fad in alternative dispute resolution. And some just want to get out of the courthouse before 3 o'clock in the afternoon.

Just as it is a mistake to start an opening statement without knowing who is on the jury, it is inviting disaster to walk into a court without scouting the judge. Particularly if he has some secondary agenda—such as using videotaped testimony or conducting minitrials—you need to know what it is.

Watch the Clock

Lack of time and resources is a common thread that touches nearly every trial judge. State courts, in particular, may be understaffed, even to the point of judges' having to type their own letters or place their own telephone calls.

This should have a serious impact on how you approach a case. Do not take half an hour to argue a pretrial motion when fifteen minutes will do the job. Understand that most of a forty-page brief will probably go unread. Small wonder; pages of string citations are not nearly as impressive as a single paragraph that cites a leading case. And besides, the subliminal message sent by your work is just as important as the research and the writing itself. The long brief says the question could go either way and begs that you be rewarded for doing your homework. The short brief says there is an answer to the problem and you have found it.

Keep a Civil Tongue

As James W. Jeans from the University of Missouri at Kansas City says, most law students do not need to be taught to be respectful to judges. They usually start out being downright obsequious, as if law schools offered classes in aerobic groveling. Young lawyers at the National Institute for Trial Advocacy sometimes even ask for permission to approach the easel, as if it were a timid witness who might be overpowered if they got too close.

But not all of them. Some lawyers seem to have a need to challenge the judge at almost every turn, in ways that are sure to give offense. And so there are lawyers who go through their professional careers at war with the bench—a war that is usually financed more by the clients than by the lawyers themselves.

Sometimes the problem is that the same quick tongue that seems to help on cross-examination or final argument gets turned on the wrong target.

But usually not. Usually it is the tone that rankles, rather than the words, and it is almost always a mistake. The jury thinks the judge is the smartest lawyer in the room, and lack of respect from you will almost always cost a lot of goodwill.

Do Not Make Faces

One of the quickest ways to make a judge angry is to show visible or audible disgust with his rulings. Moans, scowls, grimaces, rolling your eyes, or slamming your books on the counsel table are the kinds of things to avoid.

On the other hand, try not to look like a whipped dog when the judge rules against you. Not that you should thank the judge for an adverse ruling in the forlorn hope that the jury will think you won the argument. Chances are they will not buy that one. But on the other hand, if you look like you just lost the case, there is a good chance the jury will believe you.

Do Not Interrupt the Judge

Cutting off a witness or the other lawyer is bad enough, but interrupting the judge is a disaster. If you absolutely have to interrupt, do it the right way. There is a difference between asking whether you may be heard and simply starting in while the judge is already talking.

Help the Judge Save Face

You always want it to be easy for the judge to rule in your favor. That is especially true if you are trying to get the judge to change his mind. If the court has seemingly painted itself in a corner, show it the easy way out. Do not insist that the judge admit he was wrong. Start from the judge's position and show how his concern supports your argument whenever you can. Trying to convince the judge that his entire line of analysis is wrong is usually not productive.

Know When It Is Over

When you have won the argument, stop. Going on will not improve your victory, it will only put it at risk.

When you have lost the argument, stop. "Beating a dead horse" became a cliché precisely because it is such a vivid image. When the horse is dead, it is only civil to let it rest in peace.

Be Prompt

The rule is simple. Lawyers who are late to court do not win. Make it a habit to be at least ten minutes early to the simplest hearing or conference—much earlier for trials or important arguments. The lawyers who are habitually late (and always have some emergency to justify it) do not want to be late. They simply underestimate the time their other commitments will take, or have let so many things go that they are always putting out fires.

Be Scrupulously Honest

The judges at the luncheon table saved their strongest words for lawyers they cannot trust. And the stories they told ranged from simple broken promises and unreliable arguments to outright lies and misrepresentations of the law.

There are some rules to follow to avoid getting into trouble:

- Do not misstate the law. Personally read every case you cite, every rule you rely on. Even if you use the rule all the time, re-read it before you make your argument. Never conceal adverse rules or cases.
- Do not overstate any fact. Understatement, not overstatement, is the key to credibility.
- If you find you have made a mistake, correct it at the earliest opportunity.

Do Not Cave In

The dictates of professional civility do not require you to back off from legitimate positions or withdraw honest arguments. Being polite does not mean you cannot be tough.

Confront Injustice

Not every problem can be solved with good manners. There are some bullies on the bench who need to be taken to task. It is one of the most difficult conflicts of interest you can face. Your duty to the profession says blow the whistle, while your duty to your client says let it go.

There are times when you have no choice. When the judge whistles in derision at your economist's testimony, when he turns his back while your defendant testifies, when he rolls his eyes in response to your medical expert, it is time to make a record.

I hear too many complaints about judges' making telephone calls from the bench, imposing absurd limitations on discovery, or so restricting the time for argument as to take away the right to be heard.

The response to these abuses needs to be civil, but it needs to be made.

CHAPTER 54

Judge Trials

> *You have to adjust the sermon when there is only one person in the congregation.*
>
> —Angus

There is a question that is asked at every trial advocacy training program. "All these trial techniques are fine for the jury, but what do you do when you are trying the case to the judge?"

And the typical answer is not bad—as far as it goes. "The principles of advocacy do not really change. Don't let the judge bully you out of your opening statement or closing argument. You've got a case to try, and the judge needs to hear what you've got to say as much as anybody."

While it is obvious that you don't treat a lone judge the same as you would a six- or twelve-person jury, the question, "What do you change?" is worth serious consideration.

The starting point is to understand your jury as well as you can. You have only one person to persuade, and he is sure he has heard it all before. You do not have the safety in numbers that even a six-member jury provides.

You are stuck with the biases and prejudices of a single individual. In fact, some of them are probably why he is on the bench in the first place. But knowledge is power. One of the most valuable things you can do in jury selection is to get a feeling of what kind of people will be deciding your case. With a judge trial, you have a chance to scout the "jury" from the start.

What you know about your "jury" is going to influence everything you do during the course of the trial. Not that you are going to pander; but, knowing to whom you are talking makes a difference in what you say and how you say it.

And now is your opportunity to talk to the court in your opening statement—at least that is what you thought when you walked over to the lectern and said, "May it please the court. . . ." That's when the judge interrupted and said, "Counsel, I've read the pleadings and your briefs and I'm familiar with the issues in the case. You may proceed and call your first witness."

What do you do?

The teacher at the trial advocacy training program told you to go ahead and give your opening statement. But does that make any sense when the only juror in the case—the one who is going to decide the facts—just told you to forget it?

There is an administrative judge in the Midwest, who regularly teaches at the National Institute for Trial Advocacy, who takes both sides of the question. In the classroom, he tells lawyers never to waive the opening statement, but in court he always suggests they dispense with their opening and call their first witness.

Hypocrisy?

Not at all. While an opening statement is an essential part of the trial, this judge figures that lawyers who are willing to dispense with their openings were probably just going to waste the court's time anyway, while lawyers who really want to give an opening are probably going to do a pretty good job.

Chicago U.S. District Judge Ann Williams takes a different approach. She often asks the lawyers in bench trials to make opening statements, and insists on final arguments. "Even though I've gone over the whole case before trial, I want to hear it all put together. My biggest complaint with bench trials is they tend to be dry. Don't treat me like a computer. I need to have my interest piqued.

"While lawyers need to cut out the simplistic explanations and melodramatic statements, I want the heart of the case argued to me as if they care—as if the result makes a difference."

For Douglas Connah of Baltimore, a bench trial gives you an opportunity to win before the hearing ever starts. "The judge must be won over to your point of view before you walk into court. You do that with your statement of facts in the trial brief. That's your opening statement. The first three pages are an opportunity to win the case.

"That, of course," says Connah, who had been on the editorial staff of the *Baltimore Sun* before becoming a lawyer, "is an old newspaperman's instincts."

William Pannill, from Houston, agrees. "The first one to explain what the case is really all about has a tremendous advantage. The bench brief is an opportunity to do that. I may spend three weeks writing the statement of facts. It won't be more than ten or fifteen pages long, but it will really sing."

It is important not to exaggerate, says Pannill. "No purple prose. If anything, be understated. Above all, make sense. The point is to make the judge understand the case from your point of view."

So, do you waive the opening statement?

Of course not. Always make an opening. It may be written or oral—preferably both. Take some of the edge off your histrionics, and concentrate on what is actually at issue. Care about the case. Be interested and well-organized. Tell the story so that it makes sense. If you can focus the inquiry in four or five minutes, no one will think you have wasted their time.

Next come the witnesses. And it is a time to be careful. Too many lawyers figure that a bench trial is an opportunity to relax and call the witnesses in any order that happens to be convenient.

Wrong.

Why should you expect the lone juror to unscramble the facts for you? Just as with a jury trial, you want the progression of facts to be as coherent and persuasive as possible. A bench trial is no place to abandon the simple rules of witness order: Start strong and end strong. Avoid weak witnesses when you can, and don't call any unnecessary witnesses. There is no need to clutter your case with irrelevancies and uncertainties.

A bench trial is an opportunity to get right to the point. Denver U.S. District Judge Jim Carrigan has an effective way to do it. Both sides present proposed findings of facts and conclusions of law before trial. About a week before the hearing, counsel meet with Carrigan and go over the proposed findings and conclusions. Everything counsel agree on is underlined in green. Those are trial stipulations and need no proof. Everything they disagree on is underlined in red.

Only the red facts are tried.

Despite doing everything he can to streamline bench trials, Carrigan likes maps, exhibits, and blowups. In environmental cases he and the lawyers take helicopter rides, cross-country jeep trips, and hikes so he can see for himself what the witnesses are talking about.

When an English double-decker bus that was shipped to Denver was the subject of a suit, he even held the trial in the bus.

Cross-examination is a special problem in bench trials, partly because the typical American courtroom is set up all wrong for the task.

With the witness on the stand, the judge usually has to crane his neck just to get a side view of the back of the witness's head. So, ordinarily, the only juror in the case has to depend on tone of voice to interpret the witness's demeanor on cross-examination. Don't try to make up for that with sarcasm or argumentative questions. Remember that the purpose of cross-examination is not to develop information from the witness, but rather to give you a chance to tell your side of the witness's story in your way, so that the witness must agree that what you say is true.

With an evasive witness, sometimes a short, sharp glance toward the bench to make sure the judge knows what the witness is doing will be as effective as some of the witness-control techniques you may use. Be especially careful not to be rude or overbearing. You do not want the only juror to side with the witness instead of with you.

Next is the paradox of objections. The rules of evidence are intended to shape the information that goes to the fact-finder. In the bench trial, that means the lone juror is the one who decides what he gets to hear during the course of the trial.

As Christopher Lutz of Washington, D.C., says, "In a lot of bench trials, the rules of evidence don't really exist." Lutz is right. To keep things moving, many judges virtually ignore solid objections and admit improper evidence "for what it's worth." Those decisions are virtually unreviewable because most judges know how to clean things up with their findings of fact and conclusions of law.

Lutz says that is not so bad. After all, in a bench trial the need to protect the jury from improper information is gone. And the judge has to consider the evidence just to determine whether it is admissible.

But Lutz warns that you should not let these casual rulings allow you to become complacent. "You still must make your record," he says. Inadmissible evidence that is properly objected to cannot be used to support a verdict. But if you waive your objection, improper evidence can be taken into account for any logical purpose. "Besides," says Lutz, "objecting doesn't hurt you as much at a bench trial. The judge understands you have to do it."

One of the advantages of bench trials is that the "juror" gets a chance to ask questions and talk back to the lawyers and witnesses. With a jury, you have to guess what may be bothering it about the case. But with a judge, by the time for final argument, you should know. That lets you focus on what is really concerning your finder of fact instead of wasting your time with civic lectures or recapitulating what all the witnesses said.

One last point. Tell the whole story, not just part of it. Argue the entire case. Just because the "red facts" are the only ones in dispute doesn't mean you should ignore the others. Sometimes the "green facts" are the best proof of what the case is all about.

CHAPTER 55

Games Judges Play

Judge Wallop from the Court of Common Pleas was beside himself. "No, I mean it. No more Mr. Nice Judge. I may have been a judicial cream puff once, but no longer."

"Cream puff?" I said. "No one who has ever been in your courtroom could possibly call you a cream puff. What in the world are you talking about?"

"Order, decorum, efficiency, respect for the dignity of the law. That's what I'm talking about," he said.

"Except for its being a little stuffy, that's pretty much how I would describe your courtroom," I replied. "What would you want to change?"

"Listen, I just got back from one of those judicial conferences. First one I've been to, and did I learn a thing or two about how to run a courtroom. We had a whole seminar on evidentiary rulings, and I have discovered that I am way too easy about the way I treat lawyers, how I schedule hearings, the way I run my docket—everything. But especially how I conduct trials and make rulings. That's what I am going to reform.

"We even did game-playing, and I got an extra copy of the rules for you. You are welcome to them—just don't tell anyone where you got them."

Here they are—unedited and unabridged. And I broke a serious confidence to share them with you. While we have only Judge Wallop's word that "Courtroom Control" was actually a handout at a judicial conference, you may recognize some of them as games your judges play, which is certainly circumstantial evidence of something.

No Speaking Objections

Sustain an objection to any argument that might really be a speech to the jury. **1 point**

On your own motion, cut off any argument or objection on the grounds that it is really a speech to the jury. **2 points**

On your own motion, cut off any argument or objection that could be understood by the jury. **3 points**

Require all objections to be made at sidebar even though neither lawyer requests a bench conference. **5 points**

Do not permit offers of proof at the time an objection is sustained; wait until the next recess. **5 points**

Refuse to permit offers of proof until the next day of trial. **7 points**

Commentary

Making a record is essential to preserving error for appeal. If you can force lawyers to waive objections or forget to make offers of proof under the guise of courtroom order and efficiency, it will improve your batting average with the court of appeals.

Waiting for Exhibits

Admit exhibits "subject to cross-examination." **2 points**
Only admit exhibits at the end of a party's case. **3 points**
Insist that all exhibits be offered and admitted at the end of the entire trial. **4 points**

Commentary

It is improper to have testimony about exhibits until they are admitted in evidence. So technically, not admitting exhibits until the end of the trial should cut off all testimony about them except for what is required to lay the proper foundations. But that is not the purpose of this rule. Its real value is threefold:

First, it keeps the lawyers from showing the exhibits to the jury until the end of the trial. That makes everything harder to understand, but it saves time.

Second, it forces lawyers to waive most of their evidentiary objections about exhibits. At the end of trial they are thinking about their final arguments, not about foundations or rulings.

Third, if something is missing from a foundation, it is nearly impossible to cure the omission once all the witnesses have gone home.

If you do not want that much chaos, at least you can admit exhibits "subject to cross-examination." That can confuse the lawyers for several minutes just trying to figure out what it means.

Simon Says

Keep your briefcase off counsel table.	**2 points**
Stand behind the lectern for all examinations.	**2 points**
Do not approach the witness without permission.	**3 points**
Hand exhibits to the bailiff for him to give to the witness.	**5 points**
Sit at counsel table for the entire trial except opening statements and closing arguments.	**7 points**

Commentary

Lawyers are professional communicators. Their job is to present facts and make them understandable to the jury. Keeping lawyers from moving around the courtroom tends to keep things dull and uninteresting. Besides, a lawyer who can be forced either to sit or stand (it does not matter which) is psychologically much less likely to challenge the judge.

Dodge'em Rulings

Ignoring objections and arguments.	**1 point**
Inaudible rulings.	**1 point**
Incomprehensible rulings.	**2 points**
Weasel rulings, such as "I'll let it in for what it's worth."	**3 points**
Noncommittal rulings such as "I've heard enough, let's proceed," or "All right, I understand your positions; let's move along."	**4 points**

Commentary

It may be the judge's job to make a ruling, but not unless the lawyer forces the issue. Generally, if you make no ruling, you make no error. The point of this routine is to learn how to avoid taking a position on objections unless you must.

Magic Words

Require lawyers to make objections with the same words you would use. **3 points**

Treat the assertion of one basis for an objection as a deliberate waiver of all other grounds. **5 points**

Commentary

As a matter of principle, it is not enough that you know what a lawyer means when he or she makes an objection. Lawyers should not only use the same rules, but also the same terms that you would use if you were objecting. Thus, if you prefer "best evidence" to "original document rule," stick to your guns (and your words).

The second part of this routine is more difficult to play, but brings greater rewards. Of course, failing to assert ground for an objection generally is a waiver of those grounds unless admitting the evidence amounts to plain error. So it may seem to you that this is just a standard waiver.

But done properly, counsel can be enticed into objecting on the ground and then left puzzling over an adverse ruling. Extra points can be awarded if counsel does not know he has been manipulated, as in the following. Assume the defense offers a copy of a business letter into evidence. It looks like it may have both hearsay and best evidence problems. You express your interest:

"Counsel for the plaintiff, I am concerned about this letter being offered by the defense. Do you object to its admissibility?"

"Yes, Your Honor, we do."

"Your objection is the memorandum is hearsay?"

"Yes, Your Honor."

(Musing for a moment) "Hearing no other grounds, the objection is overruled."

Unless the lawyer is prompt, his best evidence objection will disappear even as you speak.

Zap

Rule on objections so it appears that counsel is taking advantage of a technicality. **2 points**

Give limiting instructions so they are self-defeating. **5 points**

Commentary

The first routine is simple to perform, but requires a little boldness. For example: "I have always felt that particular objection was a little unfair, Counsel, but until the legislature does something about it, I will have to rule in your favor."

The second routine can have even more sting. "Ladies and gentlemen of the jury: I have sustained counsel's objection to evidence of his client's membership in the organization called the Aryan Brotherhood. You are to put that fact from your minds and treat the case as if you had not heard it."

The lawyer may try to block a move like this by waiving your instruction. But if you are on your toes, you can give it anyway. In *Lakeside v. Oregon*, 435 U.S. 33 (1978), the defendant did not take the stand to testify on his own behalf. Because of the attention a cautionary instruction would focus on his silence, the defendant asked the trial judge not to say anything at all on the subject. But the trial judge gave a cautionary instruction anyway, and Lakeside was convicted.

The Supreme Court thought Lakeside's complaint about the instruction was "speculative" and said the court's instruction was proper since it was meant for defendant's benefit.

Zap.

Scoring

  0–19: Cream Puff.
20–29: Judicial Wimp.
30–39: Easy.
40–49: In Charge.
  50+: Judge Roy Bean Award.

CHAPTER 56

Staying Out of Jail

Angus was giving a talk on ethics to the young lawyers' section of the bar association. "Before we get started," he said, "I want all of you to do a little exercise. First, put both hands out in front of you. Now make fists with both of your hands. Next, bring the heels of your hands together. Now point both of your index fingers straight up. So far, so good. Now, keeping your hands like that, touch the tip of your nose with both of your thumbs."

Everybody did what Angus said, and by the time he finished his instructions, the whole audience was sitting, both hands in front of their faces, with their index fingers sticking straight up in front of their eyes.

"Okay," said Angus, "that's how it looks behind bars. My job this afternoon is to keep you from getting a better picture of what it's like. There is a motto I want you to remember that should help. Edward Bennett Williams used to say, 'If anybody is going to jail, make sure it's your client—not you.'

"At this point in your careers," Angus said, "you probably think that being disbarred, going to jail, or having to pay some huge judgment is not a realistic worry. So let's do a quick survey. How many of you do not know or have never met a lawyer who has been disbarred, suspended, or disciplined?"

Even I was surprised. Out of the 140 lawyers in the audience, only one raised his hand. He had been admitted to practice only two months earlier and had just moved to town. Angus had certainly gotten everybody's attention before he started going through his rules for staying out of trouble.

It's not your money

It's not just a technical accounting problem. Your client's money is not your money, and you have to keep it separate from your own. It is easy enough to do. All of your client's money goes into the special trust account. Then, no matter how tight your personal cash flow gets, you never borrow a penny from that trust account. It doesn't matter how valid your emergency is or how quickly you are going to return it. It's not your money.

If it's that simple, how do thousands of lawyers get in trouble every year by commingling their clients' money with their own?

There may actually be some lawyers who don't know any better—legal education being what it is these days. But most of them know that using their clients' money is like a store clerk taking an informal "loan" from the cash register.

So why do they do it?

One of the most common causes is substance abuse. The same powder, pills, or liquid courage that has diminished their capacity as lawyers (and cut their incomes or cost them their jobs) has clouded their judgment and increased their need for quick money.

For a while they get away with it. But as the debt grows and clients start pressing for their money, someone eventually calls the bar association. That's why the list in the back of the state bar bulletin that names lawyers who have had their licenses suspended or revoked for commingling their clients' funds with their own is actually a list of personal tragedies, usually involving drugs, alcohol, and debt.

It sounds pretty depressing, and it is. But there is hope. If you're a lawyer with a substance problem, get in a twelve-step program. It's a lot smarter than taking money out of your clients' trust accounts. It's not your money.

Only take one side of a case

There is an important rule of thumb to remember: The more complex and intricate the rules that govern your conflict-of-interests problem, the closer you are to getting in trouble. If it's going to take a twenty-page memo to justify your situation, you are probably better off not representing this new client who was on the other side of an earlier, "distinguishable" case.

Even if the latest case law vindicates your position completely, it may not be worth it. You don't want your clients to think you are willing to switch sides and turn against them. It is no excuse to say that clients find new lawyers all the time. Lawyers simply have to be more loyal to their clients than their clients are to them.

Know whom you represent

You have a duty to your client—everybody knows that. But sometimes that duty extends to people who aren't paying your bill.

How can that happen?

Say management hires you to do an investigation and evaluation of the way they are doing business. You come back with a detailed list of what they are doing wrong and what they have to do to fix it.

You've done everything you were supposed to do, haven't you? You don't have to blow the whistle on management and notify the shareholders of what's been going on—do you?

The $51 million settlement paid by one of the country's finest law firms in the savings and loan scandal suggests that the shareholders may be your clients, too.

Watch yourself in the woodshed

Witness preparation and client interviewing—what goes on in the woodshed—used to be one of those areas that was off-limits to everybody except the lawyer, the witness, and the gods of litigation. In the 1950s movie *Anatomy of a Murder,* defense lawyer "Polly" Beigler (played by Jimmy Stewart) gave defendant Lieutenant Manion (Ben Gazzara) the "lecture" on the law of temporary insanity that was designed to shape everything that Manion said.

Close to the line? You bet. But that's not the point. The chances of Polly Beigler ever being called to task for how he prepared his witnesses back in the 1950s were slim. Today, you never know who is wearing a miniature transmitter that is sending the entire conversation out to the "auto parts" truck that is parked in the alley.

Exaggerated concern? Not at all. Today, lawyers are being attacked in record numbers. We are being called to the grand jury to testify against our clients, having our fees attached by the prosecutor, and actually being indicted because of whom we represent. State and federal prosecutors have learned that lawyers are convenient pressure points.

What does it mean? If your ethical sense is not enough to keep you turning square corners in the woodshed, maybe self-interest will help.

Don't stonewall on discovery

If you ask lawyers anywhere in the country what is the most troublesome ethical problem they see in the practice of law, the answer is almost always the same: how other lawyers obstruct discovery in trial preparation. Lawyers have created so many ways of kicking sand in each other's faces, it is embarrassing.

It got so bad that one federal district judge actually issued the following order:

> Defendant's Motion to Dismiss or in the Alternative to Continue Trial is denied. If the recitals in the briefs from both sides are accepted at face value, neither side has conducted discovery according to the letter and spirit of the Oklahoma County Bar Association Lawyer's Creed. This is an aspirational creed not subject to enforcement by this Court, but violative conduct does call for judicial disapprobation at least. If there is a hell to which disputatious, uncivil, vituperative lawyers go, let it be one in which the damned are eternally locked in discovery disputes with other lawyers of equally repugnant attributes.
>
> It is so ordered this 24th day of February 1989.
>
> Wayne E. Alley
> U.S. District Judge

Just being obnoxious is enough to get the judge down on you. But if you really want to get in trouble, try obstructing justice. Destroy evidence, alter documents, stonewall on discovery. But before you do, read *Berkey Photo, Inc. v. Eastman Kodak Co.*, 74 F.R.D. 613 (S.D.N.Y. 1977).

Keep your mouth shut

The attorney-client privilege is designed to keep lawyers from having to testify about their clients' confidences, and it works pretty well. The ethical obligation to respect a client's confidences is a bit different. It's supposed to keep us from telling our clients' secrets even though we are not in court—and it doesn't work quite so well.

Why not?

For some reason, lots of lawyers who would rather go to jail than reveal a client's confidence on the witness stand get pretty careless when they talk with friends, family, and other lawyers. They need to learn the slogan that was on the World War II posters: "Loose Lips Sink Ships."

Respect your clients' confidences all of the time. It is one of the marks of a true professional.

Don't be a safety deposit box for anything improper

Your job is to represent people, not to help them commit crimes or frauds or to participate in concealing evidence. If your client murders her husband and brings you the gun, tell her to take it away. What she tells you is confidential, but what she gives you is different. If it is the instrumentality or the fruits of a crime or fraud, you don't want it. You would have to turn it over to the prosecution, and you don't want to try to walk the tightrope of giving it to the government and not telling who gave it to you.

And don't advise your client to get rid of the gun either. Destroying evidence is an obstruction of justice that you want no part of. And remember, the attorney-client privilege does not apply to conversations about future crimes or frauds.

Don't do business with your criminal clients

Doing business with any client is a touchy proposition in the first place (Rule 1.8 of the ABA Model Rules of Professional Conduct). But doing business with a client you represent in a criminal case is an invitation to have your office searched, your files subpoenaed, to be called before the grand jury, and maybe even be indicted.

It's not worth it.

Don't have sex with any client

If you need to ask why, you need moral recycling.

Never misrepresent the facts or the law

The ABA Model Rules of Professional Conduct talk about knowingly making a false statement of fact or law. And how could it be otherwise? Everybody makes honest mistakes.

But understand an important distinction. Whether you make a knowing misstatement is the test of whether you are guilty of an ethical violation. But your effectiveness as a lawyer depends on what judges and other lawyers think of you, not whether they can prove you violated an ethical rule.

If you develop the reputation of a lawyer who can't be trusted, it will cost you throughout your entire professional life in ways you will never see or understand.

When in doubt, shout

When sticky situations arise—and they will—don't try to tough them out alone. Call another lawyer. Talk to a judge. Ask the grievance committee for an advisory opinion. Try to put your problem in a procedural posture that will let your conduct be evaluated before the fact, not when it's too late to do anything about it.

PART EIGHT

Tactics

Trial tactics does not mean quick tricks and clever ploys. As the most important witness in the case, the lawyer has to be careful to never do anything inconsistent with his theory of the case. But absolutely consistent with that idea are some wonderful techniques that will help your case come alive.

CHAPTER 57
Seeing the Facts

CHAPTER 58
It's Happening Now

CHAPTER 59
Creating Tension

CHAPTER 60
Say it Again

CHAPTER 61
Focus

CHAPTER 62
Highlighting

CHAPTER 63
Clutter

CHAPTER 64
Cover Yourself

CHAPTER 65
Taking the Blame

CHAPTER 66
Mootcourtitis

CHAPTER 67
The Giggle Test

CHAPTER 68
Rehabilitation

CHAPTER 57

Seeing the Facts

The actual photographs would come a little later. First was a verbal snapshot of the crash that literally took the jury to the scene:

"Ladies and gentlemen, go back in time to the 14th of December, 1984. If you had been standing by the side of Highway 487 just at noon—about thirteen miles east of Carthage, Mississippi—you would have seen Linda Jackson in her 1984 GMC Jimmy 4X4, taking Amanda, her six-week-old baby girl, to the doctor for her first checkup after she was born.

"Linda and Amanda had dropped off Mr. Jackson at work and started to go on to the doctor's office just before they passed where you're standing. If you look quickly, you can see Amanda in her new safety car seat—the backward-facing kind that has been federally approved. Then right after they pass where you are, as they go around a gentle curve at about 50 to 55 miles per hour, you hear a bang—almost as if they hit another car. Only there's no other traffic, and there's nothing in the road they could hit.

"So you look at the back of the car as it is going away from you and you see the left rear wheel strangely folded underneath the car, scraping the asphalt as it's being dragged along. The car starts to fishtail back and forth on its one rear wheel. Then it swerves and starts to flip over and over. One, two, three, four—five times. You see Momma—Linda—thrown from the car and land at the side of the road, crumpled in an odd, awkward angle, her left leg broken into the shape of 'Z.'

"You run down the road to check on Amanda, to get her out of the car if you can. The GMC Jimmy 4X4 is on its back, its three remaining wheels spinning in the air. When you look inside, there is Amanda, still strapped in her seat—her head jammed between the back of her safety seat and the bottom of the dashboard. What you see dripping on her face is acid coming from the upside-down battery."

That "picture" is based on the opening statement by Tommy Rayburn from Oxford, Mississippi, in a products liability case against General Motors. It is one of a series of remarkably vivid verbal snapshots that were designed to show exactly what happened to Linda and Amanda Jackson.

Everybody knows that real and demonstrative evidence makes a difference. Lawyers talk about "visual impact" and "making the case come alive," and yet too many of us trust the heart of the case to dull witnesses who utter dull transitory sounds, which look all right on paper, but which lack the power to move judges and juries.

The visual part of communication comes into play long before we need to understand sophisticated facts or unravel complicated events. It begins with the credibility of the speaker.

Bert Decker, a communications expert from San Francisco, reports about the factors that go into the credibility of any speaker. The three basic factors, says Decker, are *verbal*, the content of what you have to say; *vocal*, the way in which you say it; and *visual*, your appearance, posture, and body language. The percentage that each factor contributes to your credibility is surprising.

Decker says psychological studies show that only 7 percent of your credibility comes from your message itself; 38 percent comes from the qualities of your voice and speech; and 55 percent comes from the visual clues you give with your appearance, posture, gestures, and body language as you speak.

If you want the jury to think of you as the guide they should follow, and if you want them to believe what your witnesses have to say, you have to pay attention to the visual impression that both you and your witnesses make.

Psychologist Elizabeth F. Loftus, author of *Witness for the Defense* (St. Martin's Press 1991; now also available in paperback), says a witness's confidence level is the single most important factor in determining his or her credibility. That meshes with Decker's observations. Confidence is communicated mainly through appearance and tone of voice. "But details make a difference, too," says Loftus. " 'I saw her that afternoon. She was wearing a Moosehead beer T-shirt and pink Nike shoes' carries a lot more weight than a simple 'I saw her that afternoon.' "

Credibility is just the start. Next is comprehension. Fred Bartlit of Chicago, one of the masters of clarity and simplicity, has demonstrated how to use the overhead projector to hundreds of students at the National Institute for Trial Advocacy. With a simple map and a red marker, Bartlit traces the course of a damaged supertanker that ignored repeated opportunities to stop for repairs before foundering in a storm and being dashed against the coast of France.

Overhead projectors are just the ticket for all kinds of things. You can use most office copy machines to make transparencies. Because they use light so efficiently, you almost never have to dim the room lights so people can see. The portable machines do not even need a fan to cool the bulb (but you have to be careful not to burn yourself). And it is a perfect example of "wysiwyg"—what you see is what you get. You can point to things on the transparency (or even draw on it) while looking at it right side up. You don't have to learn to read upside down or backward.

But despite the dust, squeaking, awkwardness, and broken writing implements, I prefer the tools of the schoolteacher—a blackboard and a piece of chalk.

Use the right system for the pictures you are showing:

Video is inexpensive, is in color, has sound—but has remarkably poor resolution that gets even worse when you push the "still" button.

Thirty-five-millimeter slides have marvelous clarity, but they require perfect focus, a good screen, and a dark room.

Exhibit books let you give jurors a copy of every exhibit, which usually means you have to pre-mark and pre-admit everything.

Mounted photographic blowups are expensive, but have the advantage of letting everybody look at the same thing at the same time. Offering the blowups into evidence (and not the smaller copies) pretty much ensures that the jury will take them into the deliberation room and prop them up against the wall, where they will continue to testify. Think what that means. Even a "day in the life of" videotape is usually seen only once.

Medical illustrations do a much better job of explaining than X rays, but are a lot more expensive. Remember that the best-evidence rule applies to X rays, and you may have to introduce the X ray itself to lay the foundation for the medical illustration if your opponent refuses to stipulate to its admissibility.

Computerized reenactments can be very helpful in understanding complex evidence, but typically cost a lot of money. They can also stir up protracted opposition. Many judges are more strict about admitting computerized reenactments than other types of demonstrative evidence.

Video depositions are often cheaper and easier than bringing the real witness to court, but they tend to be deadly dull. Few things are more stultifying than watching a talking head for several hours answer questions from a disembodied voice. Besides, when the jury can't see the questioner, it can skew their evaluation of the witness's credibility.

Dr. Jeanne Fleming, a sociologist and jury research expert from Metricus in Palo Alto, California, explains why. "Suppose you have a hostile questioner," Fleming says, "who does not appear on the screen. A lot of the questioner's hostility is expressed in things that you see, but don't hear. So when you don't see the questioner, the impact of his hostility is muted.

"But the witness sees him as well as hears him, and responds accordingly. And when the witness reacts to hostility you don't know is there, it hurts his credibility."

Seeing something also makes it more memorable. According to Kenneth L. Higbee in *Your Memory* (2d ed. Prentice Hall 1988), page 38, "Picture memory exceeds word memory when measured by recall as well as by recognition." Higbee tells of a study in which the subjects were shown 2,560 different pictures over several days. Later they were shown 280 pairs of pictures. One of each pair they had seen before, the other they had not. On the average the group correctly identified 90 percent of the pictures they had seen before.

If a picture triggers a powerful reaction, the thing itself ought to be even better. That's what Tommy Rayburn figured in the Jackson case in Mississippi. At the time of trial, Amanda was six years old. She was a beautiful child who had a 39 IQ as a result of brain damage caused by the crash.

Rayburn decided to have Amanda's psychologist actually do a brief examination of her in front of the jury. When six-year-old Amanda couldn't put a three-piece wooden duck together in a duck-shaped tray, they understood what had happened to her.

Finally, imaging—creating mental pictures—can have as much or more impact as seeing the thing itself. Ask anyone who remembers listening to "The Lone Ranger," "Sky King," or "Captain Midnight" on radio.

Sarnoff A. Mednick, Howard R. Pollio, and Elizabeth F. Loftus tell about it in *Learning* (2d ed. 1973), pages 140–141. "Gordon Bower told subjects to study sentences like Horse eats banana and Cow kicks ball. Some subjects were told to visualize the scene described, while others were told simply to read the sentences. The results for one experiment showed that when the subjects imagined the scene they scored 62 percent correct recall; subjects who merely read the sentences averaged 42 percent correct recall."

Which helps explain why when Tommy Rayburn asked the jury to stand by the side of Highway 487, what they saw was so unsettling.

CHAPTER 58

It's Happening Now

"It's a gift," said Flash Magruder. "Either you've got it genetically encoded or you don't."

"Oh, sure," said Beth Golden. "And if you happen to have the magic gene, then you're persuasive. Otherwise you might as well forget trying cases and go into dentistry. Is that what you're saying?"

"Or accounting," said Flash.

Angus peered over his newspaper at Flash and snorted.

"Well, it's true," said Flash, "which is why law schools don't offer courses in how to persuade."

"Wrong," said Beth. "Virtually every law school in the country offers a course in trial advocacy, and a lot of them do a fine job in teaching how to approach basic persuasion.

"Second, there are law schools that are offering courses in the fundamentals of persuasion—both on a practical and a theoretical level—that can apply to all different kinds of settings."

"Wait a minute," said Regis McCormick. "Just because a law school offers a course in a subject is no proof that it's got something to teach."

Angus smiled. "Maybe not," he said, "but there is a lot to the subject of persuasion that the ordinary lawyer can learn without having any special talent. I know. I've done it."

"I don't know," said Regis. "I heard you do the opening statement in that products liability case last week. The jury was spellbound. Anybody who could give that opening had to have hung upside down and kissed the stone at Blarney Castle."

"Thanks for the compliment," said Angus, "but everything you heard was learned. There was nothing I did that you couldn't do."

"No way," said Regis. "I could never do an opening like that."

"Give me a chance to show you something, and I think you might change your mind," said Angus. "First of all, I'm sure we can agree that if the facts are alive and immediate, they seem more real—more believable—than if they are something that might have happened in the distant past."

"And that's just what's wrong with trying lawsuits," said Beth. "Nothing seems very alive or immediate three or four years after the fact."

"Which is all the more reason why the lawyer has to breathe some life back into the facts that time and legal tradition have been turning into emotional prunes and raisins," said Angus.

Beth saw me taking notes and said, " 'Emotional prunes and raisins'—make sure you got that one, Jimmy."

"I've got it," I said, and everyone laughed.

"Anyway," said Angus, "that's the heart of a whole series of trial techniques—the lawyer's mindset. You've got to say to yourself, 'It's alive. It's real. It's happening now.' "

"Just saying that to yourself will make you more persuasive?" said Flash. "Humbug."

But everybody ignored him.

"Beth is right," said Angus. "Here you are, three or four years after the fact, talking about something that happened to other people in another place. The easiest thing in the world is to talk about it that way.

"But there's no rule that says you have to do that. If you say to yourself, 'It's alive. It's real. It's happening now,' it becomes natural to talk about the facts so they have that kind of feeling. There are some things you can do that will make the facts come alive."

Take them there

Visualization—being able to "see" something in your mind's eye—is a powerful persuader. It's a process you want to nurture whenever there are key facts you must get across.

The place to start is in the opening statement. The easiest way is to invite the judge and jury to go to the scene:

"I want you to come with me to Erie, Pennsylvania. You are going to visit the Federal Motors Axle Factory on the shore of Lake Erie, the oldest axle factory in the United States. You are going to see them manufacture the key part of the automobile—a defective rear axle—that killed Sandra Wilson."

It will help to have pictures and diagrams, of course. But you do not need to overdo it. Mental pictures are memorable, too.

Inviting the judge and jury to come along is not the only way to do it. You can, if you wish, just put them there:

"Ladies and gentlemen, you are standing at the corner of Ninth and Euclid in Cleveland, Ohio. You are about to see a city bus run down a little girl who has gotten away from her mother while they are crossing the street."

One of the advantages of taking them to the scene is you can put them anywhere you want. You can even let them see and hear everything without being noticed:

"This morning you are going to be a fly on the wall in a room where a secret meeting is going on. You are at an innocent-looking restaurant in Waycross, Georgia, watching three men who are eating breakfast agree to murder for hire a young mother and her two children."

Show the details of reality

Details are important. They are the difference between vague generalizations and compelling pictures that demand the right verdict.

But be careful. Most lawyers drown judges and juries in meaningless trivia. Like the patient who had to have his stomach pumped out after taking a whole bottle of aspirin, we seem to figure that if two details are good, then one hundred must be better.

Never start any part of a trial with a series of unconnected facts. Judges and juries simply won't remember them. Instead, weave in the details as they become important. It is appalling to see a lawyer start or finish his case in chief by reading a series of unrelated stipulations. It virtually guarantees that even the most important information in them will be lost.

But the right detail at the right moment can have a poignancy that will make an indelible memory—like eight-year-old Mark who put on his new Disneyland shirt so he could show it to his friend Nick who lived just three blocks away. Only Mark never got to Nick's house because the bread truck ran the red light at the corner where Mark's street crosses Capitol Drive.

Which details, how many, and where to put them is what makes this part of advocacy an art. Too many and you will turn the whole trial into a maudlin tear-jerker. Too few and it all seems distant and abstract.

Use the present tense

The logic behind the use of verb tenses is pretty basic. Use the past tense for talking about something that happened in the past, the future tense for something that is going to happen in the future, and the present tense for something happening now.

For the most part, we talk about what has happened and what is going to happen. We usually save the present tense for describing what is actually going on as we speak.

The plumber has returned your call and you say, "Am I glad to hear from you. I'm in the basement right now, and I'm standing in two feet of water. How soon can you get over here?"

When you want to convey that sense of "It's happening now," that's the way you should talk.

Say you are in the middle of an opening statement in a products liability case. You want the jury to understand that the manufacturer of an automobile axle made a deliberate decision:

"When the axle for the Wilsons' car came out of the heat-treating machine, it was time to test it. And they did. Federal Motors tested the Wilsons' axle with an ultrasound machine. It tells whether there are any internal weaknesses that you can't see with the naked eye.

"And you know what happened? The Wilsons' axle didn't pass the test. It failed. It flunked. It had internal weaknesses that made it a bad axle—an unsafe axle.

"So now Federal Motors has a choice. What to do with the bad axle? It would cost $21.37 to melt it down and start over again. But it would cost only $3.06 to send it through the axle cooker a second time.

"They decide to put it through the axle cooker a second time. It saves them $18.31. But when the axle comes out of the cooker a second time, they don't bother to test it again. Why not? Because they know this time it's good?

"No. Because the ultrasound test doesn't work on an axle that has been heat-treated twice. It won't show whether it's good or bad. The test just doesn't show anything on an axle that's been through the cooker twice.

"So what do they know about the Wilsons' axle? That it flunked the test the first time, that they cooked it a second time—

which might or might not have fixed it—and they have no idea whether it's any good or not.

"And what do they do with this axle that flunked the only test it ever got? They send it to their plant in Milwaukee where it was put in the Wilsons' new car."

You can even use present tense on direct and cross-examination.

That's when Flash interrupted again. "That's ridiculous," he said. "I can see it on cross-examination because you're doing the talking. But how do you get somebody else to use the present tense unless you tell them to do it?"

"Ask somebody a question in the present tense," said Angus, "and he'll usually answer in the present tense."

Just then Mike Pirelli came in, and Angus said, "Nobody say anything to Mike about this. I want you to see how it works."

"Hey, Mike," said Angus. "Do you mind if I ask you a couple of questions about that fender-bender you had last week? I want to do a little experiment."

"Go right ahead," Mike replied.

"Where did it happen?" asked Angus.

"Third and Locust."

"What way were you going?" Angus continued.

"South," said Mike, "on Third Street."

"How fast?" said Angus.

"Oh, about 20 or 25," said Mike.

"What time of day is it?" asked Angus.

"Between 3 and 3:15 in the afternoon," said Mike.

"Okay," said Angus. "You're approaching the intersection of Third and Locust. It's between 3 and 3:15 in the afternoon. Can you see the other car?"

"Yes," replied Mike.

"What's it doing?" asked Angus.

"It's backing out of a driveway," said Mike.

"What do you do?" asked Angus.

"I slow down," said Mike.

"What does the other car do?" said Angus.

"He turns and starts backing down the sidewalk real fast, and all the pedestrians start jumping out of his way," said Mike.

"So what do you do then?" said Angus.

"I hit my brakes, and this wild man keeps backing his car over the curb and into my right front door."

"Sounds scary," said Angus.
"I'm lucky I wasn't hurt," said Mike.
"Thanks, Mike," said Angus. "No further questions."
Beth said, "I wouldn't have believed it if I hadn't seen it."
Flash said nothing at all.

CHAPTER 59

Creating Tension

It was easy to tell what was wrong. The jury was just not interested in what the lawyer was saying. They were looking out the window, staring at the ceiling, or studying their hands and feet. One or two were looking in the lawyer's general direction, but no one made eye contact with him.

It was harder to know what to do about it. The lawyer could not think of anything, except to finish what he was saying as quickly as he could. But when he sat down, a terrible sense of self-doubt came over him. "My God," he said to himself, "I am a droner."

When you think of droners, you probably picture someone so dull that no one can listen to him for more than a minute or two without suffering an attack of narcolepsy.

But that is not all there is to it. What is said is just as important as how it is said. Style is not the only ingredient to a gripping story. And style has had more than its share of attention in recent years. So we are going to set it aside for now and concentrate on content.

That means we are concerned with the role of the trial lawyer as author or playwright. That, incidentally, is not a bad way to look at our work. Obviously we cannot invent facts or create witnesses, and there are sanctions for lawyers who do not understand that. But within the limits of relevance and the constraints of ethics, the lawyer as playwright decides whether and how the trial will be a fascinating experience that will keep the judge and the jury on the edge of their seats, or a turgid, stultifying affair that will leave everyone in a stupor.

"Wait a minute," you say. "Some cases are just inherently interesting—rape, murder, awful injuries—but not mine. Mine are inherently dull. I try commercial cases. Nothing short of new facts could make them interesting."

Wrong.

And to prove the point, I want you to do an experiment. Imagine yourself at a table for one at an elegant restaurant. Undistracted by a dinner companion, you eavesdrop.

Listen to the talk at table one:

"William Paxton Malloy, how are you? Glad you were able to make it."

"My gosh, Barney, it's been five years."

"Or more. Bill, I think the last time we talked was when you were still at IBM."

"You're right. That was a long time ago."

"Okay, Bill, bring me up to date. How is everything? Are Mary and the kids all right?"

"Couldn't be better. Sandy is in the fifth grade and has started taking clarinet lessons."

If you haven't done it already, let your mind wander from table one and listen to what is happening at table two:

"Would you like to order now?"

"Yes. I think I'd like to have the swordfish with lemon butter."

"Pardon me, sir, but I cannot recommend the swordfish tonight."

"Really?"

"I really shouldn't say anything about this, but the chef and some of the waiters are having a disagreement, and some unusual things have happened to the swordfish."

"Good grief, are you serious?"

"I'm afraid so. I just don't like my customers to be disappointed."

"I'm glad you warned me. How about the stuffed flounder?"

"Caution suggests you avoid all the seafood tonight, sir."

"What on earth is going on back there?"

"I wish I were at liberty to say. May I recommend the pasta?"

Even if you loathe seafood, the chances are you are more interested in what is going on in the kitchen than in the domestic details discussed at the first table.

Why? Surely the reason is not that dead fish are more interesting than live people.

Conflict

The secret is tension. Tension comes from conflict. It says something is going to happen, and it makes you worry or wonder what it is going to be. In an article on writing dialogue, Gary Provost said that tension "makes the reader concerned enough or curious enough to keep reading even when the actual spoken words are mundane. Remember, if the reader doesn't care what happens next, the dialogue is not working."

For the lawyer as playwright, tension means making the jury care about what happens next. Tension is an essential part, not only of dialogue, but the entire trial. The question is how to create it.

Opening Statement

Start with the opening statement. You have a lot to accomplish in a short time. You want to explain the case, make the jury identify (or at least sympathize) with your client, establish yourself as a credible source of information, and make the jury find in your client's favor.

But nothing is going to work unless you make the opening statement interesting. One of the best ways to do that is to start with a crisis. Does it work? James W. Jeans of the University of Missouri at Kansas City says that novelist Louis L'Amour used to introduce his characters in the first chapters of his Westerns and would not get into any real action until about the third chapter. It was a logical way to write, but sales were lackluster.

Then L'Amour changed his approach. He began writing the third chapter first, so the story would start with a crisis. Sales skyrocketed.

Every case, no matter how mundane, has its crisis. A breach of contract is the broken promise that shuts down a production line and puts men and women out of work. Patent infringement is the theft of another's work. Breach of fiduciary duty is an act of treachery that commits economic murder.

Cross-Examination

Tension explains why cross-examination is inherently interesting. Cross-examination supplies its own tension in a contest of wills between lawyer and witness. Besides keeping the cross-examiner out of trouble, tension is another reason why the techniques of witness control are so important—they heighten the sense of tension and make the jury pay attention. But be careful. Do not rely on technique alone to create tension. Content is essential. If you try to create an unjustified sense of conflict, the jury will find you out, and the cost to your credibility will be high.

Direct Examination

If opening statements and cross-examinations are opportunities for tension, then direct examination must give you a chance to ease up, right?

Not necessarily. First of all, remember the lesson of the waiter and the swordfish. The tension does not have to be between the two speakers for it to work. It does not even have to involve either speaker. In other words, the witness does not have to be a party or even a participant in the events to have his testimony filled with tension.

But there is a special kind of tension that does involve both the lawyer and his witness, and it is one of the signs of a superior advocate. It is used when the direct examiner challenges the witness with a difficult or embarrassing question.

Why would you do that?

Do not think that if you avoid a difficult area on direct examination the cross-examiner will oblige you and stay away from the subject as well. The witness will have to face the question sometime, so it might as well come from you. You should steal your opponent's thunder if you can. One effective way to do that is with the challenge.

For example, suppose you know that your witness is going to be cross-examined about his failure to get substitute performance when he learned the seller would not deliver in March as he agreed.

> Q. Who told you this?
> A. Mr. Donaldson.
> Q. Just what did he say?
> A. He called me in February and said that Midwest Conveyor would be about two months behind in its delivery schedule.
> Q. Did you do anything about that?
> A. Well, in June I contacted another company to see if we could use their conveyor system.

Q. June? Why didn't you do something right away?

That question has some bite to it. It challenges the witness. But it also gives him a chance to explain. It is like a fast ball that the pitcher throws right down the middle and which the batter knows is coming. It is an opportunity for him to hit it out of the park.

A. Because Mr. Donaldson promised me that even though they would be late, they would deliver the new conveyor system no later than May 30—and I believed him.

CHAPTER 60

Say It Again

What I tell you three times is true.

—Lewis Carroll, *The Hunting of the Snark* (1876)

"Repetition," said Angus, "going over a point enough times that you are sure it has been hammered home is an essential part of good trial technique."

"Even on direct and cross-examination?" asked Beth Golden.

"Absolutely," said Angus. "A trial lawyer is a teacher—someone who teaches facts to judges and juries. And like any other kind of teaching, trying cases depends on repetition, emphasis, and recapitulation."

"Sure, repetition is important," said Tucker Phillips, pulling up a chair in the Brief Bag, "but you can't do it on direct or cross-examination. That's why 'asked and answered' is such a common objection. You're supposed to wait until the final argument—at least if you play by the rules."

"Oh, I don't know," said Beth. "Angus plays by the rules. He must have written half of them—and he knows all of them. It's just that the rules are different when you've got a few gray hairs and you're one of the leaders of the bar."

"I'm not talking about getting away with anything," said Angus. "Everything I have in mind is strictly inside the rules and has nothing to do with who you are, or whether you have an inattentive opponent or a sleeping judge.

"One point I will admit," said Angus. "In trial practice it usually helps to look like you know what you are doing. But that is true for almost everything else in life as well."

Angus was at it again. I had my pen, but had to borrow a pad from Beth Golden so I could take notes. Here they are.

It starts with some basic ideas about learning. First, repetition is valuable because not everybody gets something the first time around. For some people it takes a serious amount of repetition for something to stick—particularly facts or ideas that do not mean anything to them. The more foreign it is, the more times you need to hear it to remember it.

Second, different people respond to different words, different images, different pacing, different volumes, and different kinds of emphasis.

Third, truly passive education is not every efficient. The more active the student, the quicker and better he learns. Just saying something again and again is no guarantee it will take hold.

It is interesting how well these three themes mesh with the law of evidence. Take idle repetition, for example. Like Tucker said, the most common evidentiary objection probably is "asked and answered." The objection usually comes when a lawyer who understands that repetition is important (but who does not know how to do it effectively) tries to get the exact same information four or five times on direct examination. By that time the jurors are so tired of hearing the same thing, they are truly grateful when the judge tells the direct examiner to move on to a new subject.

But creative repetition—the kind that adds something new or takes a different viewpoint with each question—tends to be proper.

This is when Tucker Phillips interrupted. "Wait a minute," he said. "What are you telling us—that there is good and bad repetition?"

"Exactly," said Angus.

There are hundreds of ways to have a witness repeat testimony, and only a few of them are off-limits—like when the unimaginative lawyer pretends he is deaf so he has to have good answers repeated. The jury knows what he is doing—so does everyone else. So look what happens. Even if the "I'm sorry, I didn't hear your answer" routine appears to work, the cost is too great. It buys only a little emphasis in return for a huge dent in your credibility with the jury.

Here are some other ways to have a witness repeat testimony at a much lower cost. And notice a shared feature: They are helpful instead of just repeating something for its own sake.

Shifting Focus

When you shift focus, every question deals with a slightly different aspect of the same idea. Here is a lawyer who is examining a policeman who one day conveniently forgot to wear his gun.

- Q. You did not wear your police revolver on Aug. 6, did you?
- A. No, I did not.
- Q. You say you forgot to strap on your holster?
- A. That's right.
- Q. Sitting on your dresser?
- A. Yes.
- Q. And when you put on your uniform, you left the gun on your dresser?
- A. That's right.
- Q. And when you got to the station house at 7:00 a.m., you had to return home, didn't you?
- A. Yes.
- Q. To get your gun?
- A. That's right.
- Q. So you were unable to participate in the drug bust at 8:15?
- A. That's right.

Recycling

Sometimes the best way to repeat something is to recycle it—break it down and use it again in the next several questions:

- Q. What did he do then?
- A. Well, he just started throwing liquor bottles around the room.
- Q. Where were you when he "started throwing liquor bottles around the room"?
- A. Right by the desk.
- Q. Where did he get these liquor bottles that he was throwing around the room?
- A. He had a whole bag full of liquor bottles that he brought with him.

Jury Participation

There was a clever advertisement on television a little while ago. A man and a woman were being quizzed about a new fast-food restaurant right while it was being dragged onto a lot and set up behind them. Every question they were asked could be answered by giving the name of the restaurant.

You could see the restaurant and you knew that the man and woman could not. The results were stunning. You wanted to help them answer the questions by giving the name of the restaurant.

Jury-participation questions work in much the same way. One approach is to put a series of questions to the witness that follow the same pattern and rhythm.

Typically the questions are designed to keep getting the same answer. When you set it up right, the jurors start answering the questions in their minds even before the witness does because they know the right answer.

Clarification

Most judges have a healthy attitude about clarification questions. If a question—even though it does nothing more than restate information already developed—will help the judge and jury understand the witness's testimony, it will usually be permitted. Questions that make sense out of obscure expert testimony are particularly welcome.

But even restating a lay witness's testimony may be permitted. There are two points to remember. First, use different words. Restate—do not simply repeat—the testimony. It also helps to introduce the question with something like "Let me see if I understand this . . . ?" Second, do not overwork clarification questions. If you ask more than one every five or ten minutes, you will probably be called to task.

Recapitulation

Summarizing without adding anything new or trying to clear up any misunderstanding is typically not permitted anywhere. Yet it is the perfect way to get back on track after an interruption like an objection, a sidebar conference, or a short recess.

How do you do it?

If you ask permission to recap the witness's testimony for the benefit of the jury, it will be denied. But if you have the courtesy to remind the witness of what he had just testified to before the break, typically no one will complain.

Outlines

One marvelous way to repeat part of a witness's testimony is to put it on the chalkboard—either on direct or cross-examination. While the witness testifies, you make a chart, a calendar, an outline, or a diagram based on his testimony. Particularly with expert witnesses, it helps to have a commercial artist make attractive outlines that you can have on an easel in front of the jury while the expert is testifying.

Demonstrative Evidence

First, demonstrative evidence is its own kind of repetition. Even without any additional testimony, it shows what the witness said, and it keeps on testifying in the jury deliberation room.

Second, demonstrative evidence gives the witness a chance to go through the story a second time, hitting the highlights that are in the picture or on the map.

But while you can use demonstrative evidence to go through direct examination twice, the integrated approach is usually better. It makes more sense to use demonstrative evidence as soon as it is needed, rather than risking losing the jury's attention because there are too many things they do not understand. Seeing and hearing at the same time is the best kind of repetition.

CHAPTER 61

Focus

If you don't know where you're going, when you get there you'll be lost.
—Yogi Berra

Angus was working with Frank Logan on a trial Frank has coming up, and I was playing the part of the witness Frank was cross-examining. I was the motorcyclist who lost control of his bike, broke his back, and became a paraplegic when an irate landowner threw some branches across the street, right in his path.

Logan seemed to be doing fine. No matter how I tried to squirm out of every line of questions, Logan kept me under control and seemed to make every point he wanted.

That's why I was surprised by Angus's reaction. "What's the focus of your cross?" asked Angus.

Frank rattled off four or five points. "I want to show that the motorcyclist had no business being in that fancy neighborhood in the first place," he said. "I want to attack his claim that he couldn't see the tree limb in the street until he came around the corner. I want to undercut his story about only going the speed limit, and I want to slam him with the admission in his deposition that he could have stopped and avoided the limb entirely."

"Frank," said Angus, "I know the points you made. No one could miss them. I asked, what was the focus of your cross-examination?"

Frank was annoyed. "That Marty Drewek's testimony does not make sense, and he should lose this case," said Frank.

"Let me put it another way," said Angus. "What do you want to accomplish with this cross-examination? What do you want the jury to feel when you are finished?"

"That I am right and Drewek should lose this case," said Frank.

Angus smiled. "That's like a man I knew in the army who kept telling me how to make money in the stock market. 'Angus,' he used to say, 'buy low and sell high.' Great advice, but it doesn't tell you what to do or how to do it. And that's exactly what this cross-examination needs.

"You've got all the elements of any number of pictures. But you don't have a picture. You don't have a guiding force to pull it all together. The focus of a direct- or cross-examination is like a slice of your theory of the case. It's a viewpoint. It's a way of looking at things.

"Take Marty Drewek," Angus said. "Why do you want to come down on him so hard?"

"Because he's got it coming," said Frank. "He's dishonest."

"He's a paraplegic, isn't he?" said Angus.

"Yes."

"Maybe some folks won't like you hammering a man who has got to live the rest of his life in a wheelchair, even if they don't agree with some of his testimony," said Angus.

"Well, anyway," said Frank, "Marty Drewek is a lot more responsible for what happened to him than the guy who put some fallen branches in the street for the trash collectors to pick up."

Angus smiled. "Now you're getting somewhere. There are other ways to focus this cross, but responsibility is one of the best."

Frank was still annoyed. "Oh, sure," he said. "All I have to do is stand up and say, 'Marty, you're responsible for what happened, aren't you?'"

"No," said Angus. "That's the whole point of focusing a witness's examination. It guides what you do so that everything points toward the impression you want to make. And you don't want to make it too obvious. You want the jury to feel it is something they figured out themselves. The idea behind focusing a direct- or cross-examination is not to tell the jury what to think.

"The idea is to have a specific objective in mind for each witness and to have that objective drive the examination. You want to show, not tell. And the focus is what you want to show.

"Take the Maggie Maguire case," said Angus. "Maggie was charged with harboring Nick Marcus when there was a federal fugitive warrant out for his arrest. She also was charged with conspiracy to commit a felony and with aiding Marcus to cross a state line so he could bribe a government official in Texas.

"Now all Maggie did was put up Nick Marcus in her apartment for the weekend and then drive him to the bus station, which happened to be across the state line. If Maggie didn't know Nick was a courier for the mob with a federal fugitive warrant out for his arrest, she was perfectly innocent. But if she knew—then she was guilty.

"So knowledge was important. And the government had an immunity witness—Maggie's old boyfriend, Jessie Chilton—to tell about Maggie's knowledge. He testified that he told Maggie all about Nick Marcus—how Marcus was a courier for the mob; how he had several hundred thousand dollars on him to bribe the official down in Dallas; how he needed a place to stay; and how he needed help getting across the state line."

"So knowledge was the focus," Frank said.

"But not just knowledge about Nick," said Angus. "Proving that was relatively easy. The hard part was convincing the jury that what Maggie did was really criminal. After all, why is it so wrong to put someone up for the weekend and then drive him to the bus station?

"The answer was simple. Hiding Nick Marcus was key to the mob's work in Dallas, and Maggie knew it. Maggie Maguire was working for the mob—which has a whole different ring to it than whether she knew a few facts about Nick's background.

"Back to Marty Drewek and his motorcycle," said Angus. "Why is it his fault he got hurt? Your defendant put the tree limb in the street, didn't he?"

"Well, Drewek should have never been out in Fox Hills in the first place," said Frank. "He had no business being on Shadow Bend Road."

"Sorry, Frank," said Angus. "It won't wash. Unless there is something dangerous about Fox Hills that Drewek should have known—besides your client's throwing things in the road—there was nothing wrong with going there. Like people used to say when I was a kid, 'It's a free country.' The more you try to make a point out of Drewek's being in the wrong neighborhood, the more snobbish you and your defendant look."

"Why not refine the focus a little more?" said Angus. "Knowing about a risk and then going ahead anyway is more irresponsible than just stumbling into a dangerous situation, right?"

"Right," said Frank. "So what?"

"Well," Angus said, "look at the choices—the decisions—that Marty Drewek made:

"First, he decided to ride a motorcycle.

"He knew the streets were wet, but he decided to go anyway. He wanted to listen to his motor, so he decided to take his helmet off.

"It was getting near dusk, but he decided to keep on riding up and down Shadow Bend Road.

"He knew people were carrying out trash to the street, but he decided to cut the corner and come close to the curb anyway.

"When he came around the corner, he saw the limb jutting into the street. He could have stopped, but he decided to keep going.

"He could have slowed down and put his feet out for stability, but he decided to do a quick S turn to get around the branch.

"And then he lost control of his motorcycle."

Frank finally smiled. "I like the way you tell it, Angus. No question about it, you've got the gift."

"It's not a gift," said Angus. "It's a principle. Every examination—direct or cross—needs a focus.

- "You should have a focus sheet for every witness in the case. It is not the outline for your questions. That comes later. The focus sheet is just one page. Put it at the front of the materials for your examination. It will have the name of the witness, his relationship to the case, and a few notes about his strengths and weaknesses as a witness.
- "Next, list the essential facts you need to bring out during the examination.
- "Then right in the center of the page comes the most important part: one or two sentences that give the focus of your examination. They state your objective: what you want to accomplish with this witness.
- "Finally, have a short list of the key words you will use in pursuing that objective. In Marty's case they would probably be words of comprehension—'saw,' 'heard,' 'understood,' 'realized,' 'recognized'—and words of responsibility like 'chose' and 'decided.'
- "Then the last thing you do before you rise to examine the witness is read that focus sheet.

"That way you'll know where you're going."

CHAPTER 62

Highlighting

Trial practice magazines are full of ways to make the high points of a case come alive:

- Showing a "day in the life of" video that demonstrates what it means to be a quadriplegic.
- Playing a computerized reenactment of an airplane crash that shows why the plane caught on fire.
- Putting a key document on an overhead projector while you go over its contents with the people who wrote it.

Important stuff?

Without a doubt. A critical job for any lawyer is to make the central parts of the case come alive with an elegant simplicity that captures the imagination of the judge and jury.

But what do you do the rest of the time?

Some lawyers try to keep the excitement up for the whole trial—a serious mistake that is like my college roommate underlining every word on the page because "every word is important."

Unfortunately, most lawyers do not even try to maintain an emotional pitch to the case. Instead they tend to exercise what Judge Warren Wolfson of Chicago calls "their constitutional right to be boring."

But do it right and your case will take on a rhythm all its own—an ebb and flow of information and emotion that helps the judge and jurors understand and care about the case.

But it doesn't happen by choreographing every moment. It works best when you respond appropriately to what goes on in the trial.

Use the best witness

The rule applies to all kinds of situations. First are the witnesses themselves. Trying lawsuits is like dealing with fractions: Everything tends to get reduced to the lowest common denominator. It is easy enough to see that calling weak witnesses produces a weak impression. But who is a weak witness may depend on the circumstances.

A respected leader of the community may be perfect for all kinds of facts, but if she can be impeached with a prior inconsistent statement about a key point of her testimony, some lesser witness who can testify to the same point may be a better choice to prove that fact.

Using the best witness applies to documents as well as people. Say the defendant in a products liability case made a glaring admission that appeared in both a letter to a design engineer and (interestingly enough) in the instruction pamphlet that came with the product. Which should you introduce for the plaintiff—the letter, the pamphlet, or both?

If the letter does a good job of spotlighting the admission, the choice may not be hard, especially since the instruction pamphlet is probably filled with cautions, warnings, and self-serving statements. Of course, Rule 106 of the Federal Rules of Evidence—the Rule of Completeness—may let the warnings from the instruction pamphlet come in no matter which document you use, on the theory that they "ought in fairness to be considered contemporaneously" with the admission.

But there are two things to think about. First, when you attack with the letter and they defend with the pamphlet, they may look like they are reaching pretty far for help. Second, using the pamphlet virtually invites the defendant to offer the rest of the document under Rule 106, while using the letter does not.

Use reverse leading

Leading questions on direct examination send a bad signal: This witness has to be told what to say. Within reason, reverse leading has the opposite effect. When the witness refutes what your question suggests, it both highlights the answer and says the witness knows what he is talking about.

> Q. So did you get out of the car?
> A. Absolutely not. Under the circumstances it was the safest place we could possibly be.

Throw the others away

Professor James W. Jeans, of the University of Missouri at Kansas City, has a technique for letting the most important claim stand out. Say you represent a man who was hit by a car when he was riding his bicycle one Sunday afternoon. As you might imagine, he got bounced around pretty badly when he hit the street.

So when the case was filed, you listed injuries to the man's head, neck, back, and shoulder. At trial, telling how the other injuries have healed is one way to emphasize the injury that is still causing trouble:

> Q. Could you tell us about your head?
> A. Well, actually, it's come along pretty well. I had to miss some work when I was in the hospital, but as soon as they got the stitches out, my hair grew back over the cut, and it's been fine.
> Q. And your neck?
> A. I've been really lucky. They had to keep it immobilized while I was in the hospital, but after that I haven't even had a pain in my neck.
> Q. How about your back?
> A. That was painful at first, but it was actually only cuts and scrapes from being dragged on the road, and they've healed very well.
> Q. What about your shoulder?
> A. Now that's a problem. I've had six different operations, and each time it gets worse. . . .

Use the paper

Your witness is on the stand and suddenly she has a memory lapse. Something got stuck in the synapses and won't come out. You already know you have a number of options for dealing with the situation—leading questions, refreshing recollection, past recollection recorded, maybe even something more.

What should you do—take the simplest way out and do a little leading?

Maybe not.

Rule 611(c) of the Federal Rules of Evidence tracks the common law and allows leading questions to the extent "necessary to develop the witness's testimony." That means leading is permitted on preliminary matters, to get an errant witness back on track, and to refresh recollection. It is just the ticket for the name, or place, or date, or time that temporarily eludes the witness.

But leading may not be the best medicine for dealing with more substantial holes in a witness's testimony. Not because leading might not work. For now we will assume that any of the common-law remedies will work perfectly well.

The problem is the impression it makes.

Just showing the witness a piece of paper may be perfectly permissible (depending on the degree of formality the judge requires). But it can make a worse impression than leading. Showing a witness a piece of paper with no identification can look like the lawyer is showing the witness something the lawyer wrote. The law may be satisfied, but the jury is not.

Instead, you could start to lay the foundation for past recollection recorded. Have the paper marked as an exhibit for identification. Have the witness testify that he made the memorandum right after the event, that he personally witnessed everything he wrote, and that it accurately records what happened.

Then see if reading the memo refreshes his recollection. If it does, it will technically be only present recollection refreshed, but it will make a grand impression.

By the way, if the exhibit does qualify as past recollection recorded, it can only be read to the jury, and not received as an exhibit under Rule 803(5) of the Federal Rules of Evidence—unless it is offered into evidence by the opponent.

And that is a good reason for trying to get the exhibit into evidence as a business record under Evidence Rule 803(6) instead. Then it is admissible as an exhibit (and will go to the jury room where it will continue to testify all during jury deliberations), even though the one who wrote it remembers every bit of its contents and is available to testify to his own recollection.

Offer it for its truth

A well-executed impeachment coupled with a prior inconsistent statement can let a lot of air out of a witness—the same as well-done impeachment with a learned treatise can deflate an expert.

The interesting point is that under the Federal Rules of Evidence, learned treatises and many prior inconsistent statements are admissible for their truth.

So what? you ask.

Why not cap your impeachment with an offer directed to the bench that the impeaching material be received in evidence for its truth? "Your Honor, we offer the portion of Mr. Wilson's deposition that has been read to him into evidence, not only to impeach his credibility but also for the purpose of proving its truth." The impression is wonderful—that the impeaching material is true.

Share the secret

Jim Jeans tells about a lawyer in Missouri who came up with a way to introduce delicate, personal information without getting maudlin about it:

"Fred, you were telling me in my office the other day about some of the problems you had encountered because of this injury, and I wonder if you might share them with the jury?"

Make a circumstantial sandwich

Jo Ann Harris of New York City uses parallel questions to heighten the jury's awareness of some important detail. The example she uses comes from a National Institute for Trial Advocacy problem in which the point is to prove that a liquor store sold liquor to a drunk, Mr. Watkins.

The eyewitness, Officer Bier of the NITA Liquor Commission, is on the stand and has just described how Mr. Watkins staggered across the street before entering the liquor store.

> Q. Officer Bier, focus on the time right before Mr. Watkins entered the store. Does he have anything in his hands?
> A. No. His hands are empty. . . .

Then later she asks:

Q. Officer Bier, focus on the time right after Mr. Watkins left the store. Does he have anything in his hands?
A. Yes. He has a brown paper bag with a liquor bottle in it.

By using parallel questions to surround an important piece of evidence, Jo Ann Harris makes a "circumstantial sandwich" that highlights the proof.

Take us there

Visualization—seeing it in your mind's eye—makes the evidence come alive so that it seems more real. It is a process that helps both credibility and recall.

One of the best ways to make everyone visualize the evidence is to direct the witness to "take us with you" to where the action took place. A police officer, for example, is on the stand, and you want to re-create the crime scene: "Officer Jenkins, I want you to take us with you, back in time to March 24 at 3:20 A.M., when you entered Mike's Place after getting the call from the police dispatcher. What is the first thing you notice as you walk in?"

Your question can make the witness relive the event so vividly that the jury can almost hear the shots and smell the gunpowder as Officer Jenkins tells how he kicks open the door.

CHAPTER 63

Clutter

Cases collect clutter.

Worse than closets or garages, desk drawers or filing cabinets, lawsuits tend to get loaded with clutter—all sorts of legal litter that has the power to obscure a perfectly good claim or defense. In final preparation for trial, one of the most important things you can do is to get rid of the rubble that would keep you from making a simple, effective presentation of your case.

Start with your theory of the case. The best theory is not only legally sound, it is psychologically strong as well. It is an engaging way of looking at the facts from your standpoint that will make a judge or jury want you to win.

But every theory has its problems. If the case is worth trying, there is something to be said for the other side as well. And that means you must have the strength to make some difficult choices. It is the pedant without the power of judgment who says, "We have fourteen different theories on which we could proceed."

It is the trial lawyer who says, "We are going to go with the best *one*."

Not that it is always wrong to have more than one theory of the case. There are times when one theory complements another. Take a products liability case, for example. Why should the plaintiff bother with negligence (and all the problems in proving fault) when he can simply use strict liability?

The answer is that fault—moral culpability—is a tremendous persuader. Whether or not negligence opens the door to punitive damages, it helps convince the jury that the defendant is responsible for the plaintiff's injuries.

But if the additional theory offers no additional help, it probably spells trouble—especially if there is anything inconsistent between the theories you have decided to sponsor. Even a seemingly harmless alternative claim or defense can be clutter that gets in the way when you are trying to persuade.

Next are the facts that do not belong. Why is it that lots of lawyers insist on proving facts that have nothing to do with their theory of the case?

One reason is they learned to do it in law school.

Remember those essay exams that made you feel your mind had been violated by some alien force? One of the assumptions you always had was that every fact in every question was relevant to some issue you needed to discuss. It was as if the question was a puzzle in which every fact would fit at least once. There would be no leftover pieces.

The idea that there is at least one place for every fact on a law school examination is so widely accepted that teachers who throw irrelevant details into their exams are often accused of being tricky or unfair.

But in real life, cases come loaded with extra baggage. And throughout pre-trial discovery we seem intent on gathering whole steamer trunks filled with even more.

Whether or not the hunt for additional facts is worth the effort, you have to be ready to throw out anything that only gets in the way.

There is a rule to remember that will help you do this. A trial is not a law-school examination. No one will give you extra points for your effort to squeeze in extraneous facts, just as no one will reward you for making every possible objection. In trial you get no credit for squaring up round pegs or reaming out square holes. Facts that do not relate to the case are clutter.

Next comes organization. The problem is we expect judges and jurors—who are unfamiliar with the facts—to sift through material that is usually presented in the order of convenience and put it together in neat little functional packages.

Wrong.

Persuasive organization takes a lot of effort. The least you can do is try to present things so that it is easy for the judge and jury to understand the points you want to make. If you do not, some of your best evidence can look like clutter.

Some of our most useless baggage is found in the verbalizations we have picked up over the years and carry with us from case to case.

Take opening statements, for example. Thousands of lawyers are at pains to tell juries that "Nothing I say is evidence. The only thing that will justify a verdict by you is testimony from the witness stand or exhibits that are admitted by the judge during the course of the trial. Everything I say and everything that Mr. Mudger says for the defense is just lawyer's talk."

This does not just get in the way, it actually hurts. It says, "Pay no attention to what I am saying."

Why do we cling tenaciously to statements like these despite decades of work by the National Institute for Trial Advocacy and other litigation programs?

One reason is, deep down we still tend to think there is more magic than logic to the art of persuasion. So like eye of newt and wing of bat, we add little incantations during our presentations in the hope they may help cast the right spell.

Another reason is our love of precedent. We are reluctant to change any part of something that worked before.

Why else would we introduce ourselves right after the judge just finished doing that?

Why else would we explain that this is an opening statement right after the judge has just finished doing that?

To be sure, you want to be the guide whom the jury will want to follow through the trial. But good guides do not make needless explanations.

Of course, if there is some good reason for introducing yourself or explaining what you are doing when you make your opening statement, go ahead. Otherwise just get to the facts of the case.

And when you talk about the facts, forget about repeating "the evidence will show" throughout your opening. It sounds like something a law professor said in an academic demonstration decades ago—and everyone keeps saying it because they figured he knew what he was doing.

Direct examination is usually littered with unhappy words and phrases, too.

"What, if anything, happened next?" is a good example. Lawyers tend to throw in "if anything" without even noticing it. That is because they hear it all the time. But to everyone else, "if anything" catches in the ear.

If it is distracting verbal litter, why say it?

It is based on the absurd notion that the simple question, "What happened next?" may actually be leading because it implies that something happened.

Does the judge really expect the witness to say, "Nothing happened next. I was in a state of suspended animation because I was frozen in liquid nitrogen"?

The point is simple. Get rid of "if anything."

Then there are questions like, "Would you indicate, please, for the benefit of the judge and jury, where you were standing on that occasion?" when "Tell us where you were standing?" would do. Everything should be for the benefit of the judge and jury. There is no need to keep saying it. "Indicate" is a pompous substitute for "show" or "tell," and an "occasion" is something for which a juror might rent a hall.

The cure for this kind of talk is to dedicate yourself to plain, simple language. Cross-examination has its own set of needless words.

Start with the notion that you have to justify asking the witness some questions. "I have just a few points that I would like to clear up from your direct examination."

That suggests your job is to clarify and polish the witness's direct testimony when you have nothing of the sort in mind. It also says you are only going to ask a few questions, when that is not true, either.

Even worse is the false bonhomie of the cross-examiner who suggests that the trial is really a chummy reunion:

Q. Good afternoon, Ms. Morgan. I am Tucker Phillips, the lawyer for the plaintiff. You and I have met before, haven't we?
A. Yes.
Q. That was at lawyer Golden's office?
A. Yes.
Q. And now, you understand I need to ask you a few questions for the judge and jury?

For some reason known only to the gods of litigation, this kind of introduction usually precedes a vicious attack in which the witness is accused of being a corrupt, pathological liar.

Then there are the introductions and tag endings. They are meant to make cross-examination more powerful, but they backfire. Instead of making questions stronger they only take more time—giving the witness longer to think and slowing the pace of the examination. See for yourself:

"It is true, is it not, that you walked out of the store in front of Mr. Winchell?" does not have the power of "You walked out of the store in front of Mr. Winchell?"

"Isn't it a fact that you wear glasses? Isn't that correct?" does not have the punch of asking "You wear glasses?"

Remember, cross-examination is not for the witness. It is for you. It is your opportunity to tell your side of the story the way you want to. Introductions and tag endings just get in the way.

Then comes final argument. It should not surprise you that the fawning thanks some lawyers give the jury at the end of the case does a lot more harm than good. And instead of cutting and pasting together buzzwords from other lawyers' speeches, you are almost always better off spending your time in a commonsense discussion of what you think is really bothering the judge or jury.

If it is honest and simple, at least it will not be cluttered.

CHAPTER 64

Cover Yourself

Angus was educating one of the new associates in his firm. "Michael," he said, "you committed a genuine sin. By not writing that letter, you put the case, the firm, and most of all yourself at risk. There is a basic rule you must never forget: C.Y.A.—cover . . . your . . . self."

Angus is right. All lawyers—especially trial lawyers—need to learn a set of skills they do not teach in law school: how to protect your flanks against the inevitable attack.

Understand that there are no guarantees. Like life in general, trial practice is a risky business. There is no way to ward off all baseless charges. But there are things you can do that will help reduce the risk.

Rule One: Make a Record

There are times when this rule is absolute.

You tell a potential client you feel his case is not worth pursuing. Make sure you warn him in writing about the statute of limitations and tell him to get a second opinion if he likes.

Why?

Many clients are not very loyal to their lawyers—especially those clients who are sent away.

You ask your opponent for additional time to answer the complaint or to respond to his requests for admissions. He allows you the time, so it does not sit well for you to ask for written confirmation.

Instead, you write a gracious note thanking him for his courtesy—which also serves as your memorandum.

Why?

Even good friends can later disagree about the details of extensions and other accommodations.

Your opponent objects to your discovery request, saying it is too broad, or asks for privileged material. Together you hammer out a compromise without having to get a court order. You take the initiative and put the terms of your agreement in a letter to your opponent.

Why?

An extraordinary amount of squabbling centers around discovery. A memorandum will ward off a fight or help win one in a hearing.

The grand jury asks for some of your client's documents in a subpoena that is ambiguous. You do not simply interpret the subpoena; you write a letter to the prosecutor telling him your interpretation.

Why?

Failing to produce a document for a grand jury is more dangerous than dragging your feet in civil discovery. The sanction may be an indictment for obstruction of justice instead of a simple order to produce.

You request copies of all documents your opponent intends to introduce at trial. You number and log each document sent to you.

Then you send a letter that describes each document, saying this is what you received and asking if there is anything else.

Why?

Having an accurate record is the only way you will enforce discovery sanctions. If you are the one with a written record, the judge is likely to listen to you if there is a hearing.

Two pieces of equipment are invaluable in helping you make the record—a tape recorder and a date stamp. While desktop dictating equipment is fine for the office, a pocket-size tape recorder lets you dictate the memorandum wherever you are. And a date stamp, which shows the date of receipt, has settled thousands of disagreements.

Rule Two: Know Your Opponent

Just how careful you have to be depends on who is on the other side.

But even if your opponent is a friend, that still does not mean you should throw caution aside. Good memos, like good fences, make good neighbors.

You must learn quickly whom you cannot trust. Judah Best of Washington, D.C., has a one-bite rule. If an opposing lawyer fails to keep a promise, misrepresents an agreement, or cuts some other corner, then Best applies his two-lawyer procedure. That means there will be two lawyers from his office for all future meetings and discussions with the corner cutter—even telephone calls.

Rule Three: Play Fair

As Eric Kennedy of Cleveland says, one way to prevent attack is to treat other lawyers with fairness and a measure of respect. If you cooperate in taking depositions and discovery, you are more likely to be treated fairly in return. By the same token, says Kennedy, if you force other lawyers to live strictly by the rules, you had better follow them yourself.

Kennedy is right. One way to guarantee a fight at every turn is to refuse to cooperate with the lawyers on the other side.

One application of the fairness rule is in how you write the memorandum that records a discovery agreement. Some lawyers, understanding they are ultimately writing for the judge, go overboard in construing every point in their favor. What starts out as a garment of self-protection winds up being a whole new suit of clothes. Sadly, there are some national firms that are known for institutionalizing this practice.

How do you protect yourself against a ten-page pettifogging memorandum—refute it point by painful point? Surely you cannot afford to ignore it. You must do something to deal with the letter that started out as protection and wound up as attack. The problem is, responding point by point can eat up valuable time. Worse, it can take your eye off the main targets in the case.

Gerald Messerman of Cleveland has an interesting approach to the situation. When his opponent goes too far with multiple points of overstatement or overreaching, he writes a letter that says he cannot agree with the statements in the memorandum, and he does not have time to refute them in particular, but his silence does not mean he agrees with them. It is a quick, clean stroke that cuts through countless hours of a young pit bull's time.

Rule Four: Do Not Be a Witness Yourself

Careful discovery does not mean you must take the formal deposition of every potential witness. In fact, there are good reasons for not taking some depositions at all.

But you still must cover yourself. Written statements, tape recordings, and statements to investigators are all better than oral statements that are made only to you. When the witness changes his story, you do not want to be the only one who can prove what is now a prior inconsistent statement. That would probably mean withdrawing from the case so you could take the stand or abandoning the attack on a dishonest witness—an awkward choice.

Rule Five: Do Not Be Overconfident

An easy way to get in trouble is to assume your best issue in a case is so good that you can ignore the others. Say you represent the defendant in commercial litigation.

You figure your case on liability is so strong that you do not need to respond to the plaintiff's proof of damages.

Watch out. It can be a billion-dollar mistake. If the defense ignores damages, the jurors have only the plaintiff's argument to guide them on how much to award.

But be careful about how you argue damages. The danger is that you may seem to be admitting the issue of liability. As the late Bob Hanley of Denver said, the challenge is to cover yourself by putting a cap on damages while still giving away as little as possible on liability.

There is no perfect answer to the problem, but there are some good approaches. Hanley liked to attack the plaintiff's damage calculations as an example of the lawyer's lack of credibility. It let him talk about a more realistic figure without admitting the defendant might be at fault.

Ed Stein of Ann Arbor, Michigan, has a slightly different approach. In final argument he says, "Now we come to something I think you will not have to be concerned with—the plaintiff's damages. But because Mr. Wilson has spent so much time talking about it, I would be wrong if I didn't say something about it, too." It lets Stein blame the other lawyer for bringing up damages without having to attack his credibility.

Rule Six: Danger Can Lurk Even Inside Your Firm

It happened a number of years ago to a lawyer we will call Paul. He had just joined a firm that had a name partner who was known as the Artful Dodger among the junior associates.

The Dodger was a superb courtroom performer, but was not always careful with his docket. When he got in trouble, he would look for someone to bail him out.

One day the Dodger was walking down the hall with a big file under his arm. He stopped inside Paul's office and asked if he could use the phone.

Paul stood up and said, "Sure." He never thought of asking why the Dodger couldn't use his own phone.

Then, while Paul stood there, the Dodger called a circuit court judge and said, "Your Honor, I'm in the office of one of our young associates," and he put the file on Paul's desk. "He has a file on his desk in which a default judgment has just been entered. As you might imagine, Judge, he is a very red-faced young man [which was now true].

"He is on the way over to your courtroom with a motion to reopen the default, and he promises me it will never happen again."

The Dodger hung up and said, "Paul, you take it from here."

Paul learned an important lesson that day. Keep your door closed when the Dodger walks down the hall.

CHAPTER 65

Taking the Blame

It almost seems built into the creature. When something goes wrong, we blame someone else. It's as if pointing the figure is genetically encoded in some strange little twist in the double helix.

If it is learned behavior, it certainly comes early in life. Before they even talk, children know how to blame their brothers and sisters and sometimes even the dog.

But even if assigning blame has some survival benefits, it still is not an attractive trait. We are (it's part of the problem) quick to criticize people who are always blaming others. And we honor those who seem to have risen above it. We keep telling the story of George Washington and the apocryphal cherry tree, and everybody remembers that Harry Truman had a sign on his desk that said, "The Buck Stops Here."

But when Truman's "Fair Deal" had trouble getting through (of all places) the Democratic-controlled House of Representatives, Harry himself blamed it on "that no-good, do-nothing, 80th Congress."

If it is hard for the rest of the world to stop blaming others, it is almost impossible for lawyers. We are professional blamers. We spent years in training, learning to find faults that would not even occur to others. And it is our job to fix responsibility on anyone other than our client—usually the party with the fattest wallet—if it will do our side any good.

Even when the task is to "unblame" our client, we usually wind up pointing the finger at someone else.

All of this means that when we are enmeshed in the intricacies of litigation—an intensive exercise in creative finger pointing—taking the blame ourselves does not come easily. But sometimes that is exactly what we should do.

Helping the Witness

The time comes in nearly every direct examination when the witness does not know what the question means, and has no idea what the lawyer wants.

Why does it happen? There are lots of reasons. First, the witness stand itself is one of those enchanted places that has the power to destroy common sense. Once they are under oath and on the stand, all kinds of witnesses become strangely literal, confusingly technical, and uncomfortably complete.

Second, we seem compelled to ask questions that sound as if they were written by law professors—with obscure words and a word order that defies comprehension.

Third, we lawyers seem to think that every question must be complete unto itself, as if there were no context provided by the rest of the examination.

And fourth, we have the habit of trying to fix broken questions on the fly by muttering "strike that" after apparent false starts, and then not really starting over again.

So the witness launches into what she thinks is wanted, only to hear the lawyer say, "You didn't understand my question."

Already confused, now the witness feels flustered, hurt, resentful—emotions that only serve to make communication more difficult as well as tell the jury something about the lawyer.

You are the professional communicator. Take the responsibility for effective communication. No matter how wonderful you feel your question was, take the blame. "I'm sorry, I didn't put that very well. Let me start that question over again."

Keeping Control

Witness control is one of the hardest parts of cross-examination. When the witness seems intent on trying to make a fool out of you by weaseling out of the question, answering a question that wasn't asked, or arguing instead of answering, you are in no mood to take the blame for anything. After all, here is this insufferable twit who is trying to ruin your lawsuit by giving you a hard time. Who could blame you for getting angry at the witness?

The jury.

They are far more likely to identify with the witness than the lawyer. And if they think you are being unfair to the witness, you are in trouble. Remember, cross-examination is a hyphenated term. It does not mean "angry examination."

So when the witness starts giving a speech instead of answering your question, try taking the blame. Instead of some smart riposte, say, "I'm sorry, Doctor. I must not have put my last question very well. What I meant to ask you was whether you had done a spinal tap on Marvin Blattner."

It has a big advantage (besides making you look a little nicer). It lets you interrupt the witness, right in the middle of his harangue. Because you are taking the blame, no one even notices you have done something that might otherwise bring a reprimand from the judge, even without an objection.

And there is another reward. The jury knows whether you asked a simple question that the witness could have answered without an argument. When you take the blame, the jury figures out what the witness has been doing without your having to say anything more.

But a word of caution: Don't be sarcastic when you take the blame. Better to come across as stern and fair than seem nasty and insincere.

Talking to the Judge

It is hard to reverse a trial court for evidence mistakes. No matter how perfectly you make your offer of proof, unless the judge's ruling affects a "substantial right of the party," it is harmless error.

And that means the time to win the evidentiary fight is at the trial, not on appeal.

What does that have to do with taking the blame?

Two things.

First, taking the blame gives you a second bite at the apple. When the judge makes what you think is an erroneous ruling, telling him he has made a big mistake is not going to convince him that he ought to let you make an additional argument. Telling the judge he is badly wrong is more likely to produce a response such as, "I have ruled, Counsel. Go on to another matter."

But when you take the blame it's different. "If I may be heard, Your Honor, I am afraid I did not make my objection so that it made much sense. The problem is, this exhibit violates the best evidence rule because it is not the original photograph."

When you take the blame, making an additional argument does not seem like an attack on the integrity of the judge's ruling, so he is more likely to listen to what you have to say.

The second point is related to the first. Taking the blame lets the judge reverse his ruling without looking like he made a mistake.

Talking to the Jury

There is an irony in careful trial preparation that can lead to "misstating" the evidence in final argument. You know what the evidence was supposed to have been, while the jury only knows what the evidence actually was—and there is always a difference between the two.

But that does not occur to the jury.

If what you say about the evidence is different from what the jurors remember, they are likely to think you are trying to make your case look better than it is.

That's why what may just seem to be boilerplate can be worth saying:

"Ladies and gentlemen, there's something I want you to do that is very important. If anything I say about the evidence differs from your recollection, follow your recollection and not mine. You are the judge of the facts—not me. And if I make a mistake and misstate any of the evidence, please hold it against me—and not against Ron Williams."

Controlling the Damage

There is a corollary to taking the blame that goes beyond how you make objections and handle witnesses. It goes to the heart of how you try cases.

Everybody makes mistakes.

Everybody.

And when you, or your client, or your witness makes a mistake in a trial, you need to do something about it. Everyone has seen it and heard it, and how you handle it makes a difference. Almost always, the best tactical decision you can make is to fix it at once. Admit it, correct it, and go on. Offering excuses will not bring you admiration or respect. Neither will blaming someone else.

There is only one thing that is worse.

Trying to cover it up.

CHAPTER 66

Mootcourtitis

"I blame the law schools," said Judge Wallop. "The problem is in how they approach the entire business of legal education."

"Oh, come on, Judge," I said, "not again? You're always blaming the law schools for something. What have they done now?"

"It's the way they teach the advocacy system," he said. "The students all come out thinking that exaggeration is the way to win, that overstatement is the heart of good persuasion."

"Just a second," I said. "Don't you mean *adversary system*? That's what everybody calls it."

"That's just the point," said Wallop. "They've turned the advocacy system into the adversary system. They concentrate on contentiousness, instead of persuasion. They teach people to fight every possible point, to give no quarter, to concede nothing. And instead of good lawyers, the law schools are graduating malamutes and pit bulls. If they taught students to be advocates instead of adversaries, everybody would be better off."

"Judge," I said, "I don't mean to suggest you are ignoring your own advice, but don't you think you've overstated your point just a little?"

That's when Angus pulled up his chair. "I don't know, Jimmy," he said. "The judge has got a point. I was over at the law school the other evening, helping judge a practice round of moot court, and I was astonished at what I heard the law professor tell those students. 'Don't concede anything,' he said, 'or you'll give your case away.' "

"Has the professor ever argued an appeal?" Judge Wallop asked.

"How did you know I asked him that?" said Angus.

"Just a lucky guess," said Judge Wallop.

"All right," I said, "the law schools are entitled to their share of the blame. But they are not the only ones. I know some law firms who actually admit that it's their policy to inflict pain when they're involved in litigation."

"There are some clients who want their lawyers to act that way," said Judge Wallop.

"And present judges excepted," said Angus, "there are some judges who let them."

"Whatever the causes," said Judge Wallop, "I call it 'Mootcourtitis.' It's the disease of exaggerating every point, of making unreasonable arguments, and it is spreading fast."

The problem is, Judge Wallop is right. "Mootcourtitis" is a disease. It takes lots of different forms and may cause serious side effects. But whatever its other symptoms, it usually costs money, and it almost always causes pain. Here are some of the variations you will find.

Arguing Every Point

Law-school classes—and especially law-school examinations—reward the students who identify and argue every possible issue. That is not wrong in itself. The lawyer who does not know what issues are available is not in a position to pick the best ones.

But there is a dangerous message in the law-school system. It implies that whatever the law says is an issue is worth arguing.

That idea can lead to astonishing results. The example comes from Judge James J. McMonagle's courtroom in Cleveland, Ohio.

The defendant was charged with rape. His defense was alibi. He had some witnesses who were ready to testify that the defendant was some place else when the crime took place. The defendant himself was ready to take the stand and testify that not only did he not commit the crime, he had never seen the victim before in his life.

The defendant was represented by a lawyer who consulted a practice book before trial—one of those manuals that identifies every element of the crime and lists every defense that can be raised in response.

So in his opening statement, the defense counsel not only told the jury that the defendant had not committed the crime, he also made the point that it was up to the prosecution to prove every element of rape—dwelling at length on the requirement that prosecution had to prove that the victim was not married to the defendant.

Result? Guilty.

Taking the Opposite View

Some lawyers figure that whatever the other side wants must be wrong, so they always argue the opposite—whatever it is. This example comes from a defamation case.

A Midwest radio station named an unsuspecting man the "Turkey of the Year."

The man claimed he was humiliated and disgraced, and had lost his job at a local department store—all for being called a turkey on the radio.

Because the plaintiff said that calling someone a turkey was disparaging, the defense lawyer automatically took the other side. In final argument he told the jury that "turkey" was actually a friendly thing to say—a term of endearment.

That was the perfect set-up for the plaintiff's rebuttal. "You heard what the defense said. Go ahead. Take him at his word. Go home tonight and hug your husband or wife and kiss him or her on the neck while you whisper, 'You're a real turkey,' and see what happens."

Entertaining the Client

It was an impassioned argument, based on notions that had not been the law since early in the industrial revolution. It was obvious to everyone in the room—judge, jury, lawyers, clients—that the argument was an eloquent loser.

Yet the representative of the defendant—a large casualty-insurance company—was happy. "Thanks, Jack," he said. "I'm sure we're going down in flames in this one, but that doesn't matter. When you're going to take a licking, it's nice to know there's someone in your corner."

There are lawyers for whom this is the practice of law. They find it easier (or more comfortable) to engage in client entertainment than to try the case they actually have or argue the law that actually applies—whether or not it benefits their clients.

Fight to the Finish

Once you decide something is worth fighting for, it is easy to conclude it is worth finishing the fight. First, this is not necessarily true. Plenty of issues that are worth raising do not justify going to the mat. Second, even if they are, you may not know when the match is over.

The perfect example comes from U.S. District Judge Ann Williams's court in Chicago.

It was a civil case that had started out in state court. First the defendant removed the case to federal court, and then the plaintiff moved to remand the case, trying to send it back to state court.

In the meantime was the question of whether the usual pre-trial discovery and motions should go ahead, or whether they should wait for the outcome of the motion to send the case back to state court.

"No sense preparing a case that might be sent back, Your Honor," said the defendant. "It would be wasted work. We should wait until the motion to remand is decided."

"Go ahead with discovery," said the plaintiff. "This is just a ploy to delay a case that has already been delayed too long."

Judge Williams decided that discovery should wait until she had decided whether the case must go back. And instantly the defendant started to argue, haranguing the judge about wasted time and unnecessary cost.

"Counsel," said Judge Williams, "what is the problem? I have ruled *for* you." He had so programmed himself to argue that he had not noticed he had won.

Judge Williams says that one of the causes of mootcourtitis is the fear of malpractice claims. She says some lawyers raise issues they know they should not bother with simply to protect themselves from later attack. The results can be maddening, like the two lawyers who presented a proposed pre-trial order in which both lawyers objected to virtually every exhibit that the other side proposed.

Judge Williams says lawyers have no idea how this kind of advocacy hurts their credibility. "It's like E.F. Hutton," she says. "When some lawyers speak, I listen. But with some others I have to force myself to listen to give them a fair shake. You should never throw away your credibility with arguments you don't mean or with cases that don't support what you say."

U.S. District Judge Jim R. Carrigan, from Denver, thinks the real problem behind mootcourtitis is economics.

"There's no incentive to get to the point," he says. "Not when you get paid by the hour, instead of the job. The problem is running the meter. The longer you take, the more you make. If more lawyers worked for a contingent fee, or were paid by the job, instead of by the hour, a lot of the needless contentiousness would disappear."

Judge Carrigan has a point. True, some clients are unhappy with lawyers for all the wrong reasons. But there is a growing group of dissatisfied people who simply want more for their money.

Getting rid of mootcourtitis helps give them their money's worth.

CHAPTER 67

The Giggle Test

Judge Wallop, my curmudgeon friend on the Court of Common Pleas, was at it again.

"I blame the law schools," he said. "If they ever trained professionals, they don't anymore. They don't train lawyers. They don't even train people to think like lawyers. They aren't law schools, they're the law departments of universities."

"Not fair," I said. "Even the most humble law schools have courses they never dreamed of when you went to school, and a lot of them involve real skills training—trial advocacy courses, advanced litigation seminars, client counseling, negotiation and settlement, legal clinics, ..."

"Aw, Jimmy" (that's what Judge Wallop calls me when he wants to be condescending), "now you sound just like a law school dean—and you're missing the point, to boot. It's not the name of the course that counts, but what they teach that matters. And American law schools are churning out hordes of brilliant young lawyers who can spot every issue, find every case, discuss every point, but who don't have the common sense to know when an argument is a loser.

"Happened in my courtroom today," he said. "Man is suing a railroad, and his lawyer offers a photo of the same kind of locomotive that hit the man's car. Demonstrative evidence. Then the defense lawyer, young man from one of the big firms—probably was a law review editor—jumps up and objects that the photo is not the best evidence."

"He wanted the plaintiff to introduce the actual locomotive into evidence, eh? Well, at least he has a sense of humor," I said, "which is more than I can say for a lot of judges."

"Humor? If he would have cracked a smile, winked or even looked out of the corner of his eye, I would have given him a prize. But no, he was serious. Pulled out the rules and read them to me. Turns out he thought that because the railroad's name was on the side of the locomotive, the locomotive must be a 'writing' under the rules of evidence.

"Yes sir," Wallop said, "I blame the law schools. They teach these kids every possible argument in the world, but don't teach them to shut up when the argument can't pass the giggle test."

"The giggle test?" I asked.

"The giggle test," he said. "Fundamental rule of advocacy. Never make an argument unless you can say it with a straight face."

Giggle test, smirk test, straight-face test—all are different names for the same point. It is not enough that an argument makes legal sense. It has to be factually and emotionally plausible as well. Otherwise, it is a loser.

Of course there are plenty of arguments made every day that do not even make legal sense. In a recent hearing in Washington, D.C., a labor union intervening in a case wanted to show some of the problems that workers were encountering in a manufacturing plant. But instead of calling the workers to testify, they called a union representative who had gone to the plant and interviewed some of the workers.

When the union representative was asked what the workers told him, the other side objected to hearsay. Without batting an eye, the union lawyer said, "That's not hearsay, Your Honor, he heard it himself."

Five Losers

Failing the giggle test is one of five ways to lose an argument:

- Overstate the facts in your favor.
- Conceal some fact that hurts you.
- Misstate the law.
- Ignore the issues.
- Make an argument that does not pass the giggle test.

Of course there are more than five ways to lose an argument, but these have a special destructive power that goes beyond the argument. In the right situation, doing any of these things can cost you the entire case.

That is because every one of them is tied to your credibility as an advocate.

Overstate the facts and it looks like you do not believe in the case you actually have. Try to hide a damaging fact and it looks like you think it makes your case a loser. Misstate the law and the judge cannot trust your arguments. Ignore the issues and you cannot be counted on to guide the fact-finders to the right questions, much less the right answers. Make an argument that flunks the giggle test and your judgment is suspect, which clouds all your other arguments.

Look at it this way. Your credibility is the most important issue in any case you try. Every fact you prove, every point you make depends on your credibility, and one way to undercut your credibility is to make an argument that does not pass the giggle test.

Even if you have some marvelous arguments, mixing them with frivolous points can offend the most sophisticated court. In *Timken Roller Bearing Co. v. United States*, 341 U.S. 593 (1951), the court was infuriated with an appeal that was based on 206 assignments of error.

"These assignments are unduly repetitious, some are frivolous, and the excessive number obscures the actual grounds on which appellant relies for reversal. As the Government pointed out in its motion to dismiss the appeal, our prior cases justify dismissal in such situations."

Only a responsive brief that "sufficiently spelled out the few real objections" saved the case from being dismissed.

If you think you are immune from this, watch out. Even the finest lawyers occasionally make silly arguments. Just as Sir Edmond Hillary climbed Mount Everest "because it was there," there are times when you will be tempted to make an argument because it is available.

The Blinding Light

Sudden inspiration can be another trap. The stroke of brilliance that lights up the mind in the middle of the night can be an utter embarrassment in front of the jury the next day. That is the reason for using the giggle test. Actually saying the argument out loud at home or in the office before you say it in court is a good way to stay out of trouble.

Even more dangerous is the piercing shaft of light that comes in the middle of trial. It is dangerous because you do not have a chance to test the idea before you use it. You know you ought to leave it alone, but it looks so attractive that you cannot resist trying it. That is what happened to no less a lawyer than Jo Ann Harris of New York.

Harris was representing a woman charged with murdering her husband with a kitchen knife. The case was tried to the judge, and from the start the defense theory was that all the surrounding emotions and actions made the case manslaughter instead of murder.

But something happened when the medical examiner took the stand for the state. He testified that it took a considerable amount of deliberate force to drive the knife six inches into the victim's body.

So on cross-examination, Harris tried to get the medical examiner to admit that falling on the knife could have driven it six inches into the victim's body. But when she looked over at the bench, she saw both the judge and his clerk wincing in agony, distressed to see her suddenly grab at another theory in the middle of trial.

Harris knew she had to do something to regain her credibility; leaving things as they were would not be enough. She got her chance in final argument. She explained that the defense was manslaughter, and that she was making no claim of accidental death. Under the circumstances, she said, the only relevance to falling on the knife was to show that just that slight amount of force—nothing superhuman—was all it took to drive the knife into the body.

Lawyers are not the only ones who need a giggle test. There is one for judges, too. It happened in North Carolina a few months ago. The judge ruled against the plaintiff, no matter what the issue was. Finally the plaintiff's lawyer approached the bench and said, "Your Honor, may I have the basis for the court's ruling?"

The judge replied, "Why? If I tell you, you'll just appeal."

It sounds like the right thing to do.

CHAPTER 68

Rehabilitation

Sometimes the best advice is the most obvious. Henny Youngman tells about going to the doctor and saying, "Doc, it hurts when I go like this (raising his arm over his head)," and the doctor says, "Then don't go like that."

Angus was out at the school, talking to my Trial Tactics class, and he gave them the same advice. One student asked what was the best way to rehabilitate a witness. Angus said, "Don't let him get in trouble in the first place."

"Wait a minute," I interrupted. "You're fighting the problem. The question was how do you get him out of trouble—not how do you keep him from getting in."

"I know," said Angus, "but it's still the best answer. Every trial is littered with holes, snares, nets, traps, and pitfalls. And prevention is still far more valuable than cure."

"Okay," the student agreed, "but even *your* witnesses must get in trouble sometimes. The question is, what do you do about it?"

Angus smiled. "Promise you won't get mad?" he said.

"Sure," we all replied.

"First," said Angus, "you're asking the wrong question. You're focusing on how to rehabilitate the witness. Instead, you should ask how to rehabilitate your case."

"Pardon me," said the student, "but isn't that just a difference in semantics?"

"Absolutely not," said Angus. "When you concentrate on rehabilitating the witness, you tend to look at those things you can do with the witness to make up for what happened. It limits the range of your responses. But when you focus on rehabilitating the case, you multiply your possibilities.

"Sure, you need to look out for your witnesses and protect them," added Angus, "but your first concern is the trial. When your case has been hurt, you need to know what your choices are."

By this time we were all taking notes. Here are mine.

Ask another witness

Redirect examination is the most immediate response to damage that was inflicted on cross. Only sometimes it doesn't help very much. Sometimes it is more effective to cross-examine the other side's witness than it is to redirect yours.

Say you've got an expert witness on the stand—a doctor—who testifies to your plaintiff's neurological condition. Your doctor says the plaintiff got nerve damage from the automobile crash he was in. Then on cross-examination the defense hammers your expert for not having conducted any tests to see whether the plaintiff might be suffering from lead poisoning instead of having a condition that was caused by the crash.

You know it is just a red-herring cross-examination, but the jury doesn't. So what do you do?

If you just look at it from your doctor's standpoint, this is something to deal with during redirect examination.

But if your doctor already looks as if she has protested too much on cross-examination, redirect examination may not do much rehabilitating.

You may have another choice. When you cross-examine the defendant's doctor and he admits that lead poisoning is an absurd suggestion, that testing for it would be a waste of time and money, the jury is going to feel they were cheated by the defendant's attack on your witness.

And if the opponent's doctor tries to defend lead poisoning, you can still call a rebuttal witness to refute it. After all, it was the defendant's idea.

Redirect examination

A clever cross-examination sometimes creates a false impression that can be put to rest on redirect. The problem is how to keep from making things worse.

First, don't cry if you aren't hurt. A long redirect sends the message that your case was really damaged by the cross-examination. Too much bandage exaggerates the injury.

Second, set it up as quickly as possible. Just as you do not want to go over direct examination on cross, you do not want to go over cross-examination on redirect—because it repeats the other side's points.

One of the easiest ways to set up redirect is to point out what wasn't asked on cross-examination:

"Mr. Jeans didn't ask you this question, so I will: Why didn't you stay at the scene of the crash until the police came?"

And the question should usually be a "why" question—something that would have been one question too many if it had been asked on cross-examination.

Third, don't belabor the issue. Make only one or two points, and make sure they are good ones. Too often, redirect examination (and recross-examination and re-redirect and re-recross, if the judge is that indulgent) is a meaningless quibble over which word properly characterizes a transaction or an event.

Corroboration

Say your witness squirms uncomfortably on cross-examination about his connection with your client—something he was reluctant to admit, so it looks all the more damning.

At this point you are probably thinking Angus was right. You should have protected the witness by bringing up the bias yourself on direct examination rather than letting your opponent make something out of it on cross.

Save your regrets for later. Now is the time to think about how this has hurt your case and what to do about it.

The interesting thing about bias is that it seldom goes to any one part of the witness's testimony. It just makes a general attack. It goes to everything the witness said. So while it has power, it lacks focus.

Understanding that, an adroit cross-examiner (of the kind who is one in a hundred or even one in a thousand) will try to link the bias to a particular point he wants to attack:

Q. Yet you're sure Paul Hammond's car had the green light?
A. Absolutely.

Q. Wait a minute. Isn't your son engaged to marry Paul Hammond's daughter?
A. What does that have to do with it?
Q. That's going to be up to the jury, Mr. Wilson. No further questions, Your Honor.

The bias is there—there is nothing you can do on redirect examination to make it go away—even if it did not affect the witness's testimony. But suppose you have another witness who can corroborate Mr. Wilson's testimony about the light. You put him on the stand even though he has nothing else to add to the case. You might even do a little linking (or unlinking) of your own:

Q. Which car had the green light, Mr. Lundquist?
A. Mr. Hammond's car—the silver Toyota.
Q. You're sure Hammond's car had the green light?
A. Oh, yes.
Q. I'm sorry, but you don't happen to have a son who's engaged to Mr. Hammond's daughter, do you?
A. I don't even have any children. Why do you ask?
Q. Just saving defense counsel a little trouble, that's all.

Prior consistent statements

The usual excuses for a prior inconsistent statement don't amount to much: "I was tired." "I was confused." "I didn't understand the question." "I never said that." "The court reporter got it wrong."

You may be better off leaving weak excuses alone, especially if you have a prior consistent statement.

According to Rule 801(d)(1)(B) of the Federal Rules of Evidence, a prior consistent statement is admissible and may be considered for its truth when it is "consistent with the declarant's testimony and is offered to rebut an express or implied charge against the declarant of recent fabrication or improper influence or motive...."

The rule of completeness

It is an antidote to selectivity. Your opponent takes something out of context and reads it to the jury. Rule 106 of the Federal Rules of Evidence lets you force your opponent to include the missing context—not next week, but right now:

"When a writing or recorded statement or part thereof is introduced by a party, an adverse party may require the introduction at that time of any other part or any other writing or recorded statement which ought in fairness to be considered contemporaneously with it."

Limited offer

One of the most common potholes in a trial is to have a bit of important evidence excluded unexpectedly.

Later on you can think about whether another witness or some other evidence can fill the gap. Right now you need something quick to hold things together.

First, courage. You are not a cheap cardboard suitcase on a rainy Saturday night. There is no reason to fall apart.

Second, imagination. If the evidence is excluded for one purpose, it may still be admissible for another.

If one hearsay exception won't work, try another.

An inadmissible business record might still qualify as past recollection recorded.

A failed excited utterance might still be a present sense impression.

The evidence might fit one of the catchall exceptions, Rule 803 (24) or 804(b)(5).

If it is a verbal act, such as an offer, acceptance, or notice, then it is nonhearsay that is not offered for its truth.

Even a bit of failed real evidence may still be admissible. If there is a break in your chain of custody and you can't prove this is the gun the defendant used, it can still be demonstrative evidence if you can prove it "looks just like" the defendant's gun.

Rebuttal

Reopening the case and putting new witnesses on the stand can be powerful medicine—if they have something new to say. Technically, rebuttal is reserved for situations in which you are responding to something new or which you could not have anticipated. So if you use rebuttal just to have the last word, do not be surprised if the judge cuts you short.

Judicial notice

One way to make up for a hole in your proof is to ask the court for permission to reopen your case—not for rebuttal, but to fix the mistake. Whether you get it will depend on the judge.

Judicial notice is another way to make up for missing evidence. But now the court has less leeway. If it is a proper matter for judicial notice, the court has to grant your request.

So what is proper for judicial notice? The range is delightfully broad: anything that is "(1) generally known in the territorial jurisdiction of the trial court, or (2) capable of accurate and ready determination by resort to sources whose accuracy cannot reasonably be questioned." Rule 201(b) of the Federal Rules of Evidence.

One last point. Is it too late to ask for judicial notice after you have already rested and closed your case?

Nope. You can even ask for judicial notice on appeal. Under Federal Rule 201(f), it can be taken "at any stage of the proceeding."

Of course, like Angus says, you are better off staying out of trouble in the first place.

PART NINE

The Language of Persuasion

Lawyers are professional communicators. To be sure, our job is to sift and examine, to test and compare. But that is just the beginning. Then it is our task to take our ideas and present them to others. Here is where the traditional obscurity of the language of the law gets in our way. And that is why serious trial lawyers spend time training themselves to become superb communicators.

CHAPTER 69
Professionally Speaking

CHAPTER 70
Reading Out Loud

CHAPTER 71
Bilingual

CHAPTER 72
Key Words

CHAPTER 73
Bad Words

CHAPTER 74
Hollow Words

CHAPTER 75
The Real Message

CHAPTER 69

Professionally Speaking

It was humiliating. The young lawyer had put in more than a hundred hours on the brief. He had a novel interpretation of the Safety Appliance Act that he was urging his firm to adopt in an important case. One of his memos had caught the attention of their client's chief general counsel, who suggested a strategy conference to discuss the young lawyer's position.

The young lawyer knew he would have to talk about some of his ideas, but he was not ready for what happened.

"All right," said the general counsel. "Let's say that Mr. Baker and I are the court of appeals. We want to hear your argument. How are you going to convince us that sixty years of our reasoning has been wrong?"

The young lawyer was off guard. He floundered around for almost half an hour, hopping from one point to another, never really making a coherent statement. He was frankly relieved when the general counsel shifted his attention to Mr. Baker and left him out of the discussion for a while. But by the end of the morning he could see that his idea was dead. They had decided not to risk using his argument.

The ride back to the office was the worst part of it. Mr. Baker wanted to talk about the dynamics of what had happened.

"Maxwell caught you by surprise, didn't he?" Baker said. "I should have told you that's what he does. I still like your idea, but we may have to wait for a client who is willing to take more of a chance."

The young lawyer didn't say anything.

"But you still got a lot out of that meeting, didn't you?" said Baker.

"What do you mean?" asked the young lawyer.

"You learned something a lot of lawyers never understand," said Baker. "A lawyer is a professional speaker. You talk for a living. Every time you say something as a lawyer, you are making a professional presentation.

"It doesn't matter whether you are in trial, arguing to an appellate court, talking to a client, or giving a continuing legal education lecture. There are some basic rules for any kind of speech that you should follow if you are going to be an effective advocate."

Twenty-five years later the young lawyer (his name is Angus) was giving those same points to Beth Golden. This time I was there and took notes.

Bond with Your Audience

Even the simple "May it please the court" is an instinctive recognition that pleasing the audience is the key to persuading them.

And there are all kinds of bonds that tie speakers to audiences—some simple and appealing, others base, even ignoble. The psychology of the bond lies in our most primitive past. Should the cavemen gathered around the communal fire even listen to this stranger from another clan? Any lawyer who has been subjected to "home cooking" has felt the power of the cave. It can be overcome, but it takes a lot of work.

Fortunately there are other bonds. One of the most effective a lawyer can draw on is the very reason for everyone being there in the first place—to right a wrong.

Accept Responsibility for Communication

You did not design the courtroom, the bench, the jury box, or the lectern. You have only a limited responsibility for who is in the jury box and even less for who is on the bench. You have only a little control over when you start to speak and how much time you have.

The same things are true in all kinds of other settings in which you must speak as a lawyer.

But whatever the surroundings, whoever the audience, whatever your goal, however long you have, you are the one who is responsible for effective communication. It is your job to make yourself understood—not your audience's job to try to understand you. Pay particular attention to this because it is exactly the reverse of how a number of your law school teachers approached their task.

Accepting the responsibility for communication means a number of things—all of them important.

- *Focus on your audience.* Watch their faces for signs of understanding or confusion. Respond to the signals they send you. Even on very formal occasions, your job is to get ideas across, not to perform an idle litany.
- *Do not complain about the adversities you face,* such as the surrounding noise, the lateness of the hour, the fact that you were deprived of some of your time to speak, or that you only had a short time to prepare. It is up to you to overcome these obstacles, not to blame them.
- *Respect your audience.* Treat them as equals. Let them understand that getting your ideas across to them is the most important task you have.

Create the Perception of Credibility

One of the reasons lawyers try so hard to sound like lawyers is that we suppose it gives us the trappings of credibility. If we know the magic words, we must know what we are talking about.

But the problem is that the rest of the world did not learn our new vocabulary with us, so sounding like a lawyer is usually a self-defeating effort. You should choose other ways to look like you know what you are talking about.

One of the best is to make sure it is true. Talk only about what you know. Whenever you try to fake it, little verbal and nonverbal clues will give you away.

Show that you have prepared for your presentation. Sharing a few bits of interesting information or using a pertinent quotation not only grabs your audience's attention, it says you have done your homework.

Use audible and visible organization. It validates what you are saying by showing that you are not simply winging it. If you announce at the beginning that you have three main points, and then call them out as you come to them, everyone will know that you have thought through what you are saying.

Of course there are lots of ways to shoot yourself in the foot (or even some more painful place). You can show you do not know the facts or do not understand the law. Even disliking the topic can be disastrous. Imagine the unhappy first-year law students at a school in Texas who lined up to complain about a teacher who announced on the first day of class that he did not enjoy Torts, did not want to teach it, and was only there because it had been assigned to him.

Have Something to Say

There was a psychology course that I always wanted to take when I was in undergraduate school, but somehow never got around to it. Early every fall, students in the class would accost people walking through the student union and ask them to participate in an experiment. They would ask you to study the contents of a cigar box for fifteen or twenty seconds. The box would have a number of ordinary objects scattered around the bottom and glued in place so they would always be in the same pattern (or lack of it).

After the time was up and the box was closed, you would be asked to recite what you had seen in the box. It was fascinating how easy it was to forget objects you had seen—even those you had consciously noted and decided you were going to remember.

But if you linked the objects together in a story, a theme, or even a fanciful chain of absurd cause and effect, then your memory was vastly improved.

The point is simple. Never make a random cigar box presentation. Even organization is not enough. You need a point of view, a story with an object, a theme. You need to have something to say.

Show—Don't Tell

If a point is worth making, it is worth illustrating.

Good examples—apt analogies—are more precious than rubies. They have the power to persuade because they make the audience think your point through for themselves. So when they reach their conclusion, it is their idea—not yours.

But just as an apt analogy is a powerful argument, so is one that turns around on you. That means you must be careful about picking your analogies. Test them out ahead of time.

Keep It Simple

The art of simplicity is not only knowing how everything fits together, but also in knowing what can safely be discarded. And this is where lawyers have trouble.

Probably our most rigorous training as lawyers is in spotting exceptions to general propositions. So as soon as we make a simple declarative sentence, we start thinking of the situations in which it does not apply. Inevitably, we start talking about those exceptions. Or even worse, we start talking about why we are not talking about the exceptions.

Stop it.

Forget the exceptions unless they are directly relevant to what you are doing. Your function is not to cover everything, but to make a focused presentation.

Make a Memory

Usually your object is not to impress your audience with what a fine speaker you are, but rather to persuade. And that means the memories you create should be vivid word pictures—sometimes even uncomfortably vivid word pictures—that will argue your case for you.

It is said that when Demosthenes spoke, people would say, "What a wonderful speaker." But when Cato spoke, the people would rise up and say, "On to Carthage!"

You want to be Cato—not Demosthenes.

Stop

When you are done, stop. Afterthoughts, recapitulations, repetitive exhortations, and the dismal trailing off by the speaker who is not certain he has finished cost more than whatever they add.

Better to leave them thinking they want more than knowing they have had too much.

CHAPTER 70

Reading Out Loud

Listening to someone read out loud is usually painful. Remember the soporific drone of the judge who read the jury instructions verbatim for more than fifty minutes? Recall how you winced in pain at hearing the president of the bar association botch the introduction of a guest speaker by reading it so poorly? And remember yesterday at the firm meeting when someone did such a bad job of reading a few announcements that you deliberately tuned out essential information?

The truth is that Americans in general are poor readers, and lawyers are no exception.

It's a shame, because we are supposed to be professionals. Reading out loud is part of what we do for a living.

Of course there are lots of times when the last thing you should do is read a script. Opening statements and closing arguments, for example, are much better delivered extemporaneously than read verbatim.

But there are times when you have no choice—you have to read. Rule 613 of the Federal Rules of Evidence may let you cross-examine a witness about a general idea behind a prior inconsistent statement, but when you confront the witness with the statement, it better be word for word. You may be able to give the gist of a stipulation to a judge, but you've got to read it to the jury. And when a key witness disappears, you cannot just summarize his deposition. You read it—or have it read.

Not surprisingly, half the problem with bad reading is bad writing. But if you think that lets you off the hook, think again. The words you read are usually the words you wrote. So write a good story—something people will enjoy listening to.

Years ago, opening statements were not permitted in Texas state courts. Instead, you read your pleadings to the jury. For the most part that meant dull, prolix bafflegab that went right past everybody.

But some Texas lawyers knew that opening statements were important. So if they were going to have to read their pleadings, then by golly, the pleadings were going to be interesting reading.

So the first point is pay attention to your writing. Everything you write should be written as if it might be read out loud. Stipulations, like the old Texas pleadings, are not written for the judge, they're written for the jury.

Second, work on reading out loud. The first part of this is exercising your voice. Actor and director Ken Albers of the Milwaukee Repertory Theater says that most people never explore the full range of their voices. "We work," says Albers, "in an incredibly narrow envelope, never stretching or working to increase our vocal abilities. People run and jog and exercise to strengthen their bodies. They do puzzles and play games to stretch their minds. But almost no one exercises his voice."

Albers does. In the shower or getting dressed or riding to work in the morning he does vocal exercises. He starts by chewing on an imaginary lump of tar, opening his mouth as far as he can, moving his jaw in a big, circular chewing motion.

Then he exercises his tongue, first sticking it out as far as he can, and then saying the tongue twister, "Red Leather, Yellow Leather, Red Leather, Yellow Leather" for a minute or two. "Go at your own pace," says Albers. "The point is to exercise your tongue and articulate the words accurately, not tie your mouth in knots."

Other tongue twisters are actually useful exercises for particular pronunciation problems. "She sells seashells by the seashore" helps develop a clear distinction between the "s" and "sh" sound. "Through darkest mists and deepest frosts he beats his fists against the posts and still insists he sees the ghosts," was part of a reading test for prospective announcers at the Duke University Radio Station. It is also a great exercise for teaching your tongue how to handle the difference between two difficult sounds in English—"st" and "sts."

Now try something suggested by Dorothy Sarnoff's *Speech Can Change Your Life* (Dell Pub. Co., 1970). Hold your nose between your thumb and forefinger so you have to breathe through your mouth. Then say, "Why do wild women want war?" Sarnoff says there are only three legitimate nasal sounds in English—*m*, *n*, and *ng*. In "Why do wild women want war?" you should not feel a nasal buzz on any of the *w* sounds—only on the *men* and *nt*.

What if you get a nasal buzz at the wrong time? Open your mouth wider, relax your jaw, and say the sentence again. Using exercises like this will help you stop talking through your nose.

If you have a serious speech pathology, consult a specialist. But the chances are you don't. On the other hand, almost everyone I know has some sort of speech problem. Most of them will yield to intelligent self-help, and Sarnoff's book is a good source for effective diagnosis and useful exercises that will attack the problem.

Well, sure, you say. Verbal exercises are fine for someone like Albers. After all, he talks for a living.

So do you.

Next, practice putting meaning into words. One good exercise is saying words so they sound like what they mean. You are probably thinking this means onomatopoeia—using words like *clang*, *snap*, or *woof* that imitate the sounds they define.

This is different. This is saying the word so that your tone of voice conveys its meaning. For example, try saying "exciting" so it sounds exciting, or "bored" so it sounds bored. Here are some words to practice on.

execution	tired	rapid
convenience	devious	persistent
pain	electric	tangle
pleasure	relax	betray

Although you can give these words some feeling, saying them one at a time, real meaning comes with context and the sense of understanding the reader gives the words. Everybody has seen the range of meaning you can get by stressing different words. Try it again by saying "She is not going," four times—emphasizing a different word each time.

Next try something you may not have done before. This time insert a pause in a different place each time you say the sentence, instead of stressing the different words. Then try both pausing and emphasizing and see the subtleties that start to emerge.

Now start reading out loud.

Reading cold—without even glancing through the text before you start—is the most difficult, but it is invaluable practice.

Abraham Lincoln's partner complained when Lincoln used to read the newspaper out loud in his law office. Lincoln said reading out loud helped him understand by letting him hear the news as well as see it. It was a good defense for someone who had really taught himself to read—and it was great practice.

Robin Weaver of Cleveland, Ohio, reads the editorial page of the *New York Times* out loud every day. "How you say it is just as important as what you say," says Weaver. "When I took ROTC in college I used to practice my 'command voice' when no one else was around. If you can't speak with authority, people won't listen to you.

"Now I read the editorial page out loud to practice reading stipulations and exhibits to the jury. You've got to know how to stress the essential words or the exhibit won't mean anything to them."

Join a play reading group. Volunteer to be a reader at church or at a civic organization. Read out loud to your children as much for you as for them. Read books out loud to your companions on automobile trips.

Reading Shakespeare out loud is great practice for reading legal materials. Shakespeare is just obscure enough so the words will just be sounds unless you understand what they mean and put that understanding into your voice.

Don't read something cold at trial if you can help it. Practice it in the office. Learn how to pronounce the words—especially medical and scientific terms—before you walk in court. If you can't prepare and have to read something cold, do it confidently. Fill it with meaning. And when you encounter a word you do not know or cannot pronounce, do not mutter, mumble, or hedge. Use your best "command voice" and fill the room with the word. The few who know the word (and were saying it differently) will think they were pronouncing it wrong.

That technique points to the biggest obstacle to good reading. Fear.

Fear of public speaking, fear of making a mistake, or fear of looking foolish lead the great majority of people to cower in the cave of mediocrity. Eyes on the floor when not buried in the book, they hide in a rushed monotone of meaningless, indistinct words. They do not want to risk putting themselves into what they are doing.

Leave the cave; it's more fun outside.

CHAPTER 71

Bilingual

"I blame the law schools," said Judge Wallop. "It's the way they approach the entire business of legal education."

"Oh, come on, Judge," I said. "You're always blaming the law schools for something. What have they done now?"

"Language," said Judge Wallop. "It's as if they are intent on preserving the biblical gift of tongues. The law schools take reasonably articulate young men and women, and in three years turn them into monsters of obscurity, who think that incomprehensibility is persuasion.

"It happened in my courtroom today," Wallop continued. "It was in an argument on a motion for a summary judgment. The defense lawyer—just out of law school last spring—sounded like a parody of a law professor. At one point he said, 'Your Honor, the defense would contend that the conduct of the plaintiff has vitiated the performance obligation of the defendant in the instant case.' I asked him what he meant, and it took five minutes of serious questioning to figure out he was saying the plaintiff was trying to get something without paying for it."

"I'm not going to defend how law schools teach legal writing and speaking," I said. "About half of what law students learn is vocabulary training. And how they learn to speak is awful. But you know where they get it? Judicial opinions."

"I'll give you that one, Jimmy," Judge Wallop said, "but the worst judicial opinion can't hold a candle to the average law-review article."

That's when Angus joined in. "The problem is," he said, "that law is a foreign language, and once lawyers learn how to speak law, they don't go back to English."

"I'm serious," Angus continued. "In one sense the law schools are too easy a target. There is some justification for learning the language of the law—you need to know the terms of art so you can wrestle with statutes, understand old opinions, and talk with some of our judges.

"But in another sense," he said, "law schools fail miserably. They know they teach people to talk like lawyers. Some of them take real pride in it. I had a teacher who would say to students, 'If you don't know the answer, at least make a sound like a lawyer....'"

"Thus," interrupted Judge Wallop, "does the serpent of obfuscation slither into the Eden of communication."

"Not bad," I said.

"Thanks," said the judge. "I've been working on it."

"My point is," said Angus, "it may not be all bad for law schools to teach law students to talk like lawyers. We couldn't make them stop if we tried—and a lot of people have tried. The law schools' sin is their failure to understand that someone who can talk law is only half-educated. Lawyers must be able to communicate their ideas to people who speak only English. If you can't translate what you know so other people can understand it, you are not a real professional. Law schools fail because they don't teach their students to be bilingual."

Beth Golden said, "I graduated from law school five years ago, and I'm still feeling the effects in the way I speak. How long does it take to wear off?"

"It doesn't wear off," said Angus. "Unless you work at it, it gets worse with age. Plain, simple language takes a lifetime of effort, but there's a lot you can do if you follow a few basic rules."

I could tell Angus was about to do one of his famous lists, so I got out my pencil. Here are my notes.

Use the Active Voice

The active voice is used by good lawyers.

Good lawyers use the active voice.

The active voice is simple and vigorous. Use it unless you have a good reason for switching to the passive voice—and sometimes you do. The passive voice lets you change things around so you can emphasize what is important. "Justice Douglas wrote the opinion in *Palmer v. Hoffman*" is in the active voice and emphasizes the author. "The opinion in *Palmer v. Hoffman* was written by Justice Douglas" is in the passive voice and focuses on the opinion.

Avoid the Conditional Mood

We would argue.

I would contend.

The plaintiff would submit.

You may think that conditional phrases are pleasant understatements that avoid the vice of dogmatism.

Not so. The conditional mood injects a tentativeness that can make any presentation sound abstract.

Then why do we use these words?

They are phrases used by law professors in class. They talk about what they would do because they are not doing it. The fascinating thing is that students mimic their teachers and continue to talk about what they "would do" even when they are actually doing it.

Avoid Pretentious Intensifiers

This is really two rules. First, be sparing with adjectives and adverbs. They often take away rather than add. "It was very hot" does not have as much punch as "it was hot."

Second, avoid pretentious terms such as "egregious," "unconscionable" and "unwarranted." These words only tell how you feel—not why. You are more persuasive if you use the facts to make your argument rather than letting your emotions do the job.

Watch Your Words

There are some words and phrases common to lawyers that cause more trouble than they are worth. Here are some to avoid.

Instant case

"Instant" is a fine word for talking about coffee or a moment in time. But when it is used as a substitute for "this" or "particular" in referring to a case, it is stultified and archaic.

In order to

An unfortunate way of saying "to."
In order to make the machine work, it is necessary to plug it in.
Plug in the machine to make it work.

Obtain

Lawyers use it to mean "apply."
In this setting, a different rule obtains. Actually "obtain" means "to have firm footing" or "to be well-established." But most people do not know that, so unless you want to sound like a 19th-century English judge, use "apply" instead.

In terms of

The phrase has a superficial interdisciplinary ring. For example, "in terms of economics" seems to suggest that some non-economics problem is going to be discussed using economics lingo, and that somehow the borrowed words will bring new understanding (a doubtful proposition). But the phrase is almost never used that way. Instead, it is used to introduce new topics: "In terms of procedure, you must be careful about the statute of limitations." In terms of writing, it is a bad phrase. Do not use it.

The process

A pretentious way to make a noun sound thoughtful. The "decision-making process" and the "election process" are examples. Avoid this construction in the writing process and the speaking process, even when you are actually concerned about the process.

Perceive and observe

"What were you able to perceive with respect to the motor vehicle in question?"
It is almost always better to use "see" or "hear" instead.

With respect to and with regard to

These phrases are best eliminated, and the rest of the sentence rearranged:

With respect to unnecessary words, they can be eliminated.
Unnecessary words can be eliminated.

In question

Where were you on the night in question?

Roughly translated, "in question" means "I cannot remember the particular facts, but I am going to refer to them anyway." Not only is it awkward, it sends an embarrassing signal that hurts your credibility.

It must be remembered

Like "it must be not be forgotten," "it must be remembered" looks like an intensifying phrase that says important information is on the way.

But that is not why lawyers use these phrases. They are actually false connectors. They imply that there is a logical relationship between what went before and what will come next.

The trouble is, that relationship is usually not there, otherwise you would say what it is. Better to admit you are changing subjects than to use an awkward phrase to pretend you are not.

Is violative of

An awkward way to say "violates."

Manifest

A pompous way to say "obvious," which you probably should not say anyway.

State whether

A stiff way to tell a witness you want some particular information. "Tell us" works a lot better.

Strike that

Supposedly this is a direction to the court reporter to strike an awkward beginning of a question from the transcript. But they do not strike it. Instead they leave what you have already said and simply write "strike that." Under the circumstances, you are probably better off saying something like "I didn't put that very well. I'm going to start that over again."

CHAPTER 72

Key Words

Angus was sitting in the Brief Bag, going over a list. Beth Golden sat down next to him.

"What are you working on, Angus?" she said.

"Actually, it's kind of a vocabulary list," Angus said.

"Good idea," Beth said. "I do that too. When I've got a case with a lot of difficult terms, or there are some names that are hard to spell, I make a list of the words and give it to the court reporter. You have no idea how they appreciate that."

"You're right," said Angus. "Helping the court reporter is a good idea. But I'm doing something different. I'm picking the key words I'm going to use in a trial I've got next month. These are my vocabulary lists for opening statement, final argument, and direct and cross-examination. These words are for me—not the court reporter."

Beth looked at Angus. "Let me see if I've got this straight," she said. "You are making a list of words to use in your opening statement before you know what you are going to say?"

"That's right," said Angus.

"You are picking words to use on direct and cross-examination before you have organized or outlined those direct and cross-examinations?" said Beth.

"You've got it," said Angus.

"And you are choosing words for your final argument before you even write your notes on how you are going to do that final argument?" said Beth.

"Exactly," said Angus.

"Angus," said Beth, "are you okay? I mean, I have an immense amount of respect for you and how you try cases, but this is not healthy. You are turning things upside down. People pick their words as they decide what to say. It is ridiculous to start with the words and then try to figure out what to do with them later."

Angus smiled. "Beth," he said, "do we agree that it is essential to have a theory of the case?"

"Of course," said Beth.

"If you are the plaintiff, you should not just come in and randomly start calling witnesses and asking questions?" he said.

"That's why you need a theory of the case," said Beth. "So you won't do that."

"And if you are the defendant, you should not just come in and start randomly trying to refute what the plaintiff says?" said Angus.

"Well, some lawyers seem to do that," said Beth, "and it is almost a guaranteed way to lose. But you're dodging the point, Angus. The subject is when you pick words—not the theory of the case."

"In a minute or two, I think you will agree they are the same topic," Angus said.

"I'm waiting," Beth said.

"Take the case I have next month as an example," Angus said. "I'm defending a building-supply company—Tri-City Lumber—that's being sued for breach of contract. The plaintiff claims we agreed to sell them more than 100,000 board feet of lumber for $750,000—and then did not deliver. They said it cost them $250,000 more to finally get the lumber they claim they ordered from us."

"Did your defendant quote them that price—$750,000?" asked Beth.

"They did," said Angus.

"And did it cost the plaintiffs $250,000 extra to get their wood?" asked Beth.

"It did," said Angus.

"It sounds like Tri-City Lumber Company is in trouble, Angus. What is their defense?"

"That the list of prices and materials we gave the plaintiff was not an invoice or a contract, but an estimate," said Angus.

"It doesn't sound very appealing so far," said Beth. "And what does it have to do with lists of words?"

"You'll see. Let's start with the plaintiff—the Willis Construction Company. What is their theory of the case?" said Angus.

"Simple," said Beth. "You guys—Tri-City Lumber—made a contract and then breached it. The result is Willis Construction Company is out a cool quarter of a million."

"Is that what you would tell the jury?" Angus asked.

"Something like that," Beth said, "working in the names and dates."

"Well," said Angus, "I hope that is what the plaintiff says, but I am afraid I can't count on it. Think about the word choices that Willis Construction has.

" 'Contract,' for example, may not be their word. To some people, contracts are things they are forced to sign to get a job or buy a car and are later used to limit their rights. Lots of people have no problem thinking about contracts, but plenty of others do. They think of a contract as a means for taking advantage of someone else. And besides, 'contract' sounds like something ordinary people can't understand.

"So look at the other words the plaintiff can use:

word	agree
promise	deal
bond	bargain

"And now look at the other words for a breach of contract:

broke their word
broke their promise
went back on their word
went back on their promise
did not do what they promised
refused to live up to their agreement
did not keep their bargain

"Of course, there are other words you can use. These are just some of the more obvious ones. They are the words—key words, impact words—that tell the theory of the plaintiff's case in human terms.

"When you start making a list of key words, you write down every likely prospect. Then refine your list. For example, you might decide that 'bargain' sounds too much like your plaintiff was saving money and should not be able to complain if he did not get a special low price."

"But that's not the law," said Beth.

"We're not talking about the law," said Angus, "but picking the words that will affect whether the jury wants you to win. 'Deal' has secondary meanings, like playing cards or selling drugs. That doesn't mean you should throw out words like 'deal' or 'bargain'—it just means you should look at all the words from every side."

"Just a second," said Beth. "I think I see your point. I've been looking at that list, and the plaintiff's opening statement jumps right off the page at me." She stood up and faced an imaginary jury. "Ladies and gentlemen," she said, "this is a case about a promise. . . ."

Angus interrupted. "Wait one more minute," he said. "Why do we enforce contracts in the first place? What words come to mind?"

"My contracts teacher said something about predictability and the orderly flow of commerce," said Beth.

"Good grief," said Angus. "He might as well have been talking about the commerce clause in the United States Constitution. Did he say anything about the 'reliance interest'?"

"Maybe a little," said Beth. "It was pretty abstract."

"Well, how about these words," said Angus. "Are they too abstract?"

believe	count on
trust	took them at their word
rely	

"Angus," said Beth, "this is marvelous. When you think about the story with those words, it seems compelling."

"Notice," said Angus, "that we have picked nouns and verbs. Adjectives and adverbs are dangerous. Words of characterization get in the way of good advocacy. They give the judge and jury your opinion—not the facts."

"Now for a little of my side of the case," said Angus. "The defense has the disadvantage of going second. So I am going to start out telling the jury that the most unfair thing anyone could do to them would be to ask them to decide the case with only half the facts. And since the plaintiff's lawyer was selective in what he told them, it is up to me to give them the rest of the story.

"Then as soon as I have done what I can to humanize the people at Tri-City Lumber, I am going to paint the picture of how Willis turned down the opportunity to enter into a contract.

"As a matter of fact, when Maxwell Jason—he's Tri-City's sales manager—gave Mr. Willis the twenty-page estimate for the cost of the lumber, he asked, 'Do we have a deal?'

"I like that because Willis said, 'I'll have to get back to you on that.' Of course, Max Jason had heard that one before. Max told Mr. Willis that the price of lumber was going up, and he should at least make a deposit if he wanted to lock in the price, but Willis didn't want to do that.

"There's more, but that gives you an idea of what our case is like.

I am going to use words like:

offered to help	prices going up
estimate	warned
bid	said would work with
asked for order	wanted to do business with
asked for deposit	asked them to call
was turned down	Willis left to look for lower prices
was refused	

"Once you start thinking about key words for the opening statement, it leads naturally to picking words for examining witnesses. If you wanted to portray an expert witness as a teacher, for instance, you might use:

teach	demonstrate
tell	explain
show	educate us

"You could even give the witness a piece of chalk and ask him to show us something on the board," Angus said, "which is a lot better than 'Would you indicate for the benefit of the jury what determination you were able to reach on that occasion?'"

Beth said, "I think I've got it."

Angus smiled.

CHAPTER 73

Bad Words

Angus was at the law school critiquing students in my Trial Tactics class when he stopped a young woman right in the middle of her direct examination.

"The problem," said Angus, "is your language. You are using too many bad words."

The student was shocked. "Is there something wrong with me? I honestly don't remember using any word that could be remotely offensive to anyone."

Angus smiled. "I don't mean dirty words or naughty words. I mean bad words—words that get in the way, words that refuse to do their work, or, even worse, words that create serious problems right in the middle of trial.

"Of course you already know that stuffy lawyer words and phrases like 'indicate,' 'with respect to,' and 'directing your attention to' are poor communicators. They mainly say you are a lawyer, which is not the most important message to send.

"But there are other words that may look and sound harmless but that can do a lot of damage," Angus said.

I already had my pen and legal pad for taking notes for critiquing the students, so I was writing before Angus even started his list. Here are my notes.

Story

Never talk about your side of the case or your witnesses' testimony as a story. In the minds of the jury, a story is made up, concocted, untrue. So normally, "story" is a word you reserve for when you are talking about the other side's case. Even then you probably ought to save it for opening statement or final argument. When you use "story" in your questions on cross-examination, you are likely to draw an objection to your characterization of the testimony as a story.

You may think that using the word "story" on cross-examination is worth the price of a sustained objection. Maybe so. But you can get the idea across with the unobjectionable word, "say."

Like this: Q. You say you used heroin, but you've never actually sold it?

Recall, Remember

There is a seductive quality to recollection that lures even the best trial lawyers into using "recall" or "remember," even though it is almost always a mistake.

The logic seems impeccable. If a witness cannot remember an event, then he obviously cannot testify to it. So lawyers habitually ask witnesses whether they remember a time, a place, or an event before they ask questions about it.

Mistake.

Asking a witness whether he remembers risks a comment on how facts are starting to fade—even on direct examination and even from the best witnesses.

On cross-examination it is even worse. Asking a witness whether he remembers is an invitation to forget. It legitimizes letting facts disappear down the memory hole (as George Orwell put it). Asking a witness whether he remembers makes it all right to forget.

(That, by the way, is why it is improper witness coaching for the opposing lawyer to insert "Objection—if he remembers" after the question and before the answer during a deposition. It instructs the witness to forget.)

So forget about asking the witness whether he remembers something unless you know he will say it was one of those awful events that is burned in his mind forever.

Stipulation

A stipulation is a wonderful thing. It takes things out of the dispute. For the stipulated facts, the battle is over.

But the jury does not know that unless someone tells them. For the average juror, "stipulation" sounds more like a technique for texturing a ceiling with thick paint than agreeing that certain facts should be accepted as true.

Since it is your stipulation, write it the way you want—so it is understandable. Instead of "stipulates," use "admits" or "agrees."

Again

Repetition and emphasis are at the heart of good teaching. And since you are using a witness to teach the jury the facts of your case, repetition, recapitulation, summarizing, and restating are essential to good direct and cross-examination.

They are also at the ragged edge of permissible questioning.

But as long as each question and answer adds something new to the case, you will probably stay out of trouble.

Not if you use the word "again." Like an electric prod to a sleepy steer, "again" will galvanize your opponent into action.

> Q. And again, how much did you pay for the radio?
> Defense: Objection, Your Honor, asked and answered.
> The Court: Sustained.

Exactly, Precisely

Asking good follow-up questions takes some finesse.

Done well, the jury almost thinks they are asking the questions themselves, since you are picking up on the points that had interested them, and are setting to rest the little snags they had found troubling.

But some lawyers cannot resist the language of exactitude when they actually want generalities.

> Q. Just exactly what is involved in "laser verified topographical analysis"?

Fortunately, many witnesses do not say exactly what is involved. Instead, they treat the question as an invitation for a few additional details.

But other witnesses are more literal. And then everyone suffers through the pain of an accurate answer to an imprudent question.

It is like the legendary fifth-grade book report: "This book told me more about penguins than I wanted to know." The lesson is simple. Do not ask for precision unless you really want it.

Why

Everyone knows that "why" is a bad question to ask on cross-examination. It invites arguments and explanations that you really do not want. Knowing this, some lawyers ask "why" on cross-examination only when they are certain the witness can have no credible answer.

When they hear the answer, their education is swift, expensive, and humiliating. So more experienced lawyers save "why" for direct examination.

But "why" can cause trouble even on direct. It is perfect for getting the reasons for what the witness did. "Why did you call?" "Why didn't you stop?" "Why did you pay for work they didn't do?" are all fine questions.

But when you use "why" to ask the witness about someone else's conduct, it is usually improper. You are either asking the witness for hearsay, or asking him to speculate about someone else's thought processes. Either way, you are asking for trouble.

The interesting point is that this kind of "why" trouble is often easy to avoid. If you set up your direct examination properly, cause and effect is implied by the very organization:

> Q. What did Morales do then?
> A. He took off his coat and dropped into a boxer's crouch.
> Q. What did Homer Johnson do?
> A. He reached into his pocket and pulled out a knife.

Do You Think You Might Be Able to Give Us Some Idea . . . ?
Are You Able to Give an Approximation of . . . ?

Witnesses take their cues from the questioner. Ask a witness a question:

> Q. Can you give us an idea of how fast the car might have been going?

See the kind of answer you get:

> A. I guess it might have been going in the neighborhood of maybe 30 to 35 miles per hour.

Now put it differently:

> Q. How fast was the car going?
> A. 35 miles per hour.

The point is simple. If you want a tentative answer, ask a tentative question.

"You Didn't Understand My Question"

Even at its finest, human communication is filled with miscues and misunderstandings. In the artificial atmosphere of a trial, loaded with verbal oddities and arcane circumlocutions, it is a wonder that we do not have far more times when a witness simply does not know what we want.

We are in control of how we put our questions. But when the question is not understood and the witness starts giving the wrong information, whom do we blame?

The witness.

That is a serious mistake that has unfortunate fallout. First, the jury senses that you are the sort of person who always points the finger at someone else, whether it is justified or not. And that does a lot of subtle damage to your credibility with the jury.

Second, it destroys your rapport with the witness. Instead of cooperation, even your own witnesses are hurt, puzzled, confused. Instead of warm and engaging explanations, you get cold and abrupt answers with baleful looks from the witness stand.

When the witness does not understand your question, blame yourself, not the witness.

> Q. I'm sorry, I didn't put that question very well; let me restate it for you.

"I Only Have One More Question"

The promise that you are about to finish is made in the hope that it will buy you a few more minutes of attention. But it doesn't work that way because the jury never agreed to the bargain. What it really does is guarantee an end to their attention when you break your promise and keep on asking questions for another fifteen minutes or half an hour.

If you never make the promise, you will never break it. If you keep your direct and cross-examinations short, you will never be tempted to make the promise in the first place.

CHAPTER 74

Hollow Words

The first time Mike Pirelli tried his final argument, he said:

"Manifestly, ladies and gentlemen, this is an egregious example of a contumacious disregard for the safety of another person. This is more than negligence. This is more than carelessness. This is deliberate, willful misconduct—calculated to inflict harm. And the tragic truth is, it worked.

"Brewster Morris intentionally set about a course of action designed to injure Marty Drewek. It was a pernicious plan born in the malignancy of a twisted heart. Devastating physical injury was the object of Brewster Morris's conduct, and it succeeded."

"Wait a minute, Mike," said Angus, who was critiquing Pirelli's argument. "I hate to interrupt, but I have a question. Did you memorize this?"

"Why?" said Mike.

"Because it sounds like it," said Angus.

"I'm sorry, Angus," said Mike, "but I can't help it. I can't just talk off the top of my head like you do. I need a script. And since I didn't want the jury to see me reading, I memorized it."

"Mike," said Angus, "I am not as concerned that you memorized your closing argument as I am with how you wrote it."

"What do you mean?" said Mike.

"No question," said Angus, "but memorizing an opening or a closing can make it sound stiff and awkward. But the biggest problem is that when you memorize it, you teach yourself to recite—verbatim—something you wrote."

"I think that fits the definition of memorizing," said Mike.

Angus looked at Mike, but went on. "And unless you are a consummate script writer for stage or television, what you write will never sound like normal spoken language—no matter how well you recite it. The words are all wrong. They sound hollow, empty, out of place. The point is, words like 'manifestly,' 'contumacious,' 'pernicious,' and 'malignancy of a twisted heart' don't sound right in final argument. They are words you wouldn't use in normal conversation. And that means you also ought to avoid them in writing—especially when you intend to read what you write."

Angus is right. Writing any kind of speech—whether it is an opening statement, closing argument, or an argument on a motion—is dangerous. No matter how well you read your script, it will not sound natural.

Part of it is because reading out loud is extremely difficult, no matter how well the material is written. And part of it is because written English is different from spoken English—no matter how formal the occasion. When you write, word choice is different, sentence structure is different, organization is different, and emphasis is different.

And that is just the beginning. Another reason for hollow words is our tendency to puff.

Listen to Mike Pirelli's closing argument again. It sounds overblown, even though we have no idea what Brewster Morris did to Marty Drewek. Stringing all those adjectives together does not show us what Brewster Morris did—it tells us how Mike Pirelli feels about it. And unless you can see that Pirelli has a good reason for feeling so strongly, his words are bound to make you a little uncomfortable.

That explains why modifiers—adjectives and adverbs—are dangerous. They are the speaker's (or writer's) characterization of what happened—not the facts themselves. You are generally a lot better off having the facts argue for you and letting the jury pick their own adjectives than you are telling the jury how to feel.

Now see how some of Pirelli's words stick out. Does the average juror even know what "egregious" or "contumacious" means? And look at how alliteration can backfire. Say "pernicious plan" and "tragic truth" out loud and they will sound studied and contrived.

If you are already convinced that you don't want to mimic Mike Pirelli, you need to know how to avoid it.

First, you've got to stop talking like a lawyer. Of course there are terms of art that you have to use in some settings. But there are hundreds of words that lawyers use in preference to plain talk that have nothing to do with legal precision.

Carolyn Dickson of Voice-Pro, Inc., in Cleveland says lawyers confuse laypeople with awkward word choices all the time.

We Say:	*We Mean:*
relate	tell
indicate	point out or tell
previously	before
facilitate	make it easier

William Pannill of Houston says our briefs are larded with all kinds of unhappy words and phrases. In one brief he found:

absent (meaning "without")
assuming *arguendo*
clearly erroneous
dispositive of the issue
extraordinarily
fatally flawed
impacted the result
meretricious
methodology
notwithstanding the fact that
null, void, and of no effect
overinclusive and underinclusive
presumptuous
suspension of disbelief
vel non

Of course, all of us have words or phrases we hate that other lawyers seem to use all the time.

Eric Zagrans of Cleveland thinks we have actually worn out "oxymoron." He predicts something even more pretentious, like "jejune abstraction," will become the fad term of the '90s. I hope he is wrong.

Jacob Stein of Washington, D.C., wants courts to stop using "scintilla" and "progeny," but does not hold out much hope. Stein sometimes watches the Supreme Court launch fad words. Years ago, when the Court talked about "chilling" First Amendment rights, suddenly there was a lot of "chilling" going around in judicial opinions. Stein says "resonates" is one of the new judicial words, and a lot of recent opinions are busy "resonating" one idea or another.

Douglas Connah of Baltimore is tired of "the gravamen of the situation" and "clear beyond peradventure." He would also like to stop hearing plaintiff's lawyers tell juries to "send the defendant a message"—not only because it is a cliché, but also because it still seems to work.

Of course there are thousands of judicial opinions that read as if they were written by 18th-century English judges. And there are hundreds of opinions that qualify for awards for obscurity and imprecision. But it is distressing that words and phrases like "eminently clear," "not susceptible of any facile solution," "no sharp demarcation," "the instant case," "pellucid," and "a mere gossamer" are so commonplace they escape attention.

The second thing you need to do to escape Mike Pirelli's affliction is to understand why lawyers sometimes puff their cases. Paul Bardacke of Albuquerque, New Mexico, says it is because lawyers try to make their clients happy rather than try to win the case.

"What the client wants to hear is overstated and overblown," says Bardacke. "When you are outraged at what the other side did, you wave your arms and storm around the courtroom. Your client hugs you and says it is the best argument he ever heard—and then you lose. When you are filled with too much outrage, the jury does not need to get outraged, too."

Bardacke is right. Let the facts do the work—not your advanced vocabulary. When you characterize what the parties did, you are trying to sell the jury your emotional reaction to the case. But when you tell the story in simple words, the jury can develop their own outrage at what the other side did.

And now back to Mike Pirelli. Part of his problem is that he memorized his final argument. He is sure he needs the security of a written script that he has down word for word.

Mike is making two mistakes. First, he writes down every word. Lots of people do that. They feel compelled. They would never dream of giving even the simplest oral presentation any other way.

Second, Mike memorizes what he writes.

Is there any cure for this compulsion?

Absolutely. I have tried it with hundreds of students and lawyers, and it works. Go ahead and write out your argument. But do not memorize it. Instead, write an outline from the script, listing every major point in your argument and write down some key words for each point.

Then use the outline for your presentation—but take your complete script with you up to the lectern, just in case you freeze and have to start reading.

It's a good system for a number of reasons. First, memorizing almost always fails anyway. When it does, you are better off having your script right there.

Second, the outline will do a beautiful job of leading you through your talk. And if you should suddenly forget what one of the points in your outline means, you just turn to your script and start reading.

Third, you will learn that the minor omissions and grammatical errors you will make with the outline (and even lapses of memory) are better than sounding hollow and insincere when you read. The outline does a better job than the script.

Gradually you will learn to use just the outline, and you will stop even writing the script. Just like Angus.

CHAPTER 75

The Real Message

Angus was out at the law school, speaking at a continuing legal education program, when he made an observation that I wish had been mine.

"The biggest single difficulty you face as persuasive speakers," he said, "is something we all share: the burden of a legal education. Whether your law school meant to or not, it taught you to sound like a lawyer."

That drew some laughter, but the idea really wasn't new. Jim Jeans from the University of Missouri at Kansas City has been saying something like that for years. But Angus went on.

"There are two unspoken messages that are the most powerful part of any legal education. The first comes from the casebook, virtually any casebook. Whether it deals with property or torts, contracts or crimes, income tax or conflicts of law, every casebook sends the same message. It says, 'See the cases in this book? That's how you should write.'

"The second message comes from the classroom," Angus continued. "It says, 'Do you hear your law professor? Listen to those obscure and difficult words. That's how you should talk.'"

That simple idea hit home. In a flush of embarrassment, I realized that I was part of the problem. Nearly every law school casebook is loaded with poorly written decisions that read as if they were deliberate parodies of stuffy nineteenth-century English judges. The very fact that the cases are in the book sends the subliminal message that this is good stuff.

It's not.

But by having them buy and read a collection of hundreds of poorly written decisions, I was contributing to my students' miseducation. I was wondering if there was anything I could do about it even as Angus continued.

"The combined product of both book and class is dismal," he said. "Lawyers ask questions like, 'With respect to the occasion in question, what, if anything, did you do in response?' and they make arguments like, 'In contradistinction to the assertion of our opponents, we would contend that it was not unreasonable to rely on the representations of the petitioner.'

"The real message of law school helps produce men and women who don't communicate well with ordinary people," Angus said. "And if that's all there were to it, it would be bad enough.

"But there's more.

"People have preconceptions about all kinds of different groups—doctors, lawyers, police officers, accountants, computer programmers, teachers, bankers, painters, movie stars, and machinists. Sometimes those preconceptions are positive, sometimes they are negative, sometimes they are mixed.

"And it's wrong to think that an individual has just one preconception—one picture—for each group.

"Take lawyers," said Angus. "Lots of people picture lawyers as pettifogging mouthpieces whose life's work is to play verbal shell games that make wrong seem right. But those same people may also have another picture. This one is the loyal advocate who refuses to cave in to all kinds of official pressure. This is the champion who confronts injustice and who finally finds the facts that show his client is innocent.

"Now remember," said Angus, "what the jury is doing while you're asking questions during jury selection. While you're picking a jury, they're picking a lawyer—a guide they can trust who will lead them through the thicket of the case.

"Which picture do you light up when you start asking questions?" said Angus. "The answer is uncomfortable. The language of the typical American law school graduate pushes the 'pettifogging mouthpiece' button. The real message is 'Here's someone who talks bafflegab. You'd better be on guard.' "

There's a lot to what Angus says. There are all kinds of situations in which what we do, what we say, or how we say it can send the wrong message.

Will you follow the law?

Most people take jury duty very seriously. In fact, in a nationwide survey, Jeanne J. Fleming and Leonard C. Schwarz of Metricus Inc., a jury research organization in Palo Alto, California, found that 60 percent of all potential jurors view a trial as a "moral arena," in which it is more important to do the right thing than the legally correct thing.

That attitude is the vantage point from which to look at a series of jury selection questions that thousands of lawyers ask every day:

> Q. Now, Mrs. Clayton, you understand that Judge Mudrock is going to instruct the jury on the law that you are to apply at the end of the case?
> A. Well, yes.
> Q. And if you are selected to serve on this jury, will you follow Judge Mudrock's instructions?
> A. Of course.
> Q. Even if you don't personally agree with the instructions, or would write them a different way if you were the judge, or if it were up to you to make the law?
> A. Yes.
> Q. You would do what the judge says even if you don't agree with it?
> A. Yes.

Some lawyers like to use this line of questioning when they think the instructions are really going to help their case. They suppose that they are getting a "commitment" from the juror that will lock her into voting their way.

But to the juror who believes in the "moral arena," the message is a little different:

"You're not going to like our case. About the only way you could find in our favor would be to follow some legal rules that you will probably find personally repugnant."

Lawyers call it an opening statement

Once again we start with good intentions. We know the jury is looking for a guide, so we decide to give them a tour—not of the facts, but of the courtroom. So immediately after we are introduced by the judge and the jury is told we are about to give an opening statement, we stand up, give our name, and say, "Ladies and gentlemen, this is what we lawyers call an opening statement."

What could be wrong with that?

First, it's not as if "opening statement" is an arcane legalism that requires detailed translation. Second, the superficial message is hardly needed, especially since the judge just told the jury this was going to be an opening statement.

But the real message is a disaster: "There's a gulf between us, folks. I'm a lawyer making big bucks to try cases like this, while you poor schleps are probably happy to be getting $12 a day for jury duty."

Objection, Your Honor!

Every time you make an objection, it makes a withdrawal from the slim credibility account you have with the jury. Bench conferences are even worse. Juries hate them because they are picking up on the real message: "This is something I really don't want you to hear."

Leading on direct examination

Any witness—even the best—can forget something or have a temporary lapse and need reminding. That's why the common law developed a wide range of techniques for dealing with the problem—including leading questions, refreshing recollection, and past recollection recorded.

But some lawyers continually lead witnesses on direct examination when they don't need to. And wise opponents object just often enough to call the jury's attention to the real message of leading on direct: "This witness doesn't know what he's talking about. He constantly needs to be told what to say."

Not leading on cross-examination

You are cross-examining a doctor, and you know exactly what his answer will be. If he deviates one syllable from what he said in his deposition, you can nail him to the wall. Besides, you need his answer to help develop your case. So instead of asking a leading question, you say:

Q. Dr. Wharton, would you please explain to the jury what is meant by the medical term "myocardial infarction."

A. Certainly. It's what people often call a "heart attack," but it's really a more precise term. It means some heart tissue has died. If a heart attack actually kills some of the heart and leaves scar tissue, it is a myocardial infarction.

Good explanation?

Just what you wanted.

But notice what an opportunity for the doctor to make a good impression. What was the real message sent by your question?

"You want good medical testimony? Ask Dr. Wharton—I do."

Good morning, Ms. Johnson

Some lawyers like to start out cross-examination with a friendly facade:

Q. Good morning, Ms. Johnson. How are you this morning?
A. I'm fine.
Q. Good. You and I have met before, haven't we?
A. Yes.
Q. At lawyer Carter's office, when we took your deposition?
A. Yes.
Q. And now I am going to ask a few questions to clear up a few things from direct examination, okay?
A. Okay.

The superficial message seems pleasant: "You don't need to worry about me—I'm more gentle than Mr. Rogers."

But after an hour or two of grueling questions and impeachment, the real message comes through: "Don't trust my cheery words. I was only stringing her along. I'll say anything if it will help me win this case."

It's not for its truth

It is one of the badges of the initiate—understanding that hearsay is "an out-of-court statement that is offered to prove the truth of the matter asserted."

And every lawyer who learned the magic definition of hearsay also learned the antidote. It's what you say every time you claim an out-of-court statement is not hearsay: "We're not offering this for its truth, Your Honor."

The real message is in the response that some lawyers give: "If it's not true, Your Honor, then what good is it?"

David Malone of Washington, D.C., has a way to avoid the problem: Instead of saying what the evidence is *not* offered to prove, tell the judge what the evidence *is* offered to prove, such as, "This proves the plaintiff knew the price was going up," or "This is part of the agreement, Your Honor. It shows there was a contract."

When Angus finished his talk, I thought about the real message of casebooks again and decided to do something about it. It would be impossible to grapple with all the stilted, awkward judicial language in even one casebook. The students would lose sight of why they were reading it in the first place.

But suppose I had them edit one of the more poorly written cases in the book, or even rewrite it completely. Then the message would be that the stuff they were reading was not all gold.

PART TEN

Final Argument

Final argument is the advocate's art. It is no time for idle recapitulation of the testimony—the jury has already heard it. Instead, there are problems to be solved, and every trial has its share. Final argument is the advocate's opportunity to attack those problems with grace and conviction.

CHAPTER 76
Peck

CHAPTER 77
The Cat and the Mouse

CHAPTER 78
The Greased Pig

CHAPTER 79
Jumping to Conclusions

CHAPTER 80
The Trial of Henry Sweet

CHAPTER 76

Peck

Come with me—back in time—to Chicago in the 1930s. I want you to see a lawyer at work: Weymouth Kirkland of Kirkland & Ellis. You are going to watch him argue for the defendant—the insurance company in a life-insurance case.

Some lawyers' arguments are memorable because they win big verdicts. Others are remembered for their emotional impact or the social significance of the case. Weymouth Kirkland's argument in the *Peck* case is memorable because it teaches a great lesson in advocacy. It is recorded in Lloyd Paul Stryker's *The Art of Advocacy* (1954), and it is still told in litigation circles in Chicago, more than fifty years after the trial. This version draws on both the oral and the written accounts.

Peck was a sailor, a deckhand on a boat in Lake Michigan. (People who live near the Great Lakes already know that big vessels that would be called "ships" on the ocean are just "boats" on the Great Lakes.) Peck's career as a sailor was undistinguished and so was his personal life. He had no family, no wife, no children, no brothers or sisters.

But he had a life-insurance policy. And the beneficiaries were other sailors—friends of Peck's from other boats. And although it was the Depression, Peck paid the premiums promptly during the few months he had the policy.

Then Peck was suddenly and unaccountably lost overboard from the boat on which he had shipped.

Peck's friends came forward, life-insurance policy in hand. "See here," they said. "Peck was lost at sea. Here is the policy on his life. We are the beneficiaries under the policy. Pay up."

The insurance company, however, thought the sailors' claim had a bad odor to it. "We don't think Peck was lost overboard at all," they said. "Prove your case."

So there the plaintiffs' lawyer was, with a handful of claimants, a case that was thin on liability, and that just didn't have the emotional appeal it would have if Peck had left a widow and two hungry children.

It was the kind of claim that used to be called a dog case because you could hear it bark whenever you even picked up the file.

What do you do when you have a dog case—when you need to dress up your proof to make it more attractive?

The plaintiffs' lawyer did the same thing lawyers have always done with dog cases.

He called an expert witness.

The witness was an oceanographer and meteorologist from a local university who testified at great length about the intricate winds and currents on Lake Michigan. His theory was that if Peck fell overboard when the plaintiffs said he did, Peck's body would have floated to a precise spot in Lake Michigan at an exact moment in time.

Then came the plaintiffs' star eyewitness. He was a cook from another boat on Lake Michigan. He was down in the galley, fixing dinner—peeling potatoes—when he just happened to look out the porthole at the right moment.

There was Peck, floating by.

Then it was time for Weymouth Kirkland to cross-examine the cook. It was a job well done:

Q. You were an old friend of Peck's?
A. Yes.
Q. Known him for years?
A. Yes.
Q. Gone out drinking with him?
A. Well, yes.
Q. And playing cards?
A. Yes.

Q. So there was no doubt in your mind when you saw that body floating by in Lake Michigan. It was Peck?
A. That's right.
Q. What were you doing when you just happened to look out the porthole and saw Peck?
A. Why, I was in the galley, fixing dinner.
Q. What part of dinner were you fixing?
A. Well, I was . . . let me see . . . I was peeling potatoes. That's right, I was peeling potatoes.
Q. I see. You were down in the galley, peeling potatoes, when you just happened to look out the porthole and there was Peck?
A. That's right.
Q. Did you tell your captain about seeing Peck?
A. I certainly did.
Q. Would you tell the ladies and gentlemen of the jury when you told the captain you saw Peck?
A. Ah . . . well . . . it was the next day.

The significance of that answer was not lost on the Chicago jury.

By the next day the boat would be in port. The cook would have plenty of opportunity to talk to Peck's other friends to concoct a story about seeing Peck floating in Lake Michigan.

It was a small point, but it was about all that Weymouth Kirkland had. Look at the situation for a minute. While the plaintiffs' case was thin, what else were they supposed to have? There was a policy on Peck's life and the premiums were paid. Peck was missing off his boat. An expert witness said where Peck's body should have turned up, and an eyewitness saw him there.

While there was no great emotional strength to the plaintiffs' case, the defendant's case was even worse. This was an action against an insurance company. It was in the middle of the Depression. And the insurance company were people who made a living off other people by taking premiums from ordinary folks like factory workers and deckhands. But when it came time to pay, they tried to dodge their obligation by forcing the claimants to go to court to get their money.

How would Weymouth Kirkland argue the cook's credibility? It would make all the difference.

Most lawyers would make a point of telling the jury what to think. It is a task that can be done any number of ways. Take, for example, the intellectual approach—as it might be done by a law professor:

"Ladies and gentlemen of the jury, surely you cannot credit the testimony of the cook. It is palpably false in every material respect. Why, it simply staggers the imagination to assume that one might see the body of a deceased friend floating in the lake and then not render a prompt hue and cry."

If you do not like that argument, I do not blame you. Maybe it was too intellectual. So we will try it again, this time with more fire.

"Did you hear that cook, lying like a dog? His lips are blistered with perjury—you can't believe a word he says. What an awful insult to your intelligence to come in here and expect you to swallow that line of poppycock and balderdash."

That's even worse, isn't it?

But the biggest problem with both of those arguments was not their tone (which was surely bad enough), but their object. Those arguments *told* the jury what to think.

That is not what Kirkland did. He *showed* the jury what to think.

When it was his turn to talk, Kirkland put a trash can in front of the jury. Then he got a chair and put it next to the can. Then he took a potato out of one coat pocket and a peeler out of the other. He put one foot up on the chair, and in the middle of final argument, Weymouth Kirkland started peeling a potato and whistling a tune.

Then he looked out of an imaginary porthole and said, "What ho! What do we have here? Why, if it isn't my old friend, Peck!

"I've got to tell the captain about that tomorrow. Meantime I will keep on peeling my potatoes."

The jury laughed and the case was over, but the lesson of Peck continues. It was not just a bit of clever argument done by a bright Chicago lawyer. It demonstrates the difference between showing and telling.

Telling pushes your idea on the jury.

Showing makes the jury come up with their own idea. And people like their own ideas.

The lesson of Peck is what is behind demonstrative evidence. It is the reason why verbal pictures on opening statement are persuasive. It is why a good direct examination paints pictures in the jurors' minds. It is why an effective cross-examination makes a lasting impression. It is the power behind analogies in final argument.

Good teaching is not jamming things down people's throats—it is helping them see for themselves. Good advocacy is good teaching.

CHAPTER 77

The Cat and the Mouse

The young lawyer was right in the middle of final argument when he had one of those awful moments of self-awareness, and wondered if he would be able to finish what he was saying. Everything had been going along just fine when all of a sudden he felt the rush of blood to his face and became exquisitely aware that he was standing in front of the jury, talking to them, and that they were listening to what he had to say.

That is when he started listening to his own words. He knew they made sense, but he worried that they might actually be hurting the case instead of helping it.

The young lawyer was right to be concerned. He was representing the defendant in a criminal case, and he was suddenly caught in the Venus flytrap of the law—proof beyond a reasonable doubt. You can look at it, you can circle it, you can describe it, you can crawl all over the outside of it. But once you settle on it and rely on it for your defense, if you are not careful, it can eat you alive.

Wait a minute, you say. Proof beyond a reasonable doubt is a heavy burden that the prosecution has to bear throughout the entire case. It is designed to protect the defendant, to guard against the possibility of the innocent being convicted. How can it be a trap for the defense?

The answer lies in the role of lawyers and the logic of argument.

Whenever you represent a client—whether it is in a civil or a criminal case—you are literally standing up for that person. It is strictly forbidden to say it out loud, but your very presence says, "I have investigated this case. I know the facts and I understand how they relate to the law. You can take my word for it; justice is on my client's side."

Jurors understand the implication of your presence, even if they do not know that it would violate both the law and the code of professional responsibility for you to voice your personal belief in the justice of your client's cause. (*See State v. Miller*, 157 S.E.2d 335 (N.C. 1967); *ABA Code of Professional Responsibility* EC 7–24). Jurors are also suspicious of lawyers; they feel that what we say and do does not represent all that we know about the case.

So instinctively they watch us to see what our unconscious conduct reveals. And because of that, it is a terrible mistake to send the signal that you actually think your client is guilty.

How might you do that?

One way is to depend too heavily on the burden of proof. To see how this works, step outside of the law for just a minute. Go to a school yard and see if you can take sides in an argument just on the basis of what two young boys are saying to each other. There are two cases. In each one the dispute is the same. One boy says the other has his baseball glove. The only difference is in how the accused responds.

Case one:
"That's my baseball glove."
"No, it's not. Yours has a broken lace."

What do you have? A factual dispute. If you can choose between the two just on what they said, you either have an unusual gift, or you are prone to jumping to conclusions. You need more than these words just to lean one way or the other in this case, much less take sides. But consider case two:

"That's my baseball glove."
"Oh, yeah? Prove it."

If you are as fairminded as you would like to be, you will want to have more evidence in this case, too. But if you are suspicious of the one who says, "Prove it," that may color the way you look at the whole case. The words are not exactly an admission, but they have a strangely guilty ring.

Now we are ready to go back to the law. When you tell the jury that there is a "heavy burden protecting the defendant, and he is presumed to be not guilty unless and until he is proven guilty beyond a reasonable doubt," there is the risk that the jury may translate what you say into a concession that "Maybe the defendant *is* guilty, but the prosecution hasn't proved it well enough."

Like case two, talking about the heavy burden can seem almost like an admission, but why?

Proof beyond a reasonable doubt really creates three different categories:

We are certain he is guilty.
We do not know.
We are certain he is innocent.

The law makes the middle ground—we do not know—a buffer. It gives the defendant the benefit of the doubt. But telling the jury to give the defendant that benefit of the doubt implies he needs its protection—and that suggests he might well be guilty. So if the jury is listening carefully to see if you will give some sign of what you secretly know, the argument that the case is not proven may sound like you are admitting the possibility of guilt and hiding behind a technicality.

Does that mean you should not argue reasonable doubt when you are for the defense?

Hardly. But it does suggest that if you have facts of your own to prove, emphasizing them may be more effective than being too defensive. It also suggests that you ought to be careful in how you present your argument on reasonable doubt.

There are lots of ways to talk about the burden of proof without admitting the possibility of guilt, but you have to think them through before you use them. You cannot simply tell the jury not to take your argument the wrong way. Here is an argument worth think about. It was used by Peter de Manio of Sarasota, Florida, in a demonstration at the National Institute for Trial Advocacy. Remember that de Manio is for the defense, because his introduction may surprise you.

"Is it possible for the government to prove guilt beyond a reasonable doubt, just on circumstantial evidence, without any eyewitness testimony?

"Of course. Take a simple example. Suppose that you take a mouse and put him in a box. Now take a cat and put him in the box with the mouse. Then take the lid and cover the box. Now tie up the box with a string so the lid can't come off.

"Leave the room for half an hour. When you come back, untie the string, take off the lid, and look inside. There is no mouse, but there is one happy cat.

"Do you *know* what happened? You weren't there, there are no eyewitnesses. All you have is circumstantial evidence. But you *know* beyond any reasonable doubt what happened to that mouse.

"Let's do that again. Put the mouse in the box. Put the cat in the box with the mouse. Put on the lid. Tie it down. Leave the room for half an hour. Come back into the room. Untie the string. Take off the lid, look inside.

"There is the cat. No mouse.

"But look—back there in the corner of the box. There is a hole, just mouse size.

"That hole is a reasonable doubt. Now let's look at the holes in the prosecution's case."

Then by implication, every problem in the government's case is not just a hole, it is a reasonable doubt.

Another nice thing about this argument is the way that it draws on our subliminal values. From the first Mickey Mouse production to the Mighty Mouse cartoons at the neighborhood theater to the Tom and Jerry reruns on Saturday morning television, we have been rooting for the mouse—which is just what Peter de Manio wants us to do.

CHAPTER 78

The Greased Pig

It was not working. The problem was that the witness had a lot more trial experience than the lawyer, and it showed. Not that the lawyer was doing anything wrong. Far from it.

His technique was nearly perfect. He was conducting cross-examination, and he was following all the rules. He was asking short, leading questions. He was asking for facts, not opinions. He was taking one point at a time. But his cross-examination was not working.

After what seemed to him like an entire day (but what really was just an hour and half) the lawyer sat down, cursing the memory of that great believer in cross-examination, John Henry Wigmore. It was Wigmore who said cross-examination was "beyond any doubt the greatest legal engine ever invented for the discovery of truth."

And it was Wigmore who said that "cross-examination, not trial by jury, is the great and permanent contribution of the Anglo-American system of law to improved methods of trial procedure." Maybe so, thought the lawyer, but it sure wasn't working this time.

One way to stay out of trouble on cross-examination is to avoid it. There are witnesses who should not be cross-examined. If the witness has not hurt your case and there is nothing affirmative to be gained from cross-examination, leave him alone.

But avoidance has its dangers. It can create the impression that you approve of the witness or what he represents. So there are things you can do besides attacking the witness or the testimony he gave on direct examination.

You can do a constructive cross-examination. The idea is to make the witness your own on some point where you know he will support your case. The doctor who says that the plaintiff's injury was congenital and not caused by the defendant's conduct may still admit that the plaintiff has a debilitating condition.

The eyewitness who says that the other side had the green light may nevertheless concede that visibility was excellent, so there was nothing to keep the plaintiff from seeing the defendant's car.

Even if you cannot do a constructive cross-examination, you may be able to take away some of the impact of direct examination by scouring through the witness's deposition and finding all the points on which he admits having no information. Using cross-examination to list what the witness does not know can create the impression that his testimony on direct examination was seriously flawed.

But these are preventative measures, not cures. They are designed to let you do a safe, limited cross-examination, to keep you out of trouble. They do little to get you out of trouble once you are there.

And that is where the lawyer was after an hour and a half of fruitless cross-examination.

Let us put some flesh on his problem with facts borrowed from the National Institute for Trial Advocacy's problem, *United States v. Evelyn Cannon*. The charge is espionage. Evelyn Cannon is alleged to have left a container of microfilmed defense secrets in a telephone booth outside the Cove Bar and Grill to be picked up by a Russian agent. The defense is alibi and mistaken identification.

The witness is Special Agent O'Rourke of the FBI who had staked out the Cove Bar and Grill, and who has just given a positive identification of Evelyn Cannon as the woman he saw in the booth.

The cross-examination is a dismal failure. For an hour and a half, Special Agent O'Rourke thwarts every line of questioning, and the defense is in deep trouble. Is there nothing left to do?

Meet R. Eugene Pincham. He is going to deal with the problem of the elusive Agent O'Rourke in final argument. Pincham, once an appellate judge in Illinois, for years was one of the outstanding criminal defense lawyers in Chicago. And he has not lost his touch. When the Smithsonian recently decided to have trial lawyers argue cases as part of its summer American Folk Art festival, Pincham was one of those selected to demonstrate the art of argument.

You need to know just a bit more about Pincham before you see him at work in your mind's eye. He is a physically imposing man with an aura of commitment about him. A black man, he grew up on a farm in Alabama in the 1920s, and his arguments draw on his childhood experiences. Listen now as he talks about the cross-examination of Special Agent O'Rourke.

"You remember that Agent O'Rourke—Special Agent O'Rourke —from the FBI. You saw what a frustrating time I had with him. I cross-examined the man for an hour and a half. An hour and a half. And I never laid a glove on him. I never touched him. Every time I thought I had him where I wanted him, he would slip away. No matter what question I asked, he had some slick answer. He was ready for me and he slipped away.

"I wondered where I had seen that man before.

"Now understand that I did not know this O'Rourke. No one had ever introduced him to me. I had never met the man. I had no idea he was going to testify in this case. I had never talked with him before. No one had even pointed him out to me. But when I asked him questions, somehow he seemed familiar. Somehow I knew I had seen him before.

"I grew up on a farm in Alabama in the 1920s. And I want you to know that entertainment—the kinds of things that we think of as entertainment—was scarce on a farm in Alabama in the 1920s. We had no television because there was no television to be had. We did not even have a radio in my house until I was 16. We went to movies every two or three months if we were lucky. Mainly we entertained ourselves. We played catch and baseball and other games outside. And we waited all summer long for the County Fair.

"I don't mean the State Fair. We didn't have the money to travel to the State Fair. I mean the County Fair. They held it in September after the heat of summer, and they held it in the county seat.

"They had some rides they brought in on wagons and set up, but it was a small fair, so the rides were mainly for the little kids. Then they had games like the one where you throw a baseball at a pyramid of wooden milk bottles and try to knock them over. We knew that all the games were fixed. We knew that those bottles had lead weights in the bottom so that they would be hard to knock over, but we tried anyway. And we would pay to take a swing with the big wooden sledgehammers and try to ring the bell.

"But there was one game I remember especially that all the teenage boys wanted to play. You would pay ten cents for a chance to win ten dollars. They would take a little pig, and grease him up from head to toe with axle grease. And they would put him in a pen. For ten cents you could get in the pen and try to catch the pig. If you could catch that pig—and hold him—you would win ten dollars.

"I paid my dime and when it was my turn I got in the pen and tried to catch the pig. When he ran by, I quickly reached out with my hand and grabbed his leg—and he slipped away. I wrapped my arm around him, and he just squirmed one time and he was gone. He squirted out of my arms. I jumped on him and tried grabbing him by the ears. He shook his head and ran away, and I was left lying on the ground. No matter what I would do, that pig would slip away every time I thought I had him.

"That's where I've seen that O'Rourke before. He's just like that greased pig."

Part of the beauty of Pincham's story is the jury's anticipation. They sense what is coming, and they want to hear it. And when they do, they laugh. But that still does not prepare them for Pincham's last line that drives the point home about Special Agent O'Rourke.

"What I want to know is who greased him up that way."

CHAPTER 79

Jumping to Conclusions

There are lots of analogies we use in final argument that are meant to emphasize the force of circumstantial evidence.

Talking about "Footprints in the Snow" or "Dripping Umbrellas," for example, is intended to make the point that you don't always have to see the paper boy to know he's been up the walk, or go outside to know it has been raining. And if you are out in the woods and see a turtle stuck on a tree stump, you know he didn't get there by himself.

Some of these arguments have taken on lives of their own. People still talk about hearing R. Eugene Pincham tell his sugar-barrel story in the Cook County Criminal Courts at 26th and California in Chicago. Pincham would tell how his momma knew when he had been in the sugar because he always wasted a few granules on the floor.

And then Pincham would go through all the circumstantial evidence that helped his case. After every point he would say, "You know what that is? Granules on the floor."

Pincham became so famous for the sugar-barrel story that one time the prosecutor interrupted him right in the middle of his argument. "Oh, Your Honor, we're not going to hear about the sugar barrel again!"

Pincham turned and pointed his finger at the prosecutor and said, "Yes, you're going to hear it, and you're going to keep on hearing it until I lose a case." And he won.

But what about arguments that are designed to work the other way? Where are the traditional stories that are meant to take the force out of circumstances, to keep the jury from jumping to conclusions on insufficient evidence?

That was the problem facing a young lawyer from Oklahoma a few years back at a National Institute for Trial Advocacy program in Chicago. The young lawyer wanted to make the point that smoke did not always mean fire as he delivered his final argument in a case where things looked pretty grim for his client.

He found an argument, and what he said drew a round of spontaneous applause from everyone in the room—including the judge and the teachers. Here it is:

"I know there is a lot of circumstantial evidence that suggests the fire at the Flinders Aluminum Company was not accidental. I would be foolish to pretend there wasn't, and you wouldn't respect what I said if I tried.

"But that doesn't mean you should jump to a conclusion. On the contrary, it means you've got to be careful not to decide anything until you take everything into account—and that is hard to do.

"You know, our Judeo-Christian tradition is not the only one that has Moses as an important character. He is also in the Koran. And while he does not figure as prominently in the Koran as he does in the Bible, he does participate in an important story.

"Moses was speaking to an Angel of the Lord, and begged the angel to let him come along and see the angel do his works of justice.

"At first the angel refused. 'No,' he said. 'You would not understand what I must do, and you might try to interfere.'

" 'I promise,' said Moses. 'I would only watch and listen, and would not speak, or question the Angel of the Lord.'

" 'If you promise not to judge what you do not understand,' said the angel, 'then you may accompany me. But you must promise.'

" 'I promise,' said Moses, and the angel took Moses with him as he went from one village to the next.

"The first place they stopped was outside the house of two young children whose mother and father had just died. The two children were hungry and dirty and crying for their parents. When the angel saw what had happened, he called down a bolt of lightning on the house, and the children's home collapsed in ruins.

"Moses cried out in anguish, 'What have you done to those children? They are blameless. The Lord has taken their parents, why must you take their house as well?'

"And the angel rebuked Moses. 'You promised not to speak,' he said.

"Then Moses and the angel walked on until they came to a little fishing village. All the fishing boats had come in for the day and were resting in the harbor. When the Angel of the Lord saw the boats, he called down a mighty storm on the harbor. The winds came and the rain fell, and the waves rose. When the storm was finished, all of the boats had sunk.

"So Moses cried out again, 'Surely these fishermen have done no wrong, and yet you have destroyed their boats. How can the Angel of the Lord be so unjust?'

"And the angel rebuked Moses a second time. 'You promised,' he said.

"Then Moses and the angel went to a third village. When they were still a ways off, they saw a handsome young man coming toward them through the village gates. When he came close, the Angel of the Lord drew his sword, and in a flash cut off the young man's head.

"Then Moses cried out, 'Three times I have seen you bring injustice without provocation. It is hard to believe you are the Angel of the Lord.'

"And the angel rebuked Moses again. 'You promised,' he said. 'You promised not to speak and you promised not to judge what you did not understand. But you spoke anyway. And because you are a human, you judge without knowing all that has transpired.

" 'The two children we saw were orphans. They had no parents and they had no money. They did not know their father had put all his money in a secret place in the wall of their home. And unless that wall fell down, their inheritance would never be found. Now money has been found, and the children will be cared for.

" 'When we came to the fishing village, you saw the boats in the harbor. But you did not see the pirates at sea, on their way to destroy the village. Had they found the boats, they would have burned them. I have protected them from attack by sinking them under the water. When the pirates have gone, the boats can be raised, and the people can fish once more.

" 'The young man you saw outside the gate was a thief. He was about to be discovered and punished for his wrongs. His parents cherished their son. And if he were put to death for theft, they would know both grief for his death and shame for his crime. By taking his life myself, they will know grief for his death, but for their righteousness they will be spared a life of shame.'"

Then the young lawyer from Oklahoma said, "The lesson is, we must never judge without *all* of the facts. Now let's talk about what the plaintiff's lawyer left out of his argument."

And Christopher Fleming, a law student in Cleveland, Ohio, used another argument that attacks the tendency to overlook too much of the evidence.

"My little boy, Brooks, is the apple of my eye. I guess it's natural for parents to dote on their kids and pay attention to all the clever little things they do.

"When Brooks was just two years old, I took him to see his grandmother who lives in New Jersey, and one afternoon, we all went to the beach. Brooks had never been to the beach before, and he played in the sand, chased the sea gulls, played in the water, and watched the waves come in to shore. He had a wonderful time.

"Then about two or three weeks later, I was picking Brooks up at the babysitter's house. And the babysitter had a sandbox in her yard. When I went to the front door, Brooks had to show me what he had been doing all day. He took me out to the sandbox, picked up a handful of sand, and poured it back into the sandbox. He was so excited. He looked up at me and said, 'Beach, Daddy, beach.' Brooks was calling that handful of sand the beach.

"Well, what is cute for a kid is not cute for a prosecutor. The prosecutor's got a man who was shot, and he wants to call it a murder. He forgot there is something called self-defense—no sea gulls. The prosecutor forgot the defendant did not start this fight; the 'victim' broke into the defendant's house—no seashells. The prosecutor forgot the defendant honestly thought the people who broke in his place had guns—no water. He forgot the defendant had to protect his kids upstairs—no waves.

"There it is. No water, no waves, no shells, no seagulls. The prosecutor's case is just a handful of sand." Then Fleming opened his hand like Brooks had done, and let the imaginary sand fall to the floor. "And he wants you to think that handful of sand is murder."

CHAPTER 80

The Trial of Henry Sweet

Lawyers are hungry for heroes. And they are hard to find. Most of us have to be content with "mentors"—middle level or senior members of the firm—whose stars (we hope) will pull our wagons.

Like feudalism, the mentor system has some value. Good associates do extra duty for their mentors (who may take a lot of the credit if there are good results), who in turn show their associates how to survive in the castle, as well as teach them some tricks of the trade.

But are they heroes?

Only by accident.

We may model our professional lives after our mentors—not for their heroic qualities, but because it makes good business sense.

That leaves us hungry for heroes.

Clarence Darrow qualifies, partly for the cases he tried, and partly for the way he tried them.

Not that he was the Mother Teresa of the law, who devoted his entire life to pro bono cases. Once a grateful client asked, "Oh, Mr. Darrow, how can I ever thank you enough for all you've done?"

And Darrow said, "Madam, ever since the Phoenicians invented money, there has been an answer to that question."

But Darrow had a remarkable clarity of vision that recognized hypocrisy and self-delusion. He identified with the underdog. He was the champion of the oppressed. And he knew which windmills to fight.

He was born in Kinsman, Ohio, in 1857, became infected with his father's passion for books, and grew up loving the clash of ideas. After one year of college and one year of law school, he started practicing law in Ashtabula, Ohio, some fifty miles east of Cleveland. Four years later, in 1888, he moved to Chicago.

Darrow was near the end of his legal career when he defended Henry Sweet. The famous cases were behind him—Eugene Debs in 1894, Leopold and Loeb in 1924, John T. Scopes in 1925. The Sweet case started in the fall of 1925, but it wasn't over until 1926. The next year, 1927, Darrow retired from the practice of law, but he kept on arguing on the lecture circuit and in public debates for years to come.

Clarence Darrow's cases are surprisingly current for a lawyer who started practice in a small Ohio town more than 100 years ago: civil rights and race relations, freedom of speech and constraints on education, crime and punishment, opposition to the death penalty.

The Case

In September 1925, Dr. Ossian H. Sweet, his wife, and his two-year-old daughter moved into a house at Garland and Charlevoix in Detroit, Michigan. Dr. Sweet was a man of some accomplishment. He was a gynecologist who had studied in Vienna, and had worked under Madame Curie. He had received his M.D. from Howard University.

Dr. Sweet was, in the modern parlance, a man of color. And the problem was that Garland and Charlevoix were in a lower middle-class, white neighborhood.

The black population in Detroit had jumped from 6,000 in 1910 to 70,000 in 1926—largely from the boom in the automobile industry that had attracted thousands of workers from all over the United States.

They needed places to live.

The whites responded with "Improvement Associations," which were used to intimidate their new neighbors, and literally force them to move out of white neighborhoods.

The Sweets understood the situation—but they were not going to be intimidated. Dr. and Mrs. Sweet sent their daughter to stay with her grandmother, while they moved into the house at Garland and Charlevoix with the help of Dr. Sweet's brothers and several friends. Anticipating the possibility of mob violence, they brought in guns as well as furniture.

On the second night they were in the house, a large crowd gathered outside, shouting "niggers" at them. According to the police, suddenly there were gunshots from the house and Leon Breiner, a white man who was sitting and smoking his pipe out in the crowd, was killed.

Everyone in the house—eleven black people—was charged with first-degree murder.

The trial started in October 1925, and Darrow represented all eleven. The jury deliberated for forty-six hours and was unable to reach a verdict, so it ended in a mistrial.

But it wasn't over. The defendants asked if there were retrials that they be tried one at a time. So in April 1926, the trial of Henry Sweet—Dr. Sweet's younger brother—began. It was a time and place in which an impartial trial was impossible.

Darrow's final argument is not a model of structured elegance. It is sometimes disjointed and repetitive. But the simplicity of his language and the power of his ideas are unsettling even today. It is a demonstration, not of slick talk, but of ideas that touched the souls of the jury. I have taken some of Darrow's words and set them out—not as a scholar would, with all the editorial trappings, but as a playwright might, to try to capture the sense of it.

The Argument

The prosecutor says that this isn't a race question; it is a murder case. He says, "We don't want any prejudice; we don't want the other side to have any. Race and color have nothing to do with the case. This is a case of murder."

I insist that there is nothing but prejudice in this case; that if it were reversed and eleven whites had shot and killed a black while protecting their home and lives against a mob of blacks, nobody would have dreamed of having them indicted. They would have been given medals instead.

Ten colored men and one woman are in this indictment, tried by twelve jurors, gentlemen. Every one of you are white, aren't you? At least you all think so. We haven't one colored man on this jury. We couldn't get one. One was called and he was disqualified. You twelve white men are trying a colored man on race prejudice.

You need not tell me you are not prejudiced. I know better. We are not very much but a bundle of prejudices anyhow. We are prejudiced against other people's color. Prejudiced against other men's religions, prejudiced against other people's politics. Prejudiced against people's looks. Prejudiced about the way they dress. We are full of prejudices.

All I hope for, gentlemen of the jury, is that you are strong enough, and honest enough, and decent enough to lay your prejudice aside in this case and decide it as you ought to.

Here were eleven colored men, penned up in the house. Put yourselves in their place. Make yourselves colored for a little while. It won't hurt. You can wash it off. They can't but you can.

Just make yourself black for a little while, long enough to judge them. Suppose you were black. Do you think you would forget it even in your dreams? Or would you have black dreams? Suppose you had to watch every point of contact with your neighbor and remember your color, and you knew your children were growing up under this handicap. Do you suppose you would think of anything else?

There was Dr. Sweet. A white man does pretty well when he does what Dr. Sweet did. A white boy who can start in with nothing and put himself through college, study medicine, and take post-graduate work in Europe—earning every penny of it as he goes along, shoveling snow and coal, and working as a bellhop on boats, working at every kind of employment that he can get to make his way—is some fellow.

But Dr. Sweet has the handicap of the color of his face. And there is no handicap more terrible than that. Supposing you had your choice, right here this minute. Would you rather lose your eyesight or become colored? Would you rather lose your hearing or be a Negro? Would you rather go out in the street and have your leg cut off by a streetcar, or have black skin?

And what has Henry Sweet done? You may think he shot too quick. You may think he erred in judgment. You may think that Dr. Sweet should not have gone there, prepared to defend his home. I say there isn't a man in Detroit who doesn't know that Henry Sweet did his duty, and that this case is an attempt to send him and his companions to prison because they defended their constitutional rights. It is a wicked attempt, and you are asked to be a party to it.

Epilogue

On May 19, 1926—the day after Darrow delivered his final argument—the jury returned a verdict of not guilty. The charges against all the other defendants were dropped. In a final bittersweet note, Dr. Sweet and his family never moved back into the house at Garland and Charlevoix.

Note: This adaptation was drawn from the argument as it appears in Arthur Weinberg's "Attorney for the Damned" (1957). It is also available in "Classics of the Courtroom, Clarence Darrow's Summation in the Trial of Henry Sweet" (The Professional Education Group, Minnetonka, Minn., 1992).

PARALLEL TABLE

The chapters in this book were originally published in the following issues of *The American Bar Association Journal*:

Chapter	Issue
Chapter 1	February 1992
Chapter 2	August 1991
Chapter 3	January 1993
Chapter 4	January 1988
Chapter 5	December 1987
Chapter 6	May 1992
Chapter 7	December 1989
Chapter 8	June 1992
Chapter 9	July 1993
Chapter 10	July 1989
Chapter 11	July 1988
Chapter 12	August 1990
Chapter 13	September 1989
Chapter 14	February 1994
Chapter 15	May 1994
Chapter 16	March 1990
Chapter 17	April 1989
Chapter 18	November 1987
Chapter 19	October 1989
Chapter 20	September 1988
Chapter 21	August 1993
Chapter 22	March 1988
Chapter 23	February 1989
Chapter 24	April 1988
Chapter 25	August 1988
Chapter 26	April 1991
Chapter 27	January 1992
Chapter 28	November 1989
Chapter 29	November 1991
Chapter 30	December 1991

Parallel Table

Chapter 31	March 1989
Chapter 32	March 1994
Chapter 33	January 1994
Chapter 34	April 1994
Chapter 35	May 1990
Chapter 36	April 1990
Chapter 37	May 1993
Chapter 38	November 1992
Chapter 39	June 1989
Chapter 40	August 1992
Chapter 41	October 1990
Chapter 42	November 1988
Chapter 43	October 1991
Chapter 44	February 1988
Chapter 45	May 1989
Chapter 46	January 1989
Chapter 47	February 1993
Chapter 48	September 1990
Chapter 49	March 1993
Chapter 50	December 1990
Chapter 51	January 1991
Chapter 52	November 1993
Chapter 53	February 1991
Chapter 54	March 1992
Chapter 55	December 1988
Chapter 56	September 1993
Chapter 57	December 1992
Chapter 58	October 1993
Chapter 59	June 1988
Chapter 60	July 1991
Chapter 61	May 1991
Chapter 62	June 1993
Chapter 63	March 1991
Chapter 64	August 1989
Chapter 65	April 1992
Chapter 66	June 1990
Chapter 67	October 1988
Chapter 68	April 1993
Chapter 69	September 1991
Chapter 70	October 1992

PARALLEL TABLE

Chapter 71 . . . . January 1990
Chapter 72 . . . . July 1990
Chapter 73 . . . . June 1991
Chapter 74 . . . . September 1992
Chapter 75 . . . . December 1993
Chapter 76 . . . . November 1990
Chapter 77 . . . . October 1987
Chapter 78 . . . . May 1988
Chapter 79 . . . . February 1990
Chapter 80 . . . . July 1992